WHERE SOCIAL IDENTITIES CONVERGE

WHERE SOCIAL IDENTITIES CONVERGE

Latin American and Latinx Youth on Screen

Traci Roberts-Camps

VANDERBILT UNIVERSITY PRESS
Nashville, Tennessee

Copyright 2024 Vanderbilt University Press
All rights reserved
First printing 2024

This book will be made open access within three years of publication thanks to Path to Open, a program developed in partnership between JSTOR, the American Council of Learned Societies (ACLS), University of Michigan Press, and the University of North Carolina Press to bring about equitable access and impact for the entire scholarly community, including authors, researchers, libraries, and university presses around the world. Learn more at https://about.jstor.org/path-to-open.

Library of Congress Cataloging-in-Publication Data

Names: Roberts-Camps, Traci, 1975- author.
Title: Where social identities converge : Latin American and Latinx youth on screen / Traci Roberts-Camps.
Description: Nashville, Tennessee : Vanderbilt University Press, 2024. | Includes bibliographical references and index.
Identifiers: LCCN 2024018752 (print) | LCCN 2024018753 (ebook) | ISBN 9780826507204 (paperback) | ISBN 9780826507211 (hardcover) | ISBN 9780826507228 (epub) | ISBN 9780826507235 (pdf)
Subjects: LCSH: Girls in motion pictures. | Teenage girls in motion pictures. | Identity (Psychology) in motion pictures. | Motion pictures--Latin America.
Classification: LCC PN1995.9.G57 R63 2024 (print) | LCC PN1995.9.G57 (ebook) | DDC 791.43/652352--dc23/eng/20240802
LC record available at https://lccn.loc.gov/2024018752
LC ebook record available at https://lccn.loc.gov/2024018753

To Martín, Carson, Eli, and Benjamin

One can enter or exit a film, an installation, an experiment, a dance, a sculpture, or a verbal text by focusing immediately on whether or not it has a voice, as well as on where and how that voice situates itself. For me, the 'voice' is a site and an activity by which the work's social, ethical, and aesthetic positioning is conveyed to the viewer-listener.
—Trinh T. Minh-ha, *D-Passage: The Digital Way*

CONTENTS

Acknowledgments   xi

INTRODUCTION   1

CHAPTER 1. Audacity, Intelligence, and Indigenous Connections: Patricia Arriaga-Jordán's *Juana Inés*   21

CHAPTER 2. Gender, Class, Sexuality, and Ethnicity: Aurora Guerrero's *Mosquita y Mari* and Viviana Cordero's *No robarás . . . a menos que sea necesario*   52

CHAPTER 3. Intersectional Subjectivity: Gabriela David's *La mosca en la ceniza*   78

CHAPTER 4. Indigeneity and the Rural/Urban Continuum: Claudia Llosa's *Madeinusa* and *La teta asustada* and Itandehui Jansen's *Tiempo de lluvia*   104

CHAPTER 5. Intersectionality and Inter-Nationality: Kaori Flores Yonekura's *Nikkei: Un viaje extraordinario* and Cecilia Kang's *Mi último fracaso*   136

CONCLUSIONS   165

Notes   171
Bibliography   209
Index   225

ACKNOWLEDGMENTS

EVERY MANUSCRIPT IS A conversation with many people. I am humbled to be in dialogue with the luminous scholars that make up the field of Latin American and Latinx cinema.

Finishing this manuscript was only possible with the sabbatical I received from the University of the Pacific (Spring 2023). I also had the great fortune to participate in the Faculty Success Program of the National Center for Faculty Development and Diversity (2018). The knowledge and skills I gained through this program were instrumental in the completion of the following chapters. I am grateful for the funding I have received from the University of the Pacific, including Scholarly and Artistic Activities Grants (SAAG) for research in Argentina (2018) and Mexico (2015) as well as a College Research Fund Grant (CRF) for research in Ecuador (2014). Many of the materials analyzed in this book, such as secondary sources, are only available in their countries of origin. With these sources, I could interact with critics and theorists from the countries that produced the films and series examined here. I had access to the Fundación Cinemateca Argentina (Cinemateca Foundation Argentina) and the MALBA (Museo de Arte Latinoamericano de Buenos Aires) in Buenos Aires for two months. Incidentally, we saw a rare and beautiful snowfall from the windows of the latter in July 2007. In Mexico City, I was able to visit the Cineteca Nacional and the National Film Archives, and in Tijuana, the CeCuT (Centro Cultural Tijuana). I visited the Casa de Cultura Ecuatoriana Benjamín Carrión in Quito with the Cinemateca Nacional. In that city, I even enjoyed being part of the production of a short film. Of course, in all the cities I visited for my research, the bookstores and video stores (when they still existed) were invaluable to the research contained in these pages.

The conversations surrounding conference presentations enrich my research immensely. Specifically, I presented content on Ecuadorian women filmmakers at Portland State University's Cine-Lit VIII: International Conference on Hispanic Film and Literature (2015). Thank you to Stacy, Tucker, Rowan, and Harris for always giving us a loving landing place in Portland. Ignacio López-Calvo's East-West conferences in Norway (2022) and Italy (2023) gave me the chance to present and dialogue with colleagues on Kaori Flores Yonekura's and Cecilia Kang's work. Furthermore, the East-West conferences I have attended—in St. Petersburg, Russia; Delhi, India; Oslo, Norway; and Verona, Italy—have provided unique occasions for discussing Latin American film and culture with scholars worldwide. Finally, I am grateful to Mirna Vohnsen and Daniel Mourenza for inviting me to contribute a chapter to *Contemporary Argentine Women Filmmakers* and giving me such valuable feedback. I presented virtually with several of the authors of the anthology at the 2022 Latin American Studies Congress and the virtual book launch in 2023. I cherish these talks as they are a rare chance to have prolonged conversations with colleagues working on Latin American women's filmmaking. During the book launch, we were even fortunate enough to have the legendary Argentine film producer Lita Stantic in attendance and hear her words on the current state of affairs for film and cultural production in Argentina.

I have been teaching a course on Latin American women filmmakers at the University of the Pacific since 2007 and have had the great fortune to interact with outstanding students who have shared with me their perspectives on film and streaming series. As I always tell them, from the most obscure film reference to the mainstream, I welcome their nuanced viewpoints. I also want to thank my colleagues in Gender Studies and Film Studies for providing a welcoming intellectual home. On that note, I have had the great privilege of being a part of a writing and accountability group at the University of the Pacific for many years, along with my colleagues Marcia Hernandez, Jennifer Helgren, and Cosana Eram.

Personally, I want to thank Lauren, Jonathan, Mira, and Danica for welcoming me into their home and giving me a place to stay when I returned monthly to Berkeley during my sabbatical to do research in the Gardner Stacks of the UC Berkeley Library. Our late-night conversations sustained me. Parenthetically, I am thankful for the student worker who showed me the alternate way out of the Stacks when I inadvertently stayed way past closing time, deep in the library. Moreover, I am grateful to my colleague Jie Lu for providing letters to help me renew my access to the UC Berkeley library.

A portion of Chapter 2 on Viviana Cordero's film *No robarás . . . a menos que sea necesario* appeared in an article titled "El género y la interseccionalidad en las cineastas ecuatorianas Viviana Cordero y Tania Hermida" in *Kipus: Revista andina de letras y estudios culturales*. A portion of Chapter 3 on Gabriela David's film appeared in the chapter "Intersectionality in Gabriela David's *La mosca en la ceniza* (2010)" in *Contemporary Argentine Women Filmmakers*, edited by Mirna Vohnsen and Daniel Mourenza. Likewise, a portion of Chapter 4 on Claudia Llosa's films appeared in a chapter titled "'El otro' en *Madeinusa* y *La teta asustada* de Claudia Llosa" in *Cine andino: Estudios y testimonios*, edited by Julio Noriega and Javier Morales.

I am incredibly grateful to director Gianna F. Mosser, former editor Zachary S. Gresham, and editor Steven P. Rodríguez at Vanderbilt University Press. I appreciated Steven's attention to detail and meticulous notes, especially on the revisions to the introduction. The entire process with the press was remarkably supportive, positive, and respectful. I am indebted to the anonymous readers for their time and energy in reading and commenting on this manuscript. Their insights were instrumental in strengthening the arguments found in these chapters. They broadened the critical horizons of the manuscript's discussions on adolescence in Latin American and Latinx cinema. I also want to thank Veasna Ling in The Cube at the University of the Pacific Library for rescaling all of my images.

As many have expressed, the COVID-19 pandemic and lockdown gave me a new perspective. I lost my grandmother during that time and was unable to travel to her funeral. I am forever grateful for her strength, courage, love, and amazing food. I still dream about her birthday cakes. Being away from my parents during the lockdown was difficult and I relish the memories of our first get-together "in the middle," in Winnemucca, Nevada, when we could finally travel to see loved ones. I am so thankful we have been able to see you much more often in the years since. No words can express my love and gratitude for Martín, Carson, Eli, and Benjamin. Your passion, unique talents, courage, and loving hearts nurture me daily.

INTRODUCTION

IN AN INTERVIEW IN 2019 with Sheryl McCarthy on "One to One," Cherríe Moraga talks about her book *Native Country of the Heart: A Memoir*.[1] She recounts her thoughts while speaking with students at Brooklyn College: "If you can walk in the world with that knowledge of your origins ... particularly young people, they will have a counternarrative. ... They will be more fortified to move through this world with some kind of self-love and self-knowledge, you know, that they have a right to be here."[2] Moraga's thoughts hit on the most central elements I consider while viewing and analyzing the films represented in this book. First, the idea of walking in the world with a particular identity and origin is key; with their films, these directors ponder the question of what it means to walk in the world in a specific body and with a particular identity that is both self-evident and imposed by others. The films studied here consider the lived experiences of adolescent girls and young women in differing circumstances and the importance of others seeing and regarding those experiences. What is more, when thinking about the reasons why these directors made their films, part of the answer lies in the idea that knowledge is fortifying power and representation is important—it leads to self-knowledge, self-love, and identification with others. Finally, these films make a concerted claim for the value of telling the story of girls and women like the protagonists they feature, with the hope that this representation leads to awareness as well as individual and societal action.

This book examines how Latin American and Latinx directors visually represent female adolescence and young adulthood as a way of exploring issues of identity, including gender, sexuality, age, race, ethnicity, socioeconomic class, language, and national and regional origin.³ These directors use the image of adolescence and young adulthood because it is the site of early trauma that presages women's lived experiences under institutional, intersectional oppression. The films analyzed in this book explore intersectionality through young, female protagonists who represent various identity struggles in Latin America and US Latinx communities. The countries and regions represented comprise Argentina, Ecuador, Mexico, Peru, the United States, and Venezuela. Moreover, this study examines a range of genres, such as fictional film, autobiographical documentary, and streaming series. Each chapter includes a close reading of specific scenes that offer insight into the female adolescent and young adult protagonists' multiple identity markers and how they intersect. The key question in each chapter is how Latin American and Latinx directors visually and audibly represent intersectionality on screen. My argument in this book is that using an intersectional lens to analyze the films herein allows us to see how these directors present female adolescence and young adulthood as a metaphorical site for identity struggles, structural oppression, and agency.

The question of why arises with any book-length project—here, why these filmmakers, why these films and series, why adolescence and young adulthood, and why intersectionality? Considering the countries represented, Argentina and Mexico have a long history of sustained cinematic production and critical attention whereas countries such as Ecuador, Peru, and Venezuela have had a more interrupted film industry history and less critical consideration. It was imperative to include both represented and under-represented cinemas in this study to underscore the diverse lived experiences within Latin America and to illustrate how questions of identity and intersectionality vary by national and regional context. While US-mainstream filmmaking is a worldwide phenomenon, independent films in the US have largely suffered the same critical fate as their counterparts in the Andean region, for example. Likewise, the film directors addressed in this study are a blend of emerging talent (Cecilia Kang), overlooked veterans of the industry (Gabriela David), and well-known names (Claudia Llosa). In terms of genre, it was important to critically address various formats, including fictional films, fictional streaming series, and documentaries, especially considering the significance of streaming content within recent cultural production as well as the continued importance of feature-length fictional and documentary filmmaking in the Latin American and US Latinx contexts. Furthermore, the incorporation of these countries, filmmakers, and genres allowed for an in-depth comparison of the visualization of intersectionality across many different contexts and representational lived experiences.

Additionally, through years of watching and writing about films, there are certain themes and styles that continuously surface and catch my attention. The more films—and now streaming series—that I watch, the more connections I see between them. This book is the result of intellectual curiosity and finding associations in unexpected places, such as the clear similarities between Viviana Cordero's Ecuadorian film *No robarás . . . a menos que sea necesario* (Thou shalt not steal . . . . . . unless necessary, 2013) and Aurora Guerrero's Latinx film *Mosquita y Mari* (2012). I came upon the first while conducting research in Ecuador (Quito, Cuenca, and Guayaquil) in 2014 and the second while compiling a film list for my Latin American women filmmakers course. Immediately, it was clear that the two films, from such differing contexts, shared common threads and this fascinated me, enough to keep returning to them and considering what a comparative analysis would look like. Other films, such as those by Venezuelan and Argentine directors, Kaori Flores Yonekura and Cecilia Kang, respectively, became focal points of my investigation when I was preparing presentations for Ignacio López-Calvo's East-West Conferences. On the other hand, I found myself watching a significant number of streaming series during the early days of the COVID lockdown. While I had already accumulated research materials on Sor Juana during a pre-COVID research trip to Mexico City, it was when I rewatched Patricia Arriaga-Jordán's series about the seventeenth-century poet that I made the mental leap from her work to the project on intersectionality that I had been formulating.

This brings me to the ideas of adolescence, young adulthood, and intersectionality. Many of the films made by Latin American women filmmakers focus on girls and young women; furthermore, their lived experiences are a metaphorical as well as concrete site through which the filmmakers explore issues of intersectional identity, repression, and power relations. Intersectionality as a theoretical concept speaks to these directors' explorations; namely, their filmic work is a visual representation of their protagonists' intersecting identities. As a theory, intersectionality analyzes the ways in which differing identity factors traverse, thus providing a more in-depth perspective on individual and societal oppression, as will be discussed further later. Through these junctures, the filmmakers underscore the social, political, cultural, and historical power dynamics exerting influence over the young women's lives. When I think about Latin American women filmmakers and Latinx filmmakers as a whole (with clear differences due to context and lived experiences), intersectionality theory encompasses the messages they strive to communicate in their films and streaming series.

In terms of the focus on Latin American and Latinx filmmakers, as a group, they continue to produce some of the most compelling and dynamic films coming from the various regions represented. And this remains so despite the fact that challenges in funding, distribution, and marketing remain clear obstacles to the completion of their work.[4] In 2017, Deborah Shaw presented the "Latin American Women's Filmmaking Manifesto," "a vision of feminist film scholarship."[5] As calls to action, manifestos are inspiring; as guidelines, they help organize the work that must be done. Namely, scholars who focus on Latin American and US Latinx filmmakers write in a moment of great cultural production and Shaw's manifesto lays out a roadmap for various approaches to this body of work. Shaw emphasizes the following goals:

> to raise awareness, promote and critically engage with the work of Latin American and Latina women filmmakers; to analyse the work of women in Latin American film industries as directors, but also as other industry professionals; to tell and reveal untold and invisible histories of women behind and in front of the camera; to account for the transnational funding mechanisms and the role of co-productions; and to embrace intersectionality and seek to understand how gender intersects with sexuality, class, ethnicity, political discourses, and (trans)nationality.[6]

The objectives of *Where Social Identities Converge: Latin American and Latinx Adolescence on Screen* reflect Shaw's manifesto in many ways—highlighting the work of lesser-known filmmakers; revealing previously unknown women's histories; looking at both Latin American and US Latinx cultural production; and focusing specifically on intersectionality.

The chapters in this book continuously return to questions of intersectionality and compare the similar and dissimilar ways in which these directors represent issues of gender, sexuality, age, race, ethnicity, socioeconomic class, ability, language, and national and regional origin. For example, ethnicity and regional origin are central to the films of Guerrero, Llosa, and Jansen. While there are differences among the depictions of ethnicity in their films due to national context, there are also similarities in the protagonists' struggles. Meanwhile, Arriaga-Jordán, David, and Llosa observe issues of agency and subjectivity in their young, female protagonists from different perspectives, including age, power, violence, and subjection. In their films, adolescent girlhood is a site of oppression and resistance. Gender and socioeconomic status weave their way through the films and series of Arriaga-Jordán, Cordero, Guerrero, David, Llosa, and Jansen. The protagonists in their films illustrate how gender is not isolated from socioeconomic class. Language and nationality intersect with gender in the films of Guerrero, Jansen, Flores Yonekura, and Kang.

This book contributes to existing critical work on Latin American and Latinx filmmakers by addressing the visual representation of intersectionality. It also shows how differing contexts highlight similar and divergent lived experiences, structural inequalities, and possibilities for agency. Existing studies fall into three categories: The first are those that focus on Latin American women filmmakers in general (Martin and Shaw, Nair and Gutiérrez-Albilla, Trelles Plazaola).[7] The second are those that are country- or filmmaker-specific (Arredondo, Eseverri and Peña, Haddu, Hershfield and Maciel, Marsh, Rashkin).[8] And the third are those that emphasize representations of childhood or adolescence in Latin American and/or Latinx film. Of the latter, the subcategories include childhood and adolescence (MacGuire and Randall, Martin, Rocha and Seminet); childhood and agency (Ramírez Rojas and Osorio Lora, Randall); and childhood and affect (Page and Selimović, Podalsky, Selimović).[9] A final category concerns childhood in cinema writ large (Lury, Olson, Shary and Seibel).[10] Of those that address Latin American women's filmmaking as a whole, Trelles Plazaola's book is foundational and examines groundbreaking directors from across the region.[11] Nair and Gutiérrez-Albilla's edited volume uniquely includes directors from Latin America, including Brazil, as well as from Spain and Portugal. Martin and Shaw's edited volume *Latin American Women Filmmakers* offers a panoramic and comparative view of women filmmakers in several Latin American countries, looking at the turn from public to personal politics. Their anthology includes established directors (Lucrecia Martel) as well as those who have received less critical attention (US Latinx director Silvia Morales) and addresses other forces in the film industry, such as producers (Bertha Navarro).[12] The current study expands on the above-mentioned work to include directors, regions, and genres not included before, as well as a focus on intersectionality as a mode of underscoring differing lived experiences, inequalities, and agency. This manuscript specifically expands on my last book on Latin American women's film by including the streaming series genre (*Juana Inés*); Andean cinema (Ecuador and Peru); Indigenous perspectives (Jansen); US Latinx cinema (Guerrero); and Asian communities in Latin America (Flores Yonekura and Kang).

While existing studies focus on the general representation of childhood and adolescence, childhood and agency, or childhood and affect, my book focuses on the visual representation of intersectionality and how this perspective sheds light on the films' protagonists and their lived experiences, oppressions, and possibilities for agency. For example, Rocha and Seminet have edited two volumes on the topic, concentrating on subjectivity and agency and gender and class within historical political conflict, respectively. Both anthologies include a wide range of perspectives, including Central American film, which has not received much critical attention. In their introduction to *Screening Minors*, Rocha and Seminet note the relatively large percentage of Latin American films focusing on children and adolescents since the 1960s.[13] This second anthology specifically analyzes children's subjectivity and agency and "the ways in which Latin American filmmakers give voice to children in film, and capture what is unique, appealing, and profound about children's subjectivity and childhood in the region."[14] For their part, Ramírez Rojas and Osorio Lora look at youth and child agency under the guise of the "individual's capacity for action as a process of learning, negotiation, and transformation that depends on constantly fluctuating networks of relations and conditions of possibility"[15] rather than an individualistic pursuit of independence. Significantly, these ideas underline the central notion that agency is not about the will or lack thereof of the individual; it depends on various societal factors that are structural in nature. Therefore, adolescent subjectivity and agency are a process of dialogue between the young person and society. Clearly, existing intersectional oppressions will curtail an adolescent's ability to exert agency or pursue full subjectivity. In the following chapters in this book, the protagonists of the films in question face a web of intersecting oppressions that affect their agency as well as decision-making processes.

Differing from other studies, I chose to include a streaming series in this book due to their increasing popularity and importance within visual media studies. Streaming content has become an important part of global cultural production; so much so, that film directors such as Quentin Tarantino question the very nature of filmmaking and their future in it with the drastic changes the medium has experienced.[16] Questions of theater release versus straight-to-streaming are contemporary versions of decisions related to digital versus celluloid and, before that, silent versus talkies. The proliferation of streaming content and cultural producers moving to this medium is just one in a line of successive revolutions cinema has seen over its history. For Latin America, streaming series come into being within a particular context. For example, film and television have always had a close and mutually beneficial relationship in countries such as Argentina and Brazil, where many of the same players—from directors and editors to the actors themselves—seamlessly move between the two media.[17] On the other hand, in countries like the US, television has been dubbed the "small screen" and therefore inferior to film, "the big screen." However, the advent of television channels such as HBO and Showtime made way for a new way of looking at television and its relationship to filmmaking. For more recent generations brought up on Netflix, it comes as a surprise that these earlier monthly subscription channels were created in 1972 and 1976, respectively. Moreover, they billed themselves as platforms that presented content that competed head-to-head with the big screen for creative awards.

Regarding streaming services in Latin America, such as Netflix, MUBI, Amazon Prime, and Curzon Home Cinema, Niamh Thornton comments on Netflix's oversized influence on Latin American cinema's viewership. The streaming giant has created its own guarded algorithms to determine what is shown in each market region, which means companies such as Netflix govern the marketing and dissemination of a large portion of filmmaking output from Latin America. Thornton affirms that "given the growth in these services and the shrinking DVD market, what they show, where it gets seen, and how this determines the viewers' understanding of Latin American film, makes this a particularly fecund area for new research."[18] As is evident in Thornton's assertions, streaming services wield a large amount of power in determining exposure for Latin American film and series content.[19] On the other hand, these services provide filmmakers with a much wider audience, at least in Latin America and the US. For filmmakers in the US not entrenched in the Hollywood system, this solves distribution and marketing issues. Of Netflix, Cory Barker and Myc Wiatrowski refer to its role in revolutionizing the way we consume media: "From the rise of binge-watching and password-sharing to intermittent debates about spoiler etiquette and how critics should cover programs that are released all at once, Netflix is the central force in the contemporary experiences of media consumption."[20] As Barker and Wiatrowski confirm, Netflix has changed the very ways in which we view content. Whereas before we waited for new episodes, with Netflix it became possible to watch an entire series in one sitting. Moreover, for many in younger generations and particularly in the COVID era, the social experience of watch parties, for example, replaces a trip to the movie theater. Additionally, there are more options for where to watch streaming content—television, computer, tablet, and a phone, most popular with younger generations.

Ramon Lobato also looks at the cultural shift driven by Netflix, "one of the few brands of the internet era to penetrate so deeply into households and the broader popular consciousness that it has become a verb ('let's Netflix it,' 'Netflix and chill'). It is a quintessential Silicon Valley success story, bridging two of America's signature fascinations—home entertainment and e-commerce."[21] Lobato, however, distinguishes Netflix from other platforms such as YouTube and Facebook because it still works under the traditional guidelines of intellectual property and professional production.[22] Like Barker and Wiatrowski, Lobato understands the profound influence of Netflix on film, television, and popular culture. Furthermore, he marks the platform's trajectory toward producing its own content while remaining closer to traditionally and professionally produced content than other popular platforms. With all of this said, the importance of addressing streaming content in this book was clear. Thus, the first chapter examines a series acquired by Netflix from Mexico.[23]

Along with including a streaming series, another unique aspect of this book that expands the conversation on Latin American and Latinx filmmaking is the focus on intersectionality. This book engages the concept of intersectionality as a way of examining the identity encounters that Latin American and Latinx cinema and television present. Significantly, the inequality represented in the films and series discussed reveals itself in its complete form only by considering the distinct facets of the protagonists' identities and how they intersect. Moreover, this framework reveals the systems of power under which the protagonists live and exposes the ways in which they are marginalized. Intersectionality as a theory and field has expanded rapidly in recent years, especially within the field of gender studies. However, the ideas central to intersectionality have existed within gender and feminist studies for decades. The following is a review of definitions and a synopsis of and engagement with recent contributions and precursors to intersectionality studies from Latin American and US Latinx feminist and gender studies. This outline of the theory of intersectionality and decolonial feminist studies sheds light on the key concepts at work in the chapters that follow. It also provides an important overview of recent scholarship and contributions to intersectionality studies.

INTERSECTIONALITY: ORIGINS AND RECENT META-ANALYSIS

Intersectionality studies are central to many contemporary feminist and gender studies critical approaches, including those that address popular culture.[24] Patricia Hill Collins and Patrick R. Grzanka provide detailed definitions and explanations of the theoretical framework for intersectionality. In *Black Feminist Thought: Knowledge, Consciousness, and the Politics of Empowerment*, Collins defines the terms intersectionality and the matrix of domination:

> Intersectionality refers to particular forms of intersecting oppressions, for example, intersections of race and gender, or of sexuality and nation. Intersectional paradigms remind us that oppression cannot be reduced to one fundamental type, and that oppressions work together in producing injustice. In contrast, the matrix of domination refers to how these intersecting oppressions are actually organized. Regardless of the particular intersections involved, structural, disciplinary, hegemonic, and interpersonal domains of power reappear across quite different forms of oppression.[25]

Collins underscores the importance of looking at various intersecting oppressions—including race, gender, sexuality, and nation, among others—rather than focusing solely on one. According to the theorist, it is necessary to consider the structural domination that results from intersectional oppression. Moreover, Collins recognizes, "All individuals and groups possess varying amounts of penalty and privilege in one historically created system."[26] Key to this observation is the idea of historical context in which structural oppression is developed over time within specific societal conditions.

Grzanka also emphasizes the structural nature of oppression: "Intersectionality is a structural analysis and critique insomuch as it is primarily concerned with how social inequalities are formed and maintained; accordingly, identities and the politics thereof are the *products* of historically entrenched, institutional systems of domination and violence."[27] Hence, it is important to signal that these inequalities are products of dominant and violent institutional systems—either the government, education, religion, or other. Grzanka indicates that "intersectionality is foremost about studying multiple dimensions of inequality and developing ways to resist and challenge these various forms of oppression."[28] Within this methodology, developing forms of resistance is central to what Collins terms the matrix of domination. Furthermore, according to Grzanka, identity and social inequality are products of violent structural domination. Collins's and Grzanka's concepts on intersectionality, the matrix of domination, structural oppression, historical context, and resistance will form the basis for the following recent meta-analyses of intersectionality studies.

Recent work on intersectionality has focused on critiquing the interdisciplinary field's own problematic tendencies to ignore its multiple origin stories, devalue the work of scholars of color, and assume itself as a solution rather than a process. These contributions shed light on the main concerns that are at work in intersectionality studies as well as the challenges and possible future pathways for the developing field. While continuing to refine the definition of intersectionality, these authors challenge inclinations to reduce the theory to a mathematical equation of oppression. Moreover, they condemn what Ange-Marie Hancock sees as the erasure of theorists of color in the field. In *Intersectionality: An Intellectual History* (2016), Hancock addresses the theoretical framework and academic uses of the term as well as the challenges facing the study of intersectionality. The author discusses the "notion of an interpretive community being entrusted with the care of such a precious and complicated phenomenon like intersectionality" and underlines theorists' ethical duty to further develop the theory in lieu of owning it.[29] Hancock traces the origins of the current theory to international activist movements calling for an end to violence against women. Intersectionality's beginnings are not limited to the United States or Europe and certainly not to Anglo-American and European practitioners.[30] Thus, Hancock squarely places the origins and concepts of intersectionality prior to the commonly held assumption that it originated in the latter part of the twentieth century.

Another analysis of the theory is Anna Carastathis's *Intersectionality: Origins, Contestations, Horizons*, in which the author examines the possibilities and challenges of intersectionality theory. Carastathis argues that intersectionality "understood as categorical critique functions as a distal horizon, powerfully illuminating the urgent conceptual, political, ethical, and affective work to be done in the 'here' and 'now' rather than an essentialist category amenable to colonial state projects of differential inclusion, diversity management, and social control."[31] She bases her examination on lived experience and views intersectionality as a "provisional concept" that is still evolving.[32] Furthermore, the theorist highlights the problematic centering of intersectionality theory within white-dominated feminist movements. Carastathis decries the distancing of intersectionality from Crenshaw's original wording and focus on the political.[33] The theorist traces intersectionality to "a trajectory of Black feminist thought that begins in the nineteenth century" and the ideas of double jeopardy, triple jeopardy, and interlocking oppressions.[34] In addition, Carastathis carefully recenters Crenshaw's work within the concept of intersectionality and the definition of the term and re-emphasizes the original theory's focus on merging "what are now falsely separated as mutually exclusive categories" such as class, sexuality, and age.[35] Thus, Carastathis's engagement with and critique of the direction of intersectionality studies focuses on a return to Crenshaw's original concepts and a view toward the possibilities for the theory first, to resist colonial categorization and, second, to address the work to be done now by proponents of the field.

For her part, Collins returns to intersectional theory in her book co-written with Sirma Bilge, *Intersectionality*, in 2020, expanded and revised from the original 2016 edition.[36] This book is based on the two authors' previous work on the theory and ideas that arose from the convergence of their perspectives and experiences. The authors emphasize the variety of approaches and uses of the theory: "intersectionality is everywhere and it is polyglot: it speaks the language of activism and community organizing as much as it speaks that of academia or of institutions. It speaks to young people through social media and popular culture and to established scholars through journals and conferences."[37] Of course, intersectionality also literally speaks many languages. It is necessary to explore beyond English or even standard academic English to reach the many contributions to the field of intersectionality studies. Collins and Bilge further contend that "in a given society at a given time, power relations of race, class, and gender, for example, are not discrete and mutually exclusive entities, but rather build on each other and work together; and that, while often invisible, these intersecting power relations affect all aspects of the social world."[38] Similar to Hancock and Carastathis, Collins and Bilge address the problem of which histories of intersectionality are highlighted at the expense of others. They also look at the relationship between intersectionality and such global issues as climate change, reproductive justice, digital media and digital violence, human rights, and social justice activism.

As with the earlier-mentioned books, *De-Whitening Intersectionality: Race, Intercultural Communication, and Politics*, edited by Shinsuke Eguchi, Bernadette Marie Calafell, and Shadee Abdi, is an anthology of essays that decenters "the logics of whiteness that characterize intersectional research."[39] In the first essay, for example, Michelle Holling points to concepts of intersectionality specific to Chicana and Xicana feminisms, adding such voices as Ana Castillo's and Alma García's to those of Anzaldúa and Moraga. Holling clarifies: "where nationalism, machismo, capitalism, and Catholicism were identified as distinct forces that repress Xicanas and inhibit concientización, Castillo's vision of Xicanisma, along with its embrace of indigenismo, the feminine, and cultural practices and rituals, are restorative thereby providing a pathway to concientización, an awakening central to decolonizing oneself."[40] The author identifies repression based on intersectional factors as a colonial legacy. Holling's idea of intersectionality studies as a stimulus for action and resistance is reminiscent of Grzanka's call to move the field beyond identity studies toward the goal of challenging structural oppression.[41]

LATIN AMERICAN AND US LATINX CONTRIBUTIONS AND PRECURSORS TO INTERSECTIONALITY

This book focuses on Latin American and Latinx film and television; therefore, theories from Latin American and Latinx critics and theorists will be central to each chapter. This section reflects on some of the main contributions to intersectionality and decolonial feminist studies in Latin America and the US as well as important precursors that developed the same ideas before the term intersectionality existed. Along with providing a summary of the theoretical perspectives on intersectionality specific to Latin America and the US, Latinx context, the following synopsis foregrounds the subsequent chapters' conceptual frameworks. For example, *Theories of the Flesh: Latinx and Latin American Feminisms, Transformation, and Resistance*, edited by Andrea J. Pitts, Mariana Ortega, and José Medina, focuses on decolonial feminist philosophy in Latin America and the US and, as the title suggests, the authors in the anthology base their approaches to decoloniality on corporeally lived experiences.[42] In "Revisiting Gender: A Decolonial Approach," Argentine philosopher María Lugones looks at decolonial feminism from the perspectives of women of color subjectivity and intersubjectivity. Lugones affirms: "Gender as a concept cannot lead us to see coloniality because it does not take . . . into account the relation of power that erases or attempts to erase what relations constitute the people that are colonized and racialized."[43] She goes on to emphasize the close connection between gender and race and underscore the humanity of the colonized: "I am particularly interested in the modern, colonial, capitalist gender system as it constructs the meaning of gender in tense relations with very different understandings that guide the colonized in their societies."[44] As is evident, Lugones contends that it is not sufficient to only look at the concept of gender when discussing subjects from colonized communities due to the history of dehumanization of the colonized individual. Likewise, it is necessary to view gender in conjunction with race as well as to understand the differing perceptions of gender held by the colonizers versus the colonized. These ideas are clearly akin to the precepts set forth by Collins and Bilge, for example, relating to intersectionality.

In "Toward a Decolonial Feminism," Lugones proposes the colonial gender system "as a lens through which to theorize further the oppressive logic of colonial modernity, its use of hierarchical dichotomies and categorical logic. I want to emphasize categorical, dichotomous, hierarchical logic as central to modern, colonial capitalist thinking about race, gender, and sexuality."[45] Decolonial feminism proposes many of the same critiques outlined by the already mentioned books on intersectionality studies and seeks to move away from a Eurocentric, white-centered, middle-class, Western view of gender as it relates to race and other identity factors. Lugones analyzes modern identity through the guise of coloniality and, more specifically, through the dichotomies the colonizers instituted upon their arrival in the Americas.[46] For example, Lugones describes the dichotomy of colonial modernity in the following: human/

nonhuman, man/woman, and European/Indigenous.[47] Lugones examines the gender framework imposed by the colonizers, who considered themselves to be civilized and fully human: "The hierarchical dichotomy as a mark of the human also became a normative tool to damn the colonized. The behaviors of the colonized and their personalities/souls were judged as bestial and thus non-gendered, promiscuous, grotesquely sexual, and sinful."[48] Thus, for Lugones, any understanding of intersectionality in Latin America must start with recognizing its history as a colonized space.[49]

Colombian theorist Mara Viveros Vigoya directly refers to intersectional theory in her writing. In "La interseccionalidad: Una aproximación situada a la dominación," Viveros Vigoya traces the history and pre-history of intersectionality, including both US and Latin American theorists, philosophers, artists, and writers. For example, she presents Peruvian author Clorinda Matto de Turner and Brazilian artist Tarsila do Amaral as precursors to what is now known as intersectionality theory. In "Cuestiones raciales y construcción de nación en tiempos de multiculturalismo," Viveros Vigoya and Sergio Lesmes Espinel discuss the changing conceptions of race in the development of the nation in Latin America. In a critical challenge to multiculturalism, the theorists contend that this model of difference focuses on only one factor at a time, whether that be ethnicity, gender, age, or other factors, "ignorando la imbricación de las relaciones de poder y las experiencias de personas que se encuentran en la intersección de distintas opresiones" (ignoring the overlapping of relations of power and the experiences of people who are found in the interstices of different oppressions).[50] Hence, Viveros Vigoya and Lesmes Espinel recognize the importance of highlighting intersecting identity factors and power dynamics for a better understanding of subjugation. The focus is similar to that of Lugones when she states that gender alone will not clarify the oppressed position of the colonized. Likewise, these theorists' concepts directly parallel those of intersectionality studies in their attention to the structural nature of oppression and domination.

Costa Rican author Marisol Fournier-Pereira analyzes Central American lesbian feminism and, like Viveros Vigoya, directly refers to intersectionality as a tool to study oppression that is the product of the "heteropatriarcado capitalista neoliberal" (the capitalist, neoliberal heteropatriarchy).[51] Specifically, Fournier-Pereira looks at a fissure in Central American feminism that has also surfaced in feminisms around the world—the inclusion or exclusion of trans individuals. As Fournier-Pereira explains, the two theoretical metaphors used include "one's own room"—used to defend not including trans individuals and the "open garden" used to defend their inclusion.[52] To the first, Fournier-Pereira cautions that this space-making should be questioned from an intersectional perspective regarding who is included and how this is decided to avoid creating hierarchies of identity.[53] In the second metaphor, the author also uses an intersectional approach to question who is included in the supposed 'open garden.' Finally, in what encapsulates the intentional challenges brought forth by intersectionality, Fournier-Pereira asserts: "no es lo mismo autodenominarse lesbiana feminista en Matagalpa, Nicaragua, que en Montevideo, Uruguay, ser lesbiana feminista campesina en el Aguan, o ser migrante nicaragüense feminista lesbiana en Upala, Costa Rica; como no es igual ser trans en Tegucigalpa que en Buenos Aires, en los barrios del sur de San José de Costa Rica o en San Paulo, Brasil."[54] Fournier-Pereira's words reach the heart of the intersectional discussion, which underscores how categories of identity and modes of resistance function in different ways, depending on the intersections and socioeconomic context.

The work done by writers such as Cherríe Moraga and Gloria Anzaldúa in the 1980s shares the same focus as intersectionality theory; namely, one, structural oppression exists; two, individual and group identities intersect in different ways; and three, these intersections make it so that those individuals and groups experience oppression in different ways. Finally, the strategies for resistance to domination look different depending on these intersecting identity factors. In 1981, Moraga and Anzaldúa edited the groundbreaking volume *This Bridge Called My Back: Writings by Radical Women of Color*. The book is a foundational intervention in the conversation about gender, class, race, and ethnicity in the United States. Meant as a response to a predominantly white, middle-class, heterosexual feminist movement, Moraga says of the anthology: "The prism of a US Third World Feminist consciousness has shifted as we turned our gaze *away* from a feminism prescribed by white women of privilege (even in opposition to them) and turned *toward* the process of discerning the multilayered and intersecting sites of identity and struggle—distinct and shared—among women of color across the globe."[55] The anthology includes varying genres and linguistic registers, not necessarily following prescribed academic styles. The title of the collection refers at once to literal bridges connecting different countries and communities as well as the metaphorical bridges the authors create with their own lived experiences. Consequently, the title also refers to the burden of being a bridge for others in understanding and learning about those who are not like them.[56]

In *Borderlands/La Frontera: The New Mestiza*, Gloria Anzaldúa emphasizes that, along with the physical US/Mexico border, she also refers to psychological, sexual, and spiritual borders: "In fact, the Borderlands are physically present wherever two or more cultures edge each other, where people of different races occupy the same territory, where under, lower, middle and upper classes touch."[57] Language is key to the borderlands intersectionality Anzaldúa presents: "The switching of 'codes' in this book from English to Castilian Spanish to the North Mexican dialect to Tex-Mex to a sprinkling of Nahuatl to a mixture of all of these, reflects my language, a new language—the language of the Borderlands."[58] Hence, Anzaldúa's reflections reveal a concerted crossing of borders—linguistic, national, and sexual, among others. One of the book's last expressions on the borderlands touches on this idea: "To survive the Borderlands / you must live *sin fronteras* / be a crossroads."[59] Harkening back to the anthology Anzaldúa edited with Moraga, the writer returns to the image of the self as the metaphorical bridge or border.[60] The author also presupposes ideas around intersectionality as related to race, ethnicity, class, sexuality, and language.[61]

In *The Bloomsbury Handbook of 21st-Century Feminist Theory*, Aída Hurtado's entry "Intersectionality" summarizes her own and others' contributions to the field of intersectionality, focusing on its use in law, public art, and political mobilization. In her summary of the theory, Hurtado includes Crenshaw, Collins, Rosa-Linda Fregoso, and Anzaldúa. For the author, the idea of "master statuses" is key to an intersectional understanding of identity and oppression. In other words, intersectionality allows for better insight into the junctures of subjugation and power related to gender, race, ethnicity, class, sexuality, and physical ableness.[62] Hurtado further explains that "[s]tigmatized social identities based on master statuses are not additive; they do not result in increased oppression with an increased number of stigmatized group memberships. Instead, individuals' group memberships are conceptualized as intersecting in a variety of ways, depending on the social context."[63] Hurtado arrives here at an essential caution found in much of intersectionality theory; namely, the analysis of oppression is not a mathematical equation of summations but rather a context-dependent examination of intersecting identities, oppressions, and power relations. Hurtado's ideas on master statuses, context-dependent oppression, and social identities mirror those set forth by Moraga and Anzaldúa beginning in the 1980s along with those proposed by later theorists referring specifically to intersectionality, such as Collins and Bilge. In all of these cases, intersecting identities and the matrix of domination are key to understanding and combating oppression.

CHAPTER SUMMARIES

Where Social Identities Converge: Latin American and Latinx Adolescence on Screen examines six fictional feature-length films, two documentary feature-length films, and one streaming series. Each chapter either considers the work of one director or compares that of two directors, always with the primary focus on intersectionality. Specifically, the following chapters analyze how Latin American and Latinx filmmakers visually represent issues of intersectionality in particular scenes in their films. In so doing, these scene-specific discussions highlight the protagonists' multiple lived experiences as well as the structural and historical oppressions they face. In each chapter, I return to the theoretical basis of intersectionality to ground my considerations, referring to the aforementioned theorists along with other works related to the field. Moreover, I have sought to foreground critics and theorists from each of the countries represented—Argentina, Ecuador, Mexico, Peru, the United States, and Venezuela—including the work of scholars of color. Furthermore, I have included in the following chapters films and series that represent a broad range of regional and historical representations as well as overlooked aspects of intersectionality such as linguistic and rural identity. Finally, each chapter explores intersectionality through the lens of adolescence and young adulthood, recognizing youth as a metaphorical site for structural and societal oppression and a presage of future trauma.

Chapter 1 focuses on the Mexican television miniseries *Juana Inés* (co-produced by Canal Once and Bravo Films in Mexico in 2016 and acquired by Netflix in 2017), about the historical figure Sor Juana Inés de la Cruz, the seventeenth-century Mexican nun and poet. Created by Patricia Arriaga-Jordán, with episodes directed by Arriaga-Jordán and others, this series focuses on the protagonist's audacious challenge of church and societal norms through her gender, age, and gifted intelligence. As a proto-feminist, Sor Juana was an anomaly of her time: she entered the convent to pursue an intellectual life, published widely, and questioned church authority, colonial female roles, and patriarchy. This chapter underscores scenes of the young Sor Juana as independent, outspoken, and intelligent. Moreover, the chapter examines Sor Juana's connections to the Nahuatl language and Indigenous culture through the miniseries and her writings. The protagonist becomes a site through which the miniseries represents intersectional identity and power dynamics in seventeenth-century Mexico. This examination of Arriaga-Jordán's Sor Juana integrates theory and critique by Stephanie Kirk, Paul Julian Smith, Margo Glantz, Moraga, Anzaldúa, and Trinh T. Minh-ha.

Chapter 2 compares Ecuadorian director Viviana Cordero's film *No robarás . . . a menos que sea necesario* (2013) and US Latinx director Aurora Guerrero's film *Mosquita y Mari* (2012) and their representations of gender, age, sexuality, class, and ethnicity in the context of coming-of-age stories about young women. While Cordero's film is set in working-class neighborhoods of Quito, Ecuador, and Guerrero's film portrays Huntington Park in Los Angeles, there are parallels between the two films that expose adolescent girlhood as a site of socioeconomic struggle.[64] For the protagonists, the process of self-determination central to adolescence is heavily affected by socioeconomic issues. Furthermore, the protagonists' gender, sexuality, and ethnicity overlap in both films, allowing the directors to explore these issues as they relate to notions of community. Key scenes in these two films highlight how the young protagonists are forced to take on early responsibilities in order to support their families and are exploited because of their age and gender. The intersectional analysis of Cordero's and Guerrero's films incorporates the work of Hurtado, Viveros Vigoya, Moraga, Anzaldúa, Frederick Luis Aldama, Mariana Ortega, David William Foster, and Geovanny Narváez.

Chapter 3 considers the intersections of gender, adolescence, working-class socioeconomic status, rural otherness, and cognitive ability in Argentine director Gabriela David's film *La mosca en la ceniza* (The fly in the ashes; 2009). David's film is set in both rural Northwestern Argentina and Buenos Aires, highlighting the different settings as they relate to the protagonists' difficulties. More specifically, this chapter looks at how David problematizes the concepts of subjectivity and agency through young, female characters who navigate a system of structural oppression and impunity. Specific scenes in this film show how the young girls are caught in a sex trafficking ring and how others exploit them for their own benefit based on their gender, age, class, rural identities, and ability. This chapter also explores the director's use of specific spaces that reflect the protagonists' confinement. Through the protagonists, David examines the rural/urban divide and lack of social networks and resources for young, rural women in contemporary Argentina. This intersectional approach to David's film underscores theories and interpretations by Collins, Bilge, Hurtado, Daniel Omar de Lucía, Liliana Hendel, Traci Brynne Voyles, Ana Corbalán, Ana Forcinito, and Marta Boris Tarré.

Chapter 4 looks at the rural/urban continuum through the lens of gender, language, and ethnicity in Peruvian director Claudia Llosa's *Madeinusa* (2005) and *La teta asustada* (The milk of sorrow; 2009) and Mexican director Itandehui Jansen's *Tiempo de lluvia* (In times of rain; 2018). Llosa's films are set either in a mythical Andean village or Lima, Peru, while Jansen's film travels between a mountain village in Oaxaca and Mexico City. These films highlight the intersections of ethnicity, gender, national identity, regional origins, linguistic difference, and socioeconomic class as they relate to the protagonists. This chapter explores the similar and differing ways in which the two directors represent indigeneity on screen. In particular, scenes from all three films underscore different approaches to presenting Indigenous identities; Llosa's depictions tend toward the mythical whereas Itandehui's mirror current reality. Both directors explore the possibilities for agency and change in their protagonists and how intersectionality relates to questions of the "other." This chapter's assessment of intersectionality in the works of Llosa and Jansen relies on the work of Julia A. Kroll, Maria Chiara D'Argenio, Minh-ha, Paul A. Schroeder Rodríguez, Pirjo Kristiina Virtanen, Angus McNelly, Nancy Postero, Freya Schiwy, Andrea Canessa, Arturo Arias, and Kim Díaz.

Chapter 5 reflects on national identity, gender, age, race, ethnicity, socioeconomic class, and language in Venezuelan director Kaori Flores Yonekura's *Nikkei: Un viaje extraordinario* (Nikkei: An extraordinary trip; 2014) and Argentine director Cecilia Kang's *Mi último fracaso* (My latest failure; 2016). Flores Yonekura's film shows scenes both in Venezuela and Japan and Kang's in Argentina and Korea. This chapter considers the directors' depictions of the power structures that exert pressure on the subjects of the two documentary films. Additionally, the chapter explores how Flores Yonekura and Kang approach their documentary films from subjective and affective perspectives in order to explore their own and their other subjects' identities. Concepts of transculturality and internationality are key to these directors' representations of intersectionality as they explore the interstitial nature of identity and belonging to more than one national and cultural community. This final chapter's look at intersectionality in Flores Yonekura's and Kang's films highlights the ideas of Schroeder Rodríguez, Won K. Yoon, Crenshaw, Hurtado, Viveros Vigoya, Collins, Bilge, Avtar Brah, Pablo Piedras, Diana Paladino, and Beatriz Sarlo.

These five in-depth studies of Latin American and US Latinx film and television offer a wide-ranging perspective on the junctions of gender, race, ethnicity, sexuality, age, class, national and regional origin, and language in the respective creators' works. In looking at these particular films and series, this book offers a unique view of intersectionality in female adolescence and young adulthood in Latin America and the US Latinx context. Furthermore, the forthcoming analyses feature theoretical work directly from Latin American and US Latinx theorists. The analysis of visual representations of intersectionality in this book provides evidence for the importance of female adolescence and young adulthood as a metaphorical site for identity struggles, institutional and societal oppression, and agency.[65]

CHAPTER 1

AUDACITY, INTELLIGENCE, AND INDIGENOUS CONNECTIONS

Patricia Arriaga-Jordán's *Juana Inés*

AT THE BEGINNING OF *Mujer que sabe latín*... (A woman who knows Latin...), Rosario Castellanos declares that in the course of history—a record of men's accomplishments—woman has been a myth.[1] According to the Mexican writer and theorist, anything that falls outside of this history, including women's achievements, "pertenece al reino de la conjetura, de la fábula, de la leyenda, de la mentira" (belongs to the kingdom of conjecture, of fables, of legends, of lies).[2] Whether relegated to a pedestal or an enclosure, Castellanos sees women's place in history erased, waved off as unreal. Moreover, as the title of her collection of essays implies, intelligent women are not only erased from history but also punished for even attempting to be included.[3] Thus was the fate of the Mexican seventeenth-century nun and poet Sor Juana Inés de la Cruz, who in life accomplished a feat almost unknown in her time, that of transcontinental acclaim as a writer. Nevertheless, Sor Juana suffered greatly for her intelligence and fame and would not have made it into the history books had it been solely up to the men in charge of her life. Sor Juana has been the focus of many scholarly and creative works both within and outside of Mexico. This chapter examines one of the most recent representations, Mexican producer and director Patricia Arriaga-Jordán's television series *Juana Inés*. In the process, the chapter explores Sor Juana's poetry, critics' debates on her use of Nahuatl, gender, the female body, and intersectional theories; and Minh-ha's theories of speaking and listening in *D-Passage: The Digital Way* as they relate to specific scenes in the series and from the following perspectives: the protagonist's audacity, precocious intelligence, and connections to Indigenous language and culture. Accordingly, this chapter will analyze the intersectional nature of the protagonist's identity in the streaming series to understand why she was punished and made to sacrifice her passion for knowledge. The chapter argues that an intersectional lens reveals Arriaga-Jordán's depiction of the structural and societal oppression that affected Sor Juana's identity and agency. As the series is a historical biopic, this analysis underscores both Arriaga's depiction of the protagonist and the life and writing of the historical figure of Sor Juana. Including a historical biopic relates to Lugones' argument that identity in Latin America is based on historical specificity as it allows for a study of both seventeenth-century and contemporary intersectional identity factors in Mexico.[4]

Juana Inés is a seven-episode series created and produced by Patricia Arriaga-Jordán and directed by Arriaga-Jordán, Emilio Maillé, and Javier Peñalosa.[5] It was co-produced by Canal Once and Bravo Films in Mexico in 2016 and acquired by Netflix in 2017. It has received numerous awards at the Crystal Screens Festival in Mexico City, among them Best Series and Director.[6] The series portrays the life of the seventeenth-century Mexican nun and poet Sor Juana Inés de la Cruz (played by Arantza Ruiz as the younger Juana Inés in episodes 1–3 and Arcelia Ramírez starting in episode 4), and, much like Walter Salles's *Los diarios de motocicleta* (*The Motorcycle Diaries*), the first three episodes delve into the early years before she becomes an icon. While Argentine director María Luisa Bemberg's film *Yo, la peor de todas* (I, the worst of all; 1990)—also based on Sor Juana and on Octavio Paz's socio-historic essay *Sor Juana Inés de la Cruz, o, Las trampas de la fe* (Sor Juana Inés de la Cruz, or, The traps of faith; 1982)—is a closed depiction of the historical character confined within the walls of the convent, Arriaga-Jordán's version in the series is based on Sor Juana's day-to-day reality in New Spain from when she is young until her death.[7] Arriaga-Jordán's main character is bolder, and the series is more explicit about her romantic and physical relationship with the vicereine in later episodes. Arriaga-Jordán also emphasizes the protagonist's connections to Indigenous language and culture. This chapter's examination of adolescence focuses on the young Juana Inés in the first three episodes of Arriaga-Jordán's series, underscoring the character's audacity, precocious intelligence, and Indigenous connections.[8] There is a concerted intersectional connection in the series between gender, age, and Indigenous cultures.

The historical Sor Juana Inés de la Cruz was born Juana Inés de Asbaje either in 1648 or 1651 (date disputed) in San Miguel Nepantla at the feet of the two volcanoes Popocatépetl and Iztaccíhuatl to Pedro Manuel de Asbaje, a Spanish captain, and Isabel Ramírez Santillana. She spent much of her childhood at her maternal grandfather's hacienda in Panoayan. This is significant because she would have interacted daily with the Indigenous workers/slaves on the hacienda, learning the Nahuatl language and culture in the process. Georges Baudot refers to Nahuatl as "aquel idioma armonioso que acunara su infancia de niña campesina y que fuera el eco sabroso y cómplice de sus juegos al entrar en el mundo" (that harmonious language that would have cradled her countryside childhood and that would have been the rich echo and accomplice of her games entering the world).[9] Juana Inés was precocious and convinced her sister's tutor to teach her to read. While she was exposed to Indigenous culture, she also had access to her grandfather's library, which would have contained Occidental classics. The young girl read extensively, and when she visited her aunt's house in Mexico City, according to María Dolores Bravo Arriaga: "la joven Juana tiene fama de ser un portento de conocimiento, tanto, que se pensaba que su sabiduría era infusa, es decir, inspirada por Dios y no adquirida por el estudio" (the young Juana is known for being a wonder of knowledge, so much so, that it was thought that her wisdom was innate, that is to say, inspired by God and not acquired through studies).[10] As a young girl, Juana Inés joined the royal court of the viceroys, the Marquesses of Mancera. One significant event during this time was when the viceroy gathered the most important intellectuals of the time in Mexico City to examine Juana Inés's intelligence, an examination in which the young girl astonished with her powers of intellect. In 1667, Juana Inés joined the Carmelite order; however, the severity of this order and her delicate health led her to change to the convent of Saint Jerónimo in 1669. The subsequent viceroys, the Marquesses de la Laguna, were her protectors during much of her life in the convent and succored her writing through dissemination as well as political support. This support was much-needed, as the nun and poet suffered from the hostile attentions of the Archbishop Francisco Aguiar y Seijas, of whom Bravo Arriaga says: "Este personaje odiaba a las mujeres, y es lógico suponer que a Sor Juana la detestara más todavía, debido a su fama, su genio creador y por ser una religiosa que se salía de los límites" (this person hated women, and it is logical to suppose that he detested Sor Juana even more, due to her fame, her creative genius, and because she was a nun that defied limits).[11] Sor Juana's writings were well-known during her time both in New and Old Spains, as she had benefactors who disseminated her work. There was much controversy around the fact that a woman—young, at that—and a nun would receive so much attention for her intellectual contributions. As Gloria Anzaldúa says, "A woman who writes has power. And a woman with power is feared."[12] After supposedly renouncing her writings, Sor Juana died on April 17, 1695, of what is thought to have been typhus, subsequent to having contracted the disease while caring for other sisters in her convent.[13]

Arriaga-Jordán's series, *Juana Inés*, begins in 1664, in a flashback of when the protagonist arrives at the viceroys' court in New Spain to win favor as a lady-in-waiting. The first three episodes depict the young protagonist in what seem to be flashbacks of the older, ailing Sor Juana at age forty-four. The first episode of the series, "Miradme al menos" (At least look unto me), introduces many of the themes relating to gender and audacity that will be repeated throughout the series and that are the focus of much of this essay.[14] More specifically, the first episode portrays the following actions taken by Juana Inés: her audacious interactions with a priest and a clerk at court, reciting a poem in Nahuatl, entering the library without permission, and the well-known scene in which forty of the top male scholars of the time test her intelligence. This last scene celebrates Sor Juana as a proto-feminist icon for her intelligence and wit. The second episode, "Para el alma no hay encierro" (There is no confinement for the soul), explores the sensual interest that the vicereine has in Juana Inés, an exploration that is more physically explicit than in Bemberg's film.[15] This episode also includes a scene in which Sor Juana meets her confessor with her legs provocatively spread out. The third episode, "Lágrimas negras de mi pluma" (Black tears from my pen), incorporates moments in which men are behind the scenes, making decisions about women, especially regarding Sor Juana.[16] This episode also depicts how Sor Juana's fame as a writer is problematic for the Catholic Church and the male figures surrounding her. The remainder of the episodes (4–7) portray the adult Sor Juana, her struggles as a thinking woman in the convent, her life as a writer, her relationships with other women, flashbacks to her childhood, and her final and apparent denunciation of her passion for writing.[17] This chapter will focus on the first three episodes and the adolescent Juana Inés, particularly her audacity, precocious intelligence, and Indigenous connections. Adolescent Juana Inés's intersectional identity made her even more of a target; she was young, *criolla*, female, and what at the time would have been termed "illegitimate."[18] Audacity, precocious intelligence, and a connection to Indigenous culture would have been accepted and most likely celebrated in a young, male, "legitimate" son of Spain. However, for Juana Inés, her varying identity markers intersect in ways that induce disapproval and even animosity from the male religious figures who would have been considered her superiors.

THE AUDACITY AND PRECOCIOUS INTELLIGENCE OF JUANA INÉS

Arriaga-Jordán's young Juana Inés is audacious; she defies the idea of a submissive colonial Mexican woman. The protagonist challenges the social, religious, and gender norms of her time in ways that are bold and surprising, especially for contemporary viewers who have conventional ideas of what a young woman in the seventeenth-century would be like. Arriaga-Jordán accentuates this aspect of the adolescent Juana Inés in the first part of her series. Taking cues from Arriaga-Jordán's feminist treatment of Sor Juana's story, this chapter uses another contemporary lens— namely intersectionality—to analyze both the protagonist and historical figure. There are three moments in the first episode of *Juana Inés* where we hear the words "¿Me puede mirar cuando le hablo?" (Can you look at me when I speak to you?) The first corresponds to the protagonist's arrival at court when her future confessor, Antonio Núñez de Miranda (theology professor, Inquisition assessor, and the viceroys' confessor), runs into her while he is walking. The young Juana Inés says: "Vuestra reverencia, le ruego que me perdone" (Your reverence, I beg you to forgive me); however, the man will not look at her. Directly following this, we see that this is a flashback she is experiencing when she is older and sick on her death bed, with the words spoken in the background: "¿Me puede mirar cuando le hablo?" The second time we hear these words is when Juana Inés enters the palace and approaches the clerk, seeking an audience at court. The clerk ignores her, and she leans her head down level to his and directly asks him: "¿Me puede mirar cuando le hablo?" This time, Juana Inés is much more direct, and this moment presages her general attitude at court, which will be one of audacity and defiance. Finally, the third time, we hear the question rephrased when Núñez de Miranda continues to look away as they converse about her recitation. Arriaga-Jordán's young Juana Inés is much bolder than Bemberg's Sor Juana and willfully defiant of authority in general and male authority in particular. In the court, when one of the other ladies-in-waiting tells her she must not be in the library, she replies, "¿que no somos seres racionales como los hombres?" (Are we not rational beings like men?) While this reflects the same general sentiment of Sor Juana's words in Bemberg's film when she gives her final class to her young, female students, Arriaga-Jordán's protagonist is still brasher in her defiance. Not only does she insist on being in the library, but she also finds a way to take the other lady-in-waiting's position as tutor to the viceroy's daughter, providing her with almost complete access to the tomes.[19]

Taking a closer look, the first of these moments is close to the beginning of the series, when Juana Inés arrives at court. She is walking and looking up at the building when Núñez de Miranda runs into her and exclaims in an irritated voice: "¡Ay, niña!" (Oh, young lady!) This is an interesting scene because it involves either a flashforward or a flashback, depending on your perspective. When they collide, the image cuts to an older nun, sick in bed, who identifies herself as Juana Inés; it is in her voice that we hear the words "¿Me puede mirar cuando le hablo?" as we see the image cut back to the younger protagonist. After this, Núñez de Miranda waves her off with a disdainful hand gesture and moves past. This first interaction between the two characters introduces elements that will be apparent not only in their future relationship but also in Juana Inés's character in Arriaga-Jordán's series. First, the voice of the older Juana Inés expresses the initial confusion she feels about the man not being able to look her in the eyes. This will later turn into defiance, as we will see in the next scene where we hear these same words. Second, Núñez de Miranda's derision is palpable in the way he refuses to acknowledge her by looking into her face, the tone of his voice when he chastises her for his own error, and the way he dismissively waves her away. While Juana Inés is not aggressive at all in this first interaction, she seems to quickly realize that she is alone at court and must be mentally nimble and tough in order to survive. This is certainly clear in her next interaction when she enters and requests an audience, directing herself to a man sitting

FIGURE 1.1. Juana Inés asks Núñez de Miranda "¿Me puede mirar cuando le hablo?" (Can you look at me when I speak to you?) Juana Inés (2016).

at a desk. When she makes this request, the man does not look up or acknowledge her words; again, we hear the same phrase but this time the young Juana Inés says them in an assertive tone: "¿Me puede mirar cuando le hablo?" Before this, she spends a good deal of time introducing herself and outlining her connections while the man at the desk ignores her. After several attempts to explain her position and request, Juana Inés raises her voice, sets her jaw, looks directly at the man, and repeats the question. The question is repeated a third time in different wording when Núñez de Miranda awkwardly praises her for her poetry recitation. She respectfully responds to his praise, and when he still does not look at her, she says, "Su ilustrístima, ¿sí ve?" (Your Grace, can you see?), to which he responds, "Cuando hay algo que vale la pena mirar, por supuesto; que no es el caso" (When there is something worth looking at, of course; which is not the case). Arriaga-Jordán underscores a theme that recurs later in the series: the idea that women are lesser beings and, in fact, evil, and must be controlled. During the Spanish Inquisition, this sentiment was particularly acute, and the historical Sor Juana was a marked victim. Moreover, it becomes apparent in the series that Sor Juana's transcontinentally recognized talent and precocious intelligence will make her a target for the men in charge of regulating the religious aspects of New Spain and the lives of nuns in particular.

There is one more moment in the first episode that encapsulates the young Juana Inés's audacity, namely, when she enters the court library without permission. She is walking with another lady-in-waiting, and they pass a library; Juana Inés abruptly leaves the conversation and enters, astounded by the quantity of books. The other woman exclaims: "Pero, por Dios, ¿qué haces aquí? Ninguna mujer puede entrar al recinto librario" (But, for the love of God, what are you doing here? No woman can enter this library). Juana Inés responds: "¿Que no somos seres racionales como los hombres?" When she learns that only the tutor to the viceroy's daughter is allowed to enter, Juana Inés finds a way to take this job from one of the other women. On one level, this scene serves to highlight the protagonist's love of books and knowledge, showing her wonder at seeing so many books housed in one place. On another level, this scene underscores Juana Inés's audacity; she enters the room without waiting for approval and remains defiant about being in a room where women are not allowed. The boldness carries over into her general demeanor at court where, as described earlier, she must be clever and aware of her surroundings in order to endure. On a third level, this scene mirrors the historical Sor Juana's coexistence with books, first at her grandfather's estate, then through her friend Carlos de Sigüenza y Góngora, and, finally, in her own eventual, sizeable book collection. Even upon her arrival at court, Juana Inés was used to being exposed to books, reading, and learning; therefore, she saw no issue with being in the library and defied any restrictions against it.

Later in her life, the historical Sor Juana—and the protagonist of *Juana Inés*—will have her own significant library. Stephanie Kirk compares the legacies of Sor Juana Inés de la Cruz's and Juan de Palafox y Mendoza's respective libraries in the first chapter of *Sor Juana Inés de la Cruz and the Gender Politics of Knowledge in Colonial Mexico*.[20] While Palafox y Mendoza's library is a UNESCO-preserved collection, Sor Juana's was purposely dismantled and taken from her. Kirk compares the gendered realities of each of these religious historical figures, emphasizing Sor Juana's library as a transgression into the male world of knowledge and education for which the Catholic Church punished her. On the other hand, as Kirk contends: "As a powerful member of the all-male ecclesiastical elite, Palafox's library benefited from the Church's support—both economic and moral."[21] Kirk reminds the reader that Sor Juana was only able to retain her library for as long as she did because of "her globally

FIGURE 1.2. Juana Inés studies and writes in the viceroys' library. *Juana Inés* (2016).

recognized intellectual and literary talents along with the protection the viceroys afforded her."[22] The author later argues that Sor Juana "used her library to venture into intellectual territory deemed the exclusive preserve of elite white males, provoking deep fear and anxiety in the hearts and minds of some of these men."[23] Kirk also explains that Sor Juana's library was a space from which to "challenge masculine monopoly on knowledge and from where she could prepare to compete in this ambit" as she had no access to formal educational institutions as a woman.[24] Furthermore, as Kirk points out, there is no evidence of banned books in her library, so "the only inference to be drawn is that her gender rendered the books in her library dangerous."[25] Kirk's assessments of the historical Sor Juana's library underscore the temerity and the consequences of her audacity in the face of such gendered pressure. However, the historical figure Sor Juana, like the fictional character in Arriaga-Jordán's series, fought against this pressure in favor of her own natural inclination toward intellectual thought and reflection.

Sor Juana writes in "Respuesta a Sor Filotea de la Cruz": "desde que me rayó la primera luz de la razón, fue tan vehemente y poderosa la inclinación a las letras, que ni ajenas reprensiones—que he tenido muchas—, ni propias reflejas—que he hecho no pocas—, han bastado a que deje de seguir este natural impulso que Dios puso en mí."[26] This natural impulse, which began when Sor Juana was three and convinced her sister's tutor to teach her how to read, is at the heart of the writer's life as depicted in the series *Juana Inés*.[27] More to the point, for most, Sor Juana's gender meant that she should not follow this impulse as she, in fact, does to its ultimate consequences. "Respuesta" is a last attempt to clarify that she tried but failed to deny her essence as a writer and thinker. The series *Juana Inés* follows this struggle from its germ in Juana Inés's early years at court and entering the convent to Sor Juana's eventual death as a nun, apparently renouncing her earthly inclinations.

In her book, Kirk compares Sor Juana to prominent male figures of her time, focusing on such aspects as her library, her autodidactic education, her knowledge of Latin and medicine, and her views on female piety. Kirk contends: "The unquestioned exclusion of women and girls from educational institutions throughout the modern world served to mark male superiority and foster the masculine elitism that prevailed in many schools."[28] She continues: "In particular, she uses the mainstays of male elite education—Latin and demonstrated knowledge of classical authors and traditions—to showcase her 'masculine' skills."[29] In fact, Sor Juana pursued a Latinate cultural life and even surpassed many institutionally-trained men of her era.[30] Kirk also argues that Sor Juana's confessor, Núñez de Miranda, would not have approved of her intellectual pursuits and progress with Latin as a nun, which coincides with how we see him depicted in Arriaga-Jordán's series.[31] Speaking specifically about his writings on female piety, Kirk asserts: "In a number of his works destined directly for the instruction of nuns, Núñez de Miranda presents a rigidly limited model of female literacy."[32] The confessor represents the sentiment of the Church and the patriarchal societal attitude that condemned educational advancement for women, who were meant to be at home or in the convent only reading for purposes of prayer. Sor Juana transcends the confines of the convent through her writing, thus transgressing the rules set forth for women by the Catholic Church's male authorities. Kirk explains that when her work was published in Spain, she "realized the ambition that almost all colonial Mexican scholars held but few fulfilled. She thus secured a wider and more cosmopolitan audience for her intellectual and literary endeavors."[33] In so doing, she also cemented her historical status as a proto-feminist.

One of Sor Juana's most well-known poems is a sonnet about her quest for knowledge:

> En perseguirme, Mundo, ¿qué interesas?
> ¿En qué te ofendo, cuando sólo intento
> poner bellezas en mi entendimiento
> y no mi entendimiento en las bellezas?
>
> Yo no estimo tesoros ni riquezas;
> y así, siempre me causa más contento
> poner riquezas en mi pensamiento
> que no mi pensamiento en las riquezas.
>
> Y no estimo hermosura que, vencida,
> es despojo civil de las edades,
> ni riqueza me agrada fementida,
>
> teniendo por mejor, en mis verdades,
> consumir vanidades de la vida
> que consumir la vida en vanidades.

> World, in hounding me, what do you gain?
> How can it harm you if I choose, astutely
> rather to stock my mind with things of beauty,
> than waste its stock on every beauty's claim?
>
> Costliness and wealth bring me no pleasure;
> the only happiness I care to find
> derives from setting treasure in my mind,
> and not from mind that's set on winning treasure.
>
> I prize no comeliness. All fair things pay
> to time, the victor, their appointed fee
> and treasure cheats even the practiced eye.
>
> Mine is the better and the truer way:
> to leave the vanities of life aside,
> not throw my life away on vanity.[34]

In typical Sor Juanian fashion, the poet sets up a series of juxtapositions contrasting knowledge with beauty and riches, asking why she is tormented for pursuing intelligence and truth. Sor Juana wonders how it is offensive to anyone that she chooses to put her energy in her mind rather than the appearance of her body and her pursuits in truth rather than superficial vanities. This poem is an example of how Sor Juana can be easily adopted as a proto-feminist and icon for so many women in the twentieth and twenty-first centuries.[35] The ideas encompassed here echo much of Sor Juana's poetry and prose, including poems such as the one dedicated to the Portuguese intellectual, the Duchess of Aveyro, "claro honor de las mujeres, / de los hombres docto ultraje, / que probáis que no es el sexo / de la inteligencia parte."[36] Another example is in her romance "No habiendo logrado una tarde" (Not having been able to one afternoon): "Quien llega necio a pisar/de la vejez los confines,/vergüenza peina y no canas;/no años, afrentas repite."[37] This sentiment appears again in her much-acclaimed *silva* (Spanish strophe) "Primero sueño," which the subtitle introduces as an imitation of Luis de Góngora, referring to the Spanish poet's 1613 poem "Soledad primera."[38] In her long-form poem, Sor Juana scrutinizes human thirst for knowledge in the metaphor of the soul searching while the body sleeps. Here again we see the author's yearning for knowledge and her incredible capacity to narrow in on the crux of an argument, which in this case is overall triumph of reason. Of Sor Juana's pursuit of knowledge and specifically on "Primero sueño," Octavio Paz said: "The knowledge she sought was not contained in sacred books; she aspired to the integration of particular truths and insisted on the unity of all knowledge. To her the world was a problem. The universe is a vast laboratory in which the soul is lost."[39] Similarly, Melissa Fernández Chagoya, speaking of the University of the Cloister of Sor Juana, says that "Primero sueño" should be considered "la manifestación y la exigencia de libertad que surgió desde este lugar para imprimirse en la inteligencia de las mujeres" (the manifestation and exigency of liberty that arose from this place to imprint itself on women's intelligence).[40] Fernández Chagoya joins other scholars in recognizing Sor Juana's intense focus on erudition.

Each of these instances of knowledge as central to Sor Juana's writings and her vision of the world is reflected in the scene in Episode 1 of Arriaga-Jordán's series in which forty male intellectuals cross-examine Sor Juana for proof of her intelligence. The inquiry is a historical fact and also appears in Bemberg's film version. The scene in the series *Juana Inés*

FIGURE 1.3. Juana Inés sits for the cross-examination. *Juana Inés* (2016).

merges the three most salient aspects of the main character—audacity, precocious intelligence, and Indigenous connections. Juana Inés's audacity is apparent in the way she believes she is more qualified than any other to be the viceroys' daughter's tutor, even in the face of severe objections, especially from Núñez de Miranda. Her precocious intelligence is on display during this examination and delights her supporters within the narrative as well as the viewers of the series. Finally, and unlike in Bemberg's film, this sequence underscores Juana Inés's associations with Indigenous culture.

SOR JUANA'S CONNECTIONS WITH INDIGENOUS LANGUAGE AND CULTURE

Directly preceding the scene where the men test Sor Juana, there is a scene of what appears to be an Indigenous ceremony and blessing of an object that is then left at the door of the library where she is studying. She discovers the object and hides it in the bodice of her dress, which she wears to the examination. The Indigenous ceremony contrasts directly with the Catholic chapel where she prays in the palace before being examined. As Juana reaches the entrance to the large hall where everyone is waiting, the background music reflects her feelings; as an anxious-sounding melody plays, the underlying violins swell, illustrating this moment as significant and implying that she will be triumphant. When Juana enters the room, the other characters surround her, and she is encircled in an arc shot wherein the camera circles around her as the subject. The effect of this camera technique is menacing and creates a feeling of being trapped, which parallels Juana's status as a young woman with limited options. At this moment, her hope is that becoming the viceroys' daughter's tutor will afford her certain freedoms, such as unlimited access to the palace library. One of the men in the room comments: "¿Es ella? Pero, es una niña" (Is that her? But she is just a girl). Of course, this mirrors what we have heard from the Núñez de Miranda when he implies there is nothing worth looking at when he sees Juana. Another man responds to the first: "Nos preparamos para destruir un galeón de Manila y esta chalupa no va a durar ni la primera vuelta" (We prepared to destroy a Manilla galleon and this canoe will not last even the first round). As Juana sits down in the chair placed for her, alone and far from the men sitting in rows of raised seats in front of her, the camera again performs an arc shot, but this time from behind the main character, highlighting her isolation and the intimidating presence of the male scholars.[41] What follows are a series of shots of Juana successfully answering complicated questions on a great variety of academic topics, both religious and secular. In one of her answers regarding the differences between the sexes, she explains the belief at the time that the female brain was smaller and less developed than the male brain. Of course, her performance during the examination is a direct challenge to this assumption, as Arriaga-Jordán makes evident. When the cross-examination is done, the same man who said Juana would not last one round replies to the viceroy that they will not find a better tutor for their daughter. As the narrative of this scene comes full circle with these words, Arriaga-Jordán holds Juana up as an example of exceptional intelligence that proves the capabilities of women's minds. Within the context of Juana Inés' time, the young woman was seen as a dangerous exception to the rule of male intellectual superiority. In the time period of the series' release, in the twenty-first century, the main character is rescued as an icon for Latin American feminism. As viewers, we can celebrate vicariously through Juana Inés the triumph of her intellect over patriarchal and oppressive attitudes toward women, both in the seventeenth century and today. Moreover, like Arriaga-Jordán's feminist reading, a decidedly contemporary approach—intersectionality—allows us to see the various aspects of the young woman's identity and how they traverse within a specific patriarchal, racial, and colonial system.

Paul Julian Smith, in his review essay of Arriaga-Jordán's series, places *Juana Inés* within the context of Mexican television, maintaining that biopics have received little attention in Mexico. Smith compares the series to Bemberg's film, also noting the more explicit lesbian relationship in later episodes of Arriaga-Jordán's representation.[42] Moreover, Smith contextualizes the series within the current women's and queer movements in Mexico and describes the negative reactions of the clergy as well as some literary scholars to this fictionalized depiction of Sor Juana. The critic references the protagonist's use of Nahuatl as well as the series' attention to race in Mexico. He also recognizes Arriaga-Jordán's attention to Sor Juana as a cultural icon: "Like the subjects of many modern biopics, Sor Juana was a proto-celebrity in her own lifetime, praised as the 'Tenth Muse' (antiquity boasted only nine)."[43] He describes the series as "overtly feminist (or perhaps protofeminist), portraying as it does a resistant subject who lived in a macho society far more oppressive than that of modern Mexico."[44] Smith references the transparently feminist two-hundred-peso banknote: "attacking as it does 'foolish men' who blame women for the faults for which men themselves are responsible. Taking its cue from its celebrated subject and taking up its place in a Mexican television scene that can sometimes seem as claustrophobic as a colonial convent, *Juana Inés* the series, like Juana Inés the woman, is a bold and original innovator."[45] Arriaga-Jordán's depiction of Sor Juana—the poet's audacity and unapologetic intelligence—emphasizes elements of the historical figure that are celebrated today as feminist. Furthermore, the series underscores a connection to Indigenous culture that has largely been overlooked by other depictions, and which harkens to Mexico's modern-day reckoning with race and ethnicity.[46] The series pointedly emphasizes the intersectional site of the protagonist's identity to highlight the structural oppressions both of the poet's seventeenth-century society as well as contemporary Mexico.[47]

Before analyzing the scenes relating to Indigenous connections in Arriaga-Jordán's *Juana Inés*, it will be useful to consider what has been written about the historical Sor Juana's contact with Indigenous language and culture, including the two poems she wrote in Nahuatl. Many have written about Sor Juana's work, including Ángel María Garibay, Octavio Paz, Margo Glantz, Luis Leal, Georges Baudot, Sara Poot Herrera, among several others. Her extensive oeuvre includes sacred and profane poetry in various forms, including romances, *redondillas*, epigrams, *décimas*, sonnets, *liras*, *silvas*, theater, and essays. Particularly controversial for her time, Sor Juana practiced Biblical hermeneutics, traditionally attributed to only male religious scholars in the seventeenth century. She is considered a Baroque writer and her work was heavily influenced by classical Latin (she also wrote poetry in Latin) and, to a certain extent, Greek sources; her contemporaries, such as Calderón de la Barca; as well as Indigenous sources. Angelina Muñiz-Huberman explains: "Sus lecturas podían oscilar de las clásicas griegas y latinas a los textos herméticos, del estudio de los mitos prehispánicos a los sermones de los teólogos contemporáneos de Europa y de América" (Her readings could oscillate between the Greek and Latin classics to hermeneutic texts, from the study of pre-Hispanic myths to the sermons of contemporary theologians of Europe and America).[48] The critic also signals Juan de Torquemada's *Monarquía Indiana* as one of the poet's favorite works and says that she would have been familiar with the Nahuatl manuscripts collected by Carlos de Sigüenza y Góngora.[49] Moreover, Muñiz-Huberman reminds us that the first missionaries conserved the languages, legends, and histories of the Indigenous populations: "Estos libros que se escribieron sobre la historia del México antiguo fueron conocidos y estudiados por Sor Juana" (These books that were written about the history of ancient Mexico were known and studied by Sor Juana).[50] María Socorro Tabuenca examines *El cetro de José* and, referring to the pre-Colombian codices, the scholar theorizes: "Debido al carácter intelectual y americano de la jerónima, es muy probable que haya tenido en sus manos estos libros y códices, y los haya asimilado de tal manera que sutilmente nos entrega en los escritos mencionados extractos del pensamiento precolombino, sobre todo del que se refiere a la creación del mundo" (Due to the intellectual and American character of the Jerome nun, it is very probable that she would have had in her hands these books and codices, and that she would have assimilated them in such a way that she subtly offers to us in the mentioned writings extracts of pre-Colombian thought, above all from that which refers to the creation of the world).[51] The critic agrees with those who assume Sor Juana had an intimate connection with Indigenous language and culture.

All of this leads us to the two *tocotines* in question, written, performed, and published in Nahuatl. What follows is the first:

> Tla ya timohuica,
> totlazo Zuapilli,

maca ammo, Tonantzin,
titechmoilcahuíliz.
Ma nel in Ilhuícac
huel
timomaquítiz,
¿amo nozo quenman
timotlalnamíctiz?

In moayolque mochtin
huel motilinizque;
tlaca amo, tehuatzin
ticmomatlaníliz.
Ca mitztlacamati
motlazo Pilzintli,
mac tel, in tepampa
xicmotlatlauhtili.
Tlaca ammo
quinequi,
xicmoilnamiquili

ca monacayotzin
oticmomaquiti.
Mochichihualayo
oquimomitili,
tla motemictía
ihuan Tetepitzin.
Ma mopampantzinco
in moayolcatintin,
in itla pohpoltin,
tictomacehuizque.

Totlatlácol mochtin
tïololquiztizque;
Ilhuícac tïazque,
timitzittalizque;
in campa cemícac
timonemitíliz,
cemícac mochíhuaz
in monahuatiltzin.

If you leave,
our precious lady,
our mother, let it not be
that you forget us.
Although in Heaven
you will rejoice,
will you not perhaps
remember us?

All your family
will suffer greatly
if you yourself do not
reach out your hand to them
He obeys you,
your precious Son
thus for people's sake
plead with him.
If he does not want to listen
remind him
that your flesh
you gave to him.
Your breast
he drank of,
if he was to be satisfied
when he was small
Because of you
those who are your family
those who are clean
we will become deserving.

All our sins
we will throw out;
to Heaven we will go,
we will see you.
Everywhere and forever
will you live,
forever will be done
your will.[52]

The *tocotines* appeared in sets of *villancicos* composed to celebrate the feast of the Assumption in 1676 and the feast of San Pedro Nolasco in 1677 in Mexico City and were later published in Sor Juana's *Inundación Castálida* in 1689.[53] Martha Lilia Tenorio explains the format of the poems in which the *tocotines* appear, the *ensalada*, or *ensaladilla*: "Es una composición extensa que contiene un relato en el cual se van intercalando otros textos. . . . Es una especie de juego poético-musical caracterizado por su variedad: parte del juego está en los continuos cambios de tono, de metro, de estrofas, de lengua" (It is an extended composition that contains a story in which other texts are interspersed. . . . It is a type of poetic-musical game characterized by its variety: part of the game is in the continuous changes of tone, meter, stanzas, and language).[54] Within the larger composition of the *ensalada* is the *villancico*: a popular poetic composition containing hexasyllables and octosyllables inside of a type of chorus that introduces the theme of the composition. Sor Juana's *villancicos* were religious and celebratory by nature and, as Luis Leal explains, they were unique in their inclusion of popular poetic forms such as the *jácara* and the *tocotín*.[55] In particular, the *tocotín* was a musical Baroque form popular in New Spain, which was traditionally set to dance and contained either Spanish or Nahuatl or both. Of the two existing *tocotines* that we have from Sor Juana, one is entirely in Nahuatl and the other in Spanish and Nahuatl. Georgina Sabat-Rivers clarifies how the sections of Sor Juana's *villancicos* in Nahuatl performed in the Cathedral would have been for the Indigenous and *criollo* audience members and specifically for the Indigenous community members that would not have followed the rest of the *villancicos* in Spanish.[56] Beatriz M. Robinson writes of how significant the audience is for these presentations, emphasizing that Sor Juana's creations would have had to be authentic because her Indigenous audiences would have understood the texts in Nahuatl as well as the dances and rhythms: "Se tendrían que hacer los ajustes necesarios que el espacio performático catedralicio ameritara, pero no podía padecer de ninguna manera de falta de autenticidad, ya que los verdaderos críticos del momento performativo eran los propios indígenas."[57] Luis Leal and Georges Baudot see the play between the two languages in the second *tocotín* as emblematic of a purposeful interplay between Indigenous and occidental linguistic organization.[58]

The protest Baudot sees in Sor Juana's *tocotines* is at the heart of modern scholarly debates about the extent of the poet's knowledge of Nahuatl, her connection to Indigenous culture, and her intentions in presenting Indigenous voices and characters in her poetry.[59] Scholars have mixed interpretations of Sor Juana's fluency in Nahuatl, her genuine knowledge of Indigenous culture, and whether she could be considered a critic of the treatment of Indigenous communities in New Spain. According to Salvador Díaz Cintora, the Nahuatl she used in her verses was no longer the Classical version; the critic analyzes her use of the language meticulously.[60] Caroline Egan describes two sets of scholars, one that feels Sor Juana's use of Indigenous characters and Nahuatl were based on a sense of justice concerning Indigenous communities and another that feels this is more an element of introducing difference into a "universalizing Catholicism."[61] Baudot, for his part, refers to the *tocotines* and Sor Juana's "conocimiento íntimo y familiar de la lengua de Nezahualcóyotl" (intimate and familiar knowledge of the language of Nezahualcóyotl).[62] According to Muñiz-Huberman, Sor Juana is part of a period in which writers were beginning to define a Mexican nationality, including the languages and customs of different groups.[63] The critic goes even further, relating: "La monja Juana de Asbaje con su ansia de conocimiento no podía haber dejado el estudio de la lengua náhuatl y prueba de que lo dominaba es el hecho de haber escrito varios poemas en ese idioma" (The nun Juana de Asbaje with her craving for knowledge could not have left off the study of the Nahuatl language and proof that she dominated it is the fact of having written several poems in that language).[64] Baudot laments what little we do have of Sor Juana's writings in Nahuatl: "Entre las frustraciones más nostálgicas que los textos de sor Juana nos han dejado, quizá esté el no saber cuánto discurso amerindio, cuánta palabra vernácula de América han podido quedar sepultados en páginas desconocidas que no nos han llegado" (Among the most nostalgic frustrations that Sor Juana's texts have left us, perhaps is not knowing how much Amerindian discourse, how many vernacular words of the Americas could have been buried in the unknown pages that have not reached us).[65] Tabuenca, for her part, argues: "Es importante resaltar el conocimiento que tenía sor Juana de los textos precolombinos y su manera de plasmar este pensamiento tan profundo, en un público que poco o nada conocía de la herencia náhuatl" (It is important to underscore the knowledge that Sor Juana had of pre-Colombian texts and her way of portraying this profound thought, in a public that knew little or nothing of its Nahuatl inheritance).[66] For the most part, critics believe that Sor Juana had considerable knowledge of Nahuatl and a clear connection to Indigenous culture, stemming first from her early childhood relationships with Indigenous workers/slaves in her grandfather's hacienda and, second, from the co-existence during the seventeenth century of Indigenous, *criollo*, and *mestizo* cultures in New Spain.

As for Sor Juana's sense of social justice in her writings, critics are also divided. While some question whether the Catholic nun had subversive intentions, others see her as a voice for the marginalized. Caroline Egan studies the idea of lyric intelligibility and wonders if Sor Juana's inclusion of Nahuatl is more a comment on and challenge to what the poet saw as Catholicism's attempts at reaching Indigenous populations through lyrical evangelism. Tabuenca reminds us that Sor Juana squarely belongs to Occidental Christian discourse despite what readers might find that is subversive or celebratory of Indigenous culture in her writings. On the other hand, many critics see a clear intent on Sor Juana's part to criticize European dominance and violence against the Indigenous population and offer a space for the disregarded Indigenous voice. For example, in her article on Barroque parody in Sor Juana's *villancicos*, Sabat-Rivers clarifies: "su tratamiento de los personajes del indio, del negro y de la mujer, no se limita a la introducción de tipos, lenguas y formas del mundo americano, propone, a través de ellos, diferencias significativas relacionadas con el mundo social y político del Nuevo Mundo y de la metrópolis" (her treatment of the Indian, Black, and women characters, is not limited to the introduction of generic types, languages, and customs of the American world, she proposed, through them, significant differences related to the social and political world of the New World and the metropolis).[67] Sabat-Rivers goes on to say: "La poeta exige que, por su mediación, se conozca el mundo americano precolombino; obliga a su público a apreciar otros valores que le son desconocidos forzando un diálogo que pone frente a frente a una cultura antigua y valiosa agredida por la fuerza y la violencia de otra" (The poet requires that, through her mediation, the pre-Columbian American world is known; she obligates her public to appreciate other values that are unknown to them forcing a dialogue that places face to face an ancient and brave culture assaulted by the force and violence of another culture).[68] Finally, Luis Leal, looking at the idea of literary *mestizaje* in Sor Juana's work, maintains that the *mestizo* elements in her writings are enough to prove her interest in autochthonous cultures; moreover: "Con sus loas y villancicos se adelanta a su tiempo haciendo uso de recursos literarios tanto cultos como populares, lo mismo que de varias lenguas en la misma composición. Con

FIGURE 1.4. Juana Inés with habit and flower wreath. *Juana Inés* (2016).

esta literatura logra dar voz a las clases marginadas" (With her *loas* and *villancicos* she was ahead of her time making use of educated as well as popular literary means, the same as various languages in the same composition. With this literature she is able to give voice to the marginalized).[69] Leal's comments reinforce the notion that Sor Juana's writings shed light on diverse communities.

Whereas the critical debate surrounding the historical figure of Sor Juana and her knowledge and connections to Nahuatl and Indigenous cultures is still evolving, it is clear that Arriaga-Jordán's fictional protagonist in *Juana Inés* is of the second persuasion—speaking Nahuatl, displaying evident knowledge of Indigenous culture, and defending Indigenous characters as they encounter trouble in the plot. Moreover, the actress who plays the young Juana Inés, Arantza Ruiz, has darker skin and hair than other actresses who have played the role, including Assumpta Serna (a European actress from Barcelona, Spain), in the Argentine María Luisa Bemberg's version *Yo, la peor de todas*. In this way, Arriaga-Jordán emphasizes the character's American identity (in the sense of the Americas) as opposed to a European identity. The series establishes this dichotomy from the very beginning when Juana Inés arrives at court and asks for an audience with the viceroys; a Spanish lady-in-waiting looks down on her and the tattered end of her dress and asks if she is going to present "¿Así?" (Like that?), to which the protagonist replies in the same haughty tone, "Sí, así"

(Yes, like this). This coincides with what some critics have commented about Sor Juana's work in that it corresponds to a New World, *criollo* perspective of those born in the Americas and associating themselves more with what would eventually be Mexico than with Spain. As Bravo Arriaga maintains, New Spain in the mid-seventeenth century becomes less new and less Spain, in favor of its own personality.[70] Bravo Arriaga continues: "Para distinguirla de la otra España, surge entre los criollos una serie de signos de identidad que marcan esta diferencia. . . . Surge un orgullo profundo hacia las grandes culturas indígenas prehispánicas, a las que consideran una especie de pasado clásico" (To distinguish it from the other Spain, among *criollos* a series of identity signals arises that marks this difference. . . . A profound pride arises toward the grand Indigenous pre-Columbian cultures, which they consider a type of classic past).[71] In her own poetry, Sor Juana praises her homeland, as in this poem dedicated to the Duchess of Aveyro: "Que yo, Señora, nací / en la América abundante, / compatriota del oro, paisana de los metales / adonde el común sustento / se da casi tan de balde, / que en ninguna parte más / se ostenta la tierra Madre. / De la común maldición / libres parece que nacen / sus hijos, según el pan / no cuesta al sudor afanes."[72] Sor Juana's association with Indigenous culture is emblematic of this pride in the Americas and the newly forming American identity. Furthermore, it is another aspect of what contemporary critics would study as an intersectional identity paradigm in which Sor Juana's identity is at the juxtaposition of various factors that place her within a particular oppressive system as a young woman of the Americas, not from the urban elites, and with a close connection to Indigenous cultures.[73] The following paragraphs include an analysis of three specific scenes in Arriaga-Jordán's series that highlight the protagonist's connections with Indigenous culture, including when Juana Inés recites poetry in Nahuatl at the viceroys' court; defends an Indigenous man who has been accused of stealing a candle; and receives medical treatment from an Indigenous woman.

When Juana Inés recites poetry as her introduction to the court at the beginning of the series, she enters at a moment when two young women are trying to convince each other to present. The protagonist quickly takes her place at the center of the room, facing the viceroys. It is clear that her appearance is meant to contrast with the Spanish lady-in-waiting whose cleavage is visible and who glances flirtatiously at the viceroy. After reciting a poem in riddle form that makes the audience and especially the vicereine laugh, she begins one in Nahuatl. Analyzing the *mise-en-scène*,

Juana Inés is standing toward the left and we see some audience members to the right of her alternately sitting or standing. The fourth person standing is an Indigenous man, and when she ends the first line of the poem, the camera cuts to his face turning toward her in apparent recognition of Nahuatl. The camera returns to Juana Inés and then moves to a Spanish woman in the court who shakes her head at her, implying that she has committed an error. She nervously stops the recital; however, the vicereine chuckles and claps her hands as she had done for the previous poem. At first, she is the only one applauding yet the rest join in and the camera follows Juana Inés's glance at the Indigenous man, who is smiling at her, and then toward the viceroys. Ending the scene, the vicereine asks who she is and declares that she wants her as a lady-in-waiting, fulfilling the protagonist's wish to be accepted at court. This scene reveals a series of aspects present in the viceroyal court in New Spain, including the predominance and feelings of superiority of the Spanish, rather than *criolla*, ladies-in-waiting, and the simultaneous Indigenous presence in the room but disavowal of Indigenous language and culture. First, Arriaga-Jordán clearly juxtaposes Juana Inés with the Spanish lady-in-waiting who seems to be the Viceroy's favorite. This is apparent in their two distinct modes of dressing; the other woman is wearing a tight-fitting, off-the-shoulder dress that reveals much of her cleavage, whereas Juana Inés wears a dress that covers her chest. Moreover, her choice of materials for reciting is much more audacious than the other woman's; she regales them with linguistic riddles that border on inappropriate and that have the vicereine laughing loudly and even speaks in Nahuatl, a language of the Americas that the Spanish lady in waiting most likely does not understand, much less speak. In fact, one of the only people who does understand what she is reciting is the Indigenous man in the audience, who smiles at her appreciatively. It is telling that he is present but silent, and his language is silenced when Juana Inés uses it, as well. The inference is that members of the Indigenous communities were an everyday part of courtly life in New Spain; however, they were to remain silent, and their language and culture were not to be celebrated. While it appears that Juana Inés incurred in this social faux pas unintentionally, later we see her insist on her connection to the Indigenous community.

There is a scene, also in the first episode of the series, where we see a white Spaniard interrogating three people of color—a young, Indigenous woman; a man of African descent; and an Indigenous man: "¿Quién ha tomado las candelas? ¿Quién ha tomado las candelas?" (Who took the candles? Who took the candles?). The first two look down at the ground while the Spaniard frowns and holds a whip. He then moves on to the shirtless Indigenous man, kneeling with a look of agony on his face and bloody whip marks on his back. Juana Inés is studying in the library and notices a sign, which she approaches with a furtive look: "Librorum Prohibitorum" (Prohibited Books). As she is about to take one of the books off the shelf, she overhears someone being whipped and goes outside, saying: "¡Basta! No puedo permitirse cometer una injusticia" (Enough! I cannot allow an injustice to be committed). She goes on to say that she saw the candles in the pantry and took them without thinking, taking the blame. She then says to the kneeling man: "Disculpa, Jacinto, si te metí en problemas" (I'm sorry, Jacinto, if I got you in trouble). The Spaniard responds: "No tenéis que disculparse con ellos. Vos sois una dama de la corte y él es sólo un indio" (There's no reason for you to apologize. You are a lady of the court and he's a mere Indian). Clearly, there are many elements to discuss in this scene, starting with the fact that she risks her place at the court by defending the man being whipped. Secondly and most significantly, she calls him by name—Jacinto—when she apologizes to him. The deference she shows to the Indigenous man incenses the Spaniard, who does not believe that "a mere Indian" deserves her attention and courtesy. Of course, the most obvious aspect of the scene is the image of a white man cruelly interrogating the three people of color and whipping the Indigenous man relentlessly; they are simply objects from his point of view. During the Conquest of the Americas, one of the most heated debates was whether the Indigenous populations had souls and were worthy of Catholic conversion. Bartolomé de las Casas argues in his chronicle that they do have a soul; however, many of the Spaniards who arrived questioned this idea. In his book *Racismo en México*, Carrillo Trueba explains that the Europeans who arrived in Mexico based their notion that the Indigenous populations were subhuman on their understanding of humanity from the origin stories in the Bible, in which they would not have appeared, along with their resistance to adopting European ways.[74] While others, including de las Casas, refuted these ideas, many also disseminated the image of the Indigenous person as barbarian or childlike, which fostered the Spaniards' feelings of superiority. Knowing of this debate helps to better understand the dynamics in this scene; much as the humanity of slaves was questioned in the United States, the same was deliberated in New Spain. Thus, from this standpoint, it is audacious and brave of Juana Inés' character to defend the man being whipped. It is also significant that this was during the time of the Spanish Inquisition, when anything and anyone thought to be against the Catholic Church would be targeted. Here we see the protagonist purposefully connecting herself with the Indigenous community at whatever cost. She no longer silences herself as she did in the original audience with the viceroys.

A comparison could be made between this depiction of Sor Juana and the figure of Malintzin. When discussing Malintzin, Margo Glantz proposes:

> Para los indígenas ella es definitivamente la dueña del discurso, y él, Cortés, el Capitán Malinche, jefe de los españoles, un hombre despojado de repente de su virilidad; carece de lengua porque sus palabras carecen de fuerza, es decir de inteligibilidad, sólo las palabras que emite una mujer que cumple con excelencia su oficio de lengua . . . alcanzan a su destinatario: esa operación de lenguaje actúa sobre la virilidad y enturbia la que debiera ser una estricta categoría, la de lo masculino.[75]

Malintzin, Hernán Cortés's interpreter, had the power of language, as Glantz argues. This linguistic power meant that she was able to communicate with other Indigenous people in a way that Cortés could not. Glantz views her as taking on the masculine authority conferred to her by language and the ability to communicate, feminizing Cortés in the process. Moreover, Malintzin performs her job as "lengua"—interpreter, go-between, representative of language itself—well, thus setting up another confrontation not only between masculine and feminine but also between European and Indigenous. In a way, Arriaga-Jordán's Juana Inés is like Glantz's Malintzin; they are both intersectional figures. As we have seen, Juana Inés's intersectional identity as a young, *criolla* woman who was considered "illegitimate" affected the way men treated her and how they had power over her. Similarly, Malintzin's intersectional identity as a young, Indigenous woman meant that Cortés and other men had authority over her. On the other hand, both women are adept at harnessing the power of language and communication. While Malintzin interprets and communicates for Cortés during the Conquest, Juana Inés studies languages, recites, and writes during the colonial period. Both women are confined by the men who have authority over them, Cortés over Malintzin and Núñez de Miranda and other male religious figures over Juana Inés. However, both women also find a way to use their linguistic abilities for personal gain and power. In Arriaga-Jordán's series, Juana Inés speaks directly to the Indigenous peoples in the court, accepts their cultural offerings, and defends them through her use of language. As we will see in this next scene, the Indigenous characters in the series also accept Juana Inés.

The scene in which the Indigenous woman heals the protagonist appears at the end of episode three. At the beginning of this episode, the camera focuses on a woman performing a ritual with stone figures in front of a Catholic altar and speaking in Nahuatl, at one point saying Juana's name. A hooded figure is seen watching in the shadows, purportedly a nun, who then begins to shout: "¡El demonio! ¡El demonio!" (The Devil! The Devil!). The juxtaposition is clear here between the Catholic and Indigenous faiths; likewise, any remaining and open Indigenous rituals during the colonial period would have been considered sacrilege. Later in the episode, after the vicereine finds out that Juana Inés is deathly ill, we see a Spanish doctor practicing what was called bloodletting, a Western medical technique of the time. After the doctor tells her that there is nothing else he can do, we hear her whispering to a lady-in-waiting: "yo he escuchado que los indios tienen remedios que nosotros no" (I have heard that the Indians have remedies we do not have), after which the other woman expresses surprise that she would recur to "prácticas prohibidas" (prohibited practices). In the culmination of this episode, the Vicereine invites the woman who had been performing the stone ritual to help Juana Inés. The woman begins her preparations, and we see Jacinto helping in the background. This scene is directly juxtaposed with the one of Juana Inés in the bed, her blood being let by the Spanish doctor. Here, she is wrapped tightly in cloth and the woman explains that her *nahual* (personal guardian spirit) is trapped, while she asks them to undress her and proceeds to brush her with green foliage and sing the word "Tonantzin" ("Our Sacred Mother" in Nahuatl).[76] Whereas, with the European doctor, the medicine he practices is Western and male-centric, the healing practiced by this woman is Indigenous and woman-centric, connected to the goddess of earth and fertility. The healing woman drips the blood of a snake over Juana Inés's body while still softly singing "Tonantzin." The camera loses focus, and we see her bloodied hand working over the protagonist's body.

Throughout these two contrasting scenes, there are two questions that surface: first, whether Juana Inés will survive and second, who has ownership over her body. It is clear that Núñez de Miranda and the Catholic

Church, in general, feel a sense of ownership over Juana Inés's body because of her commitment to a convent. The vicereine has a sense of ownership over Juana Inés as her daughter's tutor and, moreover, would like to be her lover. Finally, there is a question throughout the series about whether Juana Inés herself is the owner of her own body. Returning to the first element, Indigenous healing does what Occidental medicine cannot, and the healing woman saves Juana Inés. As for the second, the question of ownership over her body, this will continue to be a conflict throughout Arriaga-Jordán's series and, in fact, throughout the historical Sor Juana's life. Ownership over the female body, whether metaphorical or literal, constitutes a large part of feminism's examination of gender dynamics. Within feminism, the female body is the focus of such theories as the materiality/immateriality of the female body (Susan Bordo / Judith Butler); the female body and the abject (Julia Kristeva); the gaze in film and the female body (Laura Mulvey); female spectatorship (Chris Strayer) as well as, how the image of the female body intersects with race, ethnicity, sexuality, and socioeconomic class (Cherríe Moraga, Gloria Anzaldúa); among others. Added to this is the age of the protagonist in these first episodes of the series; Juana Inés is young, and her youth contributes to the power factors at play over her body. In the current discussion of Juana Inés in Arriaga-Jordán's series, the protagonist's body is contested ground—is it meant for Occidental or Indigenous medicine, is it the crown's through the figure of the vicereine, or is it the Church's as represented by Núñez de Miranda? Moraga and Anzaldúa would recognize that Juana Inés's intersectional identity—female, *criolla*, young, "illegitimate"—affects how authority figures assume power over her.[77] Julia Kristeva would view the confessor's discomfort with the young woman's body as emblematic of the abject nature of the female body in its ambivalence of boundaries.[78] Laura Mulvey's and Chris Strayer's theories on the gaze correspond to the erotic looks that the vicereine gives to Juana Inés and how she gazes on her as one of her possessions.[79] Finally, Moraga's and Anzaldúa's intersectional theories appeal to the manner in which authority figures in the government and the Church see Juana Inés as a pawn in certain ways, because of her identity as a young, *criolla*, "illegitimate" woman. Consequently, the other characters feel that they should be the ones to decide how Juana Inés is treated medically.

Returning to the question of the protagonist's connection to Indigenous culture, in the contemporary context, critics might say that Sor Juana was monopolizing on another culture, a sort of cultural appropriation.

This may be so; however, it is important to consider the time period and social context in which Sor Juana was writing. Indigenous communities had very little cultural voice in the development of the nation that would become Mexico. In its nascent state, Indigenous voices were not elevated on the cultural stage; therefore, Sor Juana gave Indigenous language and culture a presence it would otherwise not have had. In the context of Arriaga-Jordán's series, Indigenous language and culture are clearly visible and featured throughout. Moreover, Arriaga-Jordán's audience is contemporary Mexico, and her message speaks to current socio-political tensions in the country between Indigenous and *mestizo* communities as well as Eurocentric cultural production. In this sense, it is also valid to question whether the series is an example of cultural appropriation, as most of the Indigenous characters themselves do not have significant lines. Sor Juana is able to communicate with them; however, all these verbal interactions are within the context of the writer helping them. There are many scenes that depict Indigenous women performing rituals, such as the one that produced the plants that she takes into the examination and the one of the healing woman who cures her of her illness. Nevertheless, these characters are silent. Minh-ha, in *D-Passage: The Digital Way*, asserts the following: "'Who's speaking?' is also asking 'Who's listening?' To be aware, without closing off, of where and from where one speaks, or else of how, when, and by whom one can be heard cannot be reduced to a mere question of audience and readership."[80] First, Minh-ha creates a dialogue between who is speaking, including where and from where, and who is listening, including how and when they can hear. Her theory corresponds to Gayatri Chakravorty Spivak's question of whether the subaltern can speak. Returning to Minh-ha's theory, this sets up a multitude of perspectives in Arriaga-Jordán's series, even relating to Minh-ha's perspective on multiplicity and the importance of the passage or travelling between, a space where she proposes identity can exist.[81] Along this line of thought, the question of Sor Juana's identity is important; she is Criolla, not Indigenous, and speaks for and not with Indigenous voices.

In the case of *Juana Inés*, in one sense, the protagonist is speaking, and the Indigenous characters are not; however, in another sense, when the male religious figures speak from a place of authority, Juana Inés cannot. In terms of who is listening and even who is able to hear, the Indigenous characters are listening to Juana Inés in the series and supporting her; they hear her recite poetry in Nahuatl and they hear her defending them against cruel Spaniards. Nevertheless, most of the other characters in the series and certainly the audience are unable to listen to the Indigenous characters either because they are silent or because the other characters do not speak Nahuatl. Once again, we return to the idea of Arriaga-Jordán's intent in her representation of Indigenous culture. Historically speaking, according to Kirk: "Not until 1724 and the foundation of a convent for Indigenous women of noble lineage was the native female community present in the convent in a capacity other than servant. Within the ranks of the white women who occupied the coveted position of nuns of the black veil, key distinctions were solidified between *criolla* nuns and those born in Spain."[82] Thus, there was no historically viable way for Arriaga-Jordán to give the Indigenous characters more of a voice in the series. Similarly, the dynamic between Juana Inés and the other ladies-in-waiting plays out clearly along the lines of the divide between *criollas* and women born in Spain. Even after entering the convent, Sor Juana suffers from persecution because of her identity as someone born in the Americas.[83] Lugones's emphasis on the colonial legacy of identity in Latin America is key to understanding Sor Juana's intersectional place in seventeenth-century New Spain.

There is a difference between how the protagonist Juana Inés interacts with the Indigenous characters and how Arriaga-Jordán portrays the Indigenous characters in the series. The protagonist is portrayed as having a true connection with them, reciting poetry in fluent Nahuatl, defending them against punishment, and receiving medicinal relief from them in illness. On the other hand, although the series seems to challenge the colonial views of first peoples through the character of Juana Inés, it also includes scenes of Indigenous women silently practicing what seem to be religious ceremonies. These women have no voice in the narrative and serve to perpetuate the image of Indigenous women as passive objects. Then again, one of these women is instrumental in healing Juana Inés when she becomes very ill before leaving the first convent she joined. The vicereine essentially entrusts Juana Inés to this woman and her healing practices, thus trading Occidental for Indigenous medicine or healing. In this way, Arriaga-Jordán's series also emphasizes Juana Inés's uniquely American identity as opposed to the vicereine's European identity; the vicereine evidently does not understand the woman's ritual but somehow knows that it is what the girl needs to heal. The series implies that, as a daughter of the Americas, Juana Inés could only be cured through practices native to a land often opaque to the Spaniards. This harkens back to the protagonist keeping the sprig left at the library door in the bosom of her dress when she goes to the examination. Here again, Juana Inés, a daughter of the Americas, not only speaks Nahuatl but she also clearly believes deeply in Indigenous faith and wisdom, enough to take this token with her to one of the most important moments of her young life. As we explored earlier, while Juana Inés herself is not Indigenous, Arriaga-Jordán certainly underscores the protagonist's relationship with Indigenous philosophy, culture, medicine, and faith.

It is clear in the analyzed scenes from *Juana Inés* that Arriaga-Jordán wished to emphasize the protagonist's audacity, precocious intelligence, and connections to Indigenous language and culture. In so doing, the series creator presents a compelling examination of the intersectional nature of her identity as a young, *criolla*, "illegitimate" woman who insists on her place at the court. This coincides with the historical figure of Sor Juana as a writer and theoretical philosopher who resisted the gendered restrictions of her time to become one of the most well-known figures in Mexican history. This emphasis on gender, age, and self-reliance is central to Guerrero's and Cordero's films in the following chapter, as well.

CHAPTER 2

GENDER, CLASS, SEXUALITY, AND ETHNICITY

Aurora Guerrero's *Mosquita y Mari* and
Viviana Cordero's *No robarás . . . a menos
que sea necesario*

AN INTERSECTIONAL ANALYSIS OF Aurora Guerrero's *Mosquita y Mari* (2012) and Viviana Cordero's *No robarás . . . a menos que sea necesario* (2013) reveals the two films' emphasis on the crossroads of gender, age, sexuality, class, and ethnicity in the context of coming-of-age stories about young women. The meeting point between the two films is the protagonists' struggles due to their socioeconomic statuses, reflected even in the respective filming location choices. While the settings are different— Huntington Park, California, and Quito, Ecuador—the same intersections of identity uncover the difficulties the main characters face. More specifically, each film shows the challenging decisions and sacrifices made by adolescent girls to support their families. Understanding the complexities of the protagonists' circumstances is possible through the analysis of the intersections of their identities; looking at gender, class, sexuality, or ethnicity separately would only expose a narrow view of these young women's lives. Thus, relying on intersectional theory from the US and Latin America, this chapter examines how class intersects with gender, sexuality, and ethnicity in Guerrero's *Mosquita y Mari* and Cordero's *No robarás*. In particular, this chapter references intersectionality theorists such as Hurtado and Viveros Vigoya as well as those who engaged the same concepts before the term intersectionality was coined, including Anzaldúa and Moraga. The current analysis also references studies on Latinx film (Frederick Luis Aldama), queer studies (Mariana Ortega and David William Foster), as well as youth and punk cultures (Geovanny Narváez). This chapter argues that an intersectional approach underscores the filmmakers' and their protagonists' challenges to systemic racism, sexism, classism, and heteronormativity while revealing possibilities for identity development and agency.

Set in Southeast Los Angeles's Huntington Park, Guerrero's *Mosquita y Mari* tells the story of two adolescent girls, Yolanda "Mosquita" (Fenessa Pineda) and Mari (Venecia Troncoso), and their evolving friendship.[1] The girls navigate the world of first love, but with the added difficulty of the heteronormative restrictions of their community. Yolanda is from a middle/working-class family and Mari is from a working-class family and the young women discover they have a romantic connection beyond platonic friendship.[2] Yolanda's and Mari's parents' sacrifices for their families are passed to their children; Yolanda's parents work long hours to provide for their daughter and her future and Mari's single mother works many hours as well. Whereas Yolanda's mother asks her to sacrifice certain social experiences to stay on track in school, Mari sacrifices more for the economic security of her mother and younger sibling, secretly turning to prostitution to help pay the rent when she loses her job handing out flyers for a photography studio. The film ends with the two girls reconciling and returning to a favorite hideout; one of them traces the letters "M y M" in the window of a car, cementing their relationship as the subject of the film.

Set in Quito in the neighborhoods of Cumbayá, González Suárez, and in the area surrounding the Women's Prison el Inca, Cordero's *No robarás* narrates the story of Lucía [Vanesa Alvario], the daughter of single mother Marta [Ana María Balarezo].[3] One night, when Marta's abusive boyfriend attacks her, she pushes him in self-defense, and he falls unconscious down the stairs. Marta is imprisoned and Lucía must support her three younger siblings. Essentially a child herself, Lucía begins to steal money—something that she had criticized in her friends—to buy food and pay rent. She considers becoming a prostitute for female clients but runs away before her first encounter. Her friends in her punk band help her to rob a house, and with the money she and her siblings survive until Marta gets out of prison. The film ends at the airport, with an image of the family heading supposedly toward a new life on the coast.

The main characters of Guerrero's and Cordero's films navigate a complex web of intersecting identities and social realities. For Yolanda and Mari in Guerrero's *Mosquita y Mari*, the protagonists are Latinx adolescent females from the working and middle classes. Their age, gender, class, and ethnicity collide in ways that complicate their interactions with each other and the world. Also coinciding with Lucía's experience, Mari's ability to help provide for her family is affected by her intersecting identities.[4] Both young women make drastic sacrifices to pay for basics such as food and rent. For Lucía in *No robarás*, she negotiates her life as an adolescent female from the subsistence class with apparent Indigenous heritage. Her age, gender, class, and ethnicity influence the ways in which she lives in the world; they affect how others view and treat her. Even the possibilities of providing for herself and her younger siblings are in jeopardy because of this intersection of identities. All three—Yolanda, Mari, and Lucía—see their adolescence and budding sense of self heavily influenced by their gender, class, and ethnicity. In fact, all three must navigate their adolescent sexual curiosity within the framework and restrictions of gender, class, and ethnicity. For Yolanda and Mari, this is the working-class Latinx community in Southeast Los Angeles and for Lucía, working-class Quito.[5]

An intersectional approach to analyzing film allows for an expanded focus, recognizing that directors like Guerrero and Cordero made their films in order to highlight the multiple modes of oppression their protagonists experience. Hurtado discusses intersectionality as a way of describing the "intersections of identities in the modes of their oppression."[6] Collins and Bilge relate intersectionality theory to "how intersecting power relations influence social relations across diverse societies as well as individual experiences in everyday life."[7] For Viveros Vigoya, who focuses on corporeally lived experiences, intersectionality "es una perspectiva donde ya no se habla de la mujer, sino de las mujeres porque somos conscientes de las diferencias de clase, etnicidad, raza, generación, sexualidad, entre otras" (is a perspective where one no longer talks of Woman, but women because we are conscience of the differences of class, ethnicity, race, generation, sexuality, among others).[8] Thus, Viveros Vigoya captures the foundational premise of intersectionality theory in recognizing the differences in lived experience among women of diverse class, ethnic, racial, generational, and sexuality-based backgrounds. Viveros Vigoya discusses the dangers of considering only one aspect of identity alone when discussing oppression or reducing the issues to an arithmetic equation, emphasizing that domination is historical "y que las relaciones sociales están imbricadas en las experiencias concretas que pueden vivirse de muy variadas maneras. Los parámetros feministas universales son inadecuados para describir formas de dominación específicas en las cuales las relaciones se intrincan y se experimentan de diversas formas."[9] For Viveros Vigoya, it is essential to recognize how oppression has developed through time in a particular historical context. Moreover, the Colombian theorist emphasizes the idea of lived experiences that challenge the precepts of a universal feminist approach. The power relations and oppression discussed by Hurtado, Collins, and Bilge are specific to each particular case for Viveros Vigoya, who is speaking from an Andean postcolonial society.[10]

Theorist Audre Lorde addresses these same power relations and recognizes that using the master's tools will only make the master's house stronger; therefore, it is necessary to find an alternative.[11] In this way, intersectionality theory finds an alternative to white, middle-class feminism. By taking away the focus from gender alone, intersectional theory gets at a more exacting perspective of real, lived experiences. Furthermore, early white, middle-class feminism used a language too akin to what Lorde designates the master's tools. Theorists such as Moraga and Anzaldúa literally use another language, Spanish, and at times communicate through a more informal, nonacademic language and style in order to convey their ideas. As we will see, this style is also used by the filmmakers studied in this chapter, especially regarding youth language, slang, and the use of Spanish and English (in the case of *Mosquita y Mari*). Youth culture is a focus for both films, especially in terms of music (punk music appears in both).

In Anzaldúa and AnaLouise Keating's anthology *This Bridge We Call Home* (2002), Evelyn Alsultany articulates: "My body becomes marked with meaning as I enter public space. My identity fractures as I experience differing dislocations in multiple contexts. Sometimes people otherize me, sometimes they identify with me. Both situations can be equally problematic. Those who otherize me fail to see a shared humanity and those who identify with me fail to see differences."[12] The "differing dislocations in multiple contexts" to which Alsultany refers relate directly to the concept of intersectionality. As Alsultany contends, the body is marked as it enters public spaces; intersecting identities are physically apparent due to such things as skin color, physical traits, and dress. Furthermore, use of language marks a person in terms of nationality, race, ethnicity, socioeconomic class, gender, and physical ability. The intersecting identity factors that are exposed both physically and vocally in the public space signal to others where a person fits within socially constructed systems of power. For Alsultany, as with the other discussed theorists, identity is intersectional and visible; furthermore, it marks a person and affects how others identify or not with that person. Finally, the theorist recognizes that identification or differentiation based on visible identity demarcations is problematic; certain intersectional identity factors will be overlooked, actively ignored, or enhanced based on the viewer's perceptions.

The visibility of intersectional identity is central to Guerrero's and Cordero's films. Both directors chose their filming locations carefully to reflect the subsistence- and working-class statuses of their protagonists. Guerrero filmed *Mosquita y Mari* in Huntington Park, Southeast Los Angeles. Of her filming location, Guerrero explains: "This is a mostly immigrant, Mexican community (98 percent Mexican) with a strong identity of its own. Much of the cultural trends in Mexico, especially music and fashion, have seeped into the youth scene making this a very unique blend of Mexican immigrant and American identity."[13] Guerrero also chose Southeast LA, rather than the typical Latino story set in East LA. She felt it was a forgotten area both by the film industry and politicians.[14] The vast majority of the young cast in the film is from South East Los Angeles and were non-actors.[15] Reflecting the economic status of the film's characters, 23.6 percent of the population of Huntington Park lives below the poverty line (compared to a 12.3 percent national average).[16] Likewise, Cordero filmed *No robarás* in Quito in the neighborhoods of Cumbayá, González Suárez, and in the area surrounding the Women's Prison el Inca. In general, Quito has the highest poverty index in Ecuador.[17] Certainly, the Women's Prison el Inca is most indicative of Cordero's characters' circumstances.

MOSQUITA Y MARI

Highlighting the importance of class in an intersectional analysis of *Mosquita y Mari*, toward the beginning of Guerrero's film, the camera captures slow-motion images of Huntington Park, along Pacific Avenue— people crossing the street, pedestrians on the sidewalk, small storefronts at day and night. Further into the film, Yolanda and Mari walk along the sidewalk, the camera showing shops selling tortillas and playing Mexican music. Again, later in the film, the camera shows the same street, with Mari standing outside of a photography store handing out flyers. Finally, when Yolanda's parents drive her home from school after a contentious meeting over her falling grades, they drive by several unhoused individuals on the sidewalk and her father says, "No tenemos que regresar a México para recordarte lo que es la pobreza, Yolanda" (We don't have to return to Mexico to remind you what poverty is, Yolanda). Her parents continue, reminding her of what they must endure at work so that she can go to college and have a better life "lejos de aquí" (far from here). This harkens to another moment in the film where Yolanda asks her mother about how she met her father, and her mother chastises her for thinking of these things instead of school: "No ando en chinga todo el día para que tú lo eches todo a perder" (I'm not working my ass off all day for you to throw it all away).

The trauma of near poverty haunts Yolanda's parents and paints their worldview; her parents have sacrificed their former life, spare time, and dreams in order to provide a better life for her. The weight of this responsibility lies heavy on Yolanda and affects the ways she experiences her adolescence and her budding sense of sexuality. While her parents do not directly censure a romantic relationship with Mari, they refuse the possibility of any activity that will distract her from school and a better life. Their insinuation that they left Mexico for opportunities in the United States is directly related to their socioeconomic status and goals. Thus, Yolanda's identity as a daughter of middle-/working-class Mexican immigrants affects how she experiences and perceives adolescence and sexuality; she is taught to focus only on those activities that will raise her class status and is discouraged from considering her budding sexual feelings. Furthermore, it is indicative of her Latinx background that the possibility of her friendship with Mari being sexual is not considered by her parents. In the scene in the car after the school meeting, her mother warns her about boys, "cualquier muchachito" (any young man). They think it is the negative influence of other youth on Yolanda that has made her grades fall. Both her socioeconomic status and ethnicity are factors in how she experiences or allows herself to experience this first sexually curious romance. Guerrero talks about the impetus for the film: "The core conflict in the story of *Mosquita y Mari* isn't a homophobic parent getting in the way of their experience but rather the pressures that come with surviving as an immigrant or coming from a legacy of self-sacrifice for the sake of family and status in society."[18] So, in a way, the larger pressure on Yolanda is the economic one; she is expected to live a certain way in order to respect and justify the sacrifices her parents made.

On the other hand, Mari's family's economic situation is more dire; her single mother barely makes enough money to pay the rent. Mari takes on work after school handing out flyers for a photography store to help pay for food and bills. When Yolanda first visits her apartment, we see Mari as a maternal-like figure for her younger sister as she arrives home, turns the television off, and tells her younger sister "después de la tarea" (after your homework). She then makes bowls of cereal for them all, including Yolanda. When Mari's mother arrives from work, she asks "¿Estamos ofreciendo cereal a nuestra invitada?" (We're offering cereal to our guest?) to which Mari replies: "Pues, no es como que si tuviéramos *steak* que ofrecer" [sic] (Well, it's not like we have any steak to offer). This scene's implications are that it is normal for the kids to be home alone eating snacks like cereal and that they normally do not have luxury items such as steak for dinner. Mari's single-income household also affects the ways in which she experiences adolescence; for example, she feels the need to work after school rather than focus on doing better in school and talks about the futility of studying. The immediate need of providing for her family eclipses any prospect of continuing in school. Moreover, the need to work after school precludes most of the after-school extracurricular and social activities typical of adolescence in the United States.

When Mari's mother finds the money that her daughter has been setting aside in her dresser from passing out flyers, she misinterprets where the money comes from: "Tu padre estaría muy decepcionado contigo. En la calle. Como si no tuvieras madre" (Your father would be very disappointed in you. On the streets. As if you didn't have a mother). Mari responds: "A lo mejor, estaría orgulloso de mí porque estoy asegurando que tengamos una oportunidad como él quería" (Probably he would be proud of me because I'm making sure we have an opportunity like he wanted). When the mother says she'll figure it out, meaning the finances, Mari responds: "Apenas haces suficiente para la renta" (You barely make enough for rent). The mother's response is more painful because we as viewers have seen how proud Mari is about the money she is handed for the flyers. Her sacrifice for the good of the family is downplayed by her mother's suspicions. Mari has sacrificed socializing after school and spending more time focusing on schoolwork. She has also taken on a

FIGURE 2.1. Mari stands on Pacific Avenue, where she hands out flyers. *Mosquita y Mari* (2012).

more parental role in the family, affecting how she experiences adolescence. This scene with her mother is a tipping point as it is after this that she skips out on work to spend time with Yolanda and dumps the flyers in the garbage. She eventually loses the job and will make an even more drastic sacrifice to get money for her family.

Mari offers to help a man "boletear" (pass out flyers) on the sidewalk. When he refers to her needing money, he stares at her body, seeing it as a commodity. In this initial scene together, Mari rides away on her bike, ignoring the offer. However, we later see her with him in the same garage Yolanda and Mari had "discovered" and used as their special place. Yolanda excitedly takes her an exam with a high grade but finds Mari with the man, throws the exam on the floor, and angrily leaves. Mari looks at the grade, but the man demands of her: "¿Estamos jugando pinches juegos de la primaria?" (Are we playing silly grade school games?) to which she replies no and that they had a deal. She has decided to trade her body for money, seeing it as a source of income after not being paid for the flyers. This is a clear example of Mari's economic situation interfering with her normal adolescent development. Rather than socialize with teenagers her own age and explore her budding sexuality in this way, she feels she must use her body and sex as part of a financial transaction.

The man who pays her for sex sees her body as a commodity and takes advantage of her young age and economic difficulties. Thus, gender, age, and class intersect in this moment; Mari is young, female, and working class and seen as an easy target for this man. As Alsultany declares: "My body becomes marked with meaning as I enter public space."[19] The man sees Mari and makes certain assumptions about his power over her. He even plays on her need to not be seen as too young when referring to elementary school games. She is desperate for the money and to be seen as more mature, able to be part of this transaction. Looking back to the other scenes with Mari and her mother, it is clear that she has mentally stepped into the provider role for her family and will do what needs to be done to help take care of her mother and sister. Guerrero sets Yolanda and Mari's relationship as the positive alternative to the abusive experience with the man in the garage; the girls' physical interactions with each other are gentle, affirmative, and driven by innocent adolescent sexual curiosity.

Yolanda's and Mari's stories play out within a specific sociocultural and historical context. As a coming-of-age story in a Latinx community in Southern California, *Mosquita y Mari* reflects the history of Mexican immigrants, Mexican citizens who lived in the area before it was taken by the United States, and original Indigenous populations in the region. Viveros Vigoya emphasizes the historical aspect of lived experiences and intersectionality. For the Colombian theorist, there cannot be a universal feminist ideal because women's experiences are not universal, they are specific to a region's historical development. Yolanda y Mari's story is set against the backdrop of a very specific history, and we would not understand it fully from an analysis that ignores this history. The intersections of the protagonists' race, ethnicity, language, and culture are central to their lived experiences. As young Latinx women, Yolanda and Mari speak Spanish and English, listen to music from Mexico and the United States, abide by their parents' ideals that are a mixture of traditional parenting from both countries, and move adeptly between the worlds of their homes, school, social settings, and what happens on the streets of their city. Because of Guerrero's choice to place the film in Huntington Park, the city's own reality as majority Mexican or Mexican American affects the characters' experiences in all of these settings, as well.

Reflecting on Yolanda and Mari's experience in Guerrero's film, community is a central concept. Mina Karavanta clarifies: "In colonial modernity, community is often aligned with the history of the nation-state and linked with the fixity but also fluidity of the demarcators of ethnicity, race, religion, class, language, sexuality, and gender."[20] Later, Karavanta affirms: "As the world becomes discontinuously and unevenly connected, community signifies the rise of diasporic and intercultural communities and the perseverance of the peripheral and nondominant collectives that seek recognition within the nation or as nations, struggling against their marginalization."[21] The Latinx community of *Mosquita y Mari* is evident and central to the film's message. The depictions of this community are present in the grocery store where the shopkeeper tells Yolanda's and Mari's parents about their daughters; in the school where the students are closely connected by family ties or friendships; in the after-school outings the teenagers take, listening to music in Spanish; and in the many images of Huntington Park and Pacific Avenue's shop signs in Spanish. Guerrero also portrays the community in the language that her characters speak (Spanish and English); the music they play (mariachi, banda, norteño, and cumbia along with styles from the US); the clothing they wear; and the lessons they give their children (moving from Mexico for better opportunities). This Latinx community is diasporic and original at the same time. Moraga, speaking of her own community of San Gabriel in East Los Angeles, proclaims: "I am one among millions of delusional *Mexican*Americans, who has pretended we immigrated to (and were not born of) these lands."[22] Moraga talks of her Tongva heritage and the fact that many of the ancestors of the Latinx community today were, in fact, original inhabitants of the Southern California lands. While *Mosquita y Mari* is focused on the story of two girls, the setting and surrounding characters tell the story of a larger community with its own distinct characteristics. Furthermore, Guerrero purposely chose this setting and these characters to represent the Latinx community of Huntington Park.[23]

In terms of representation, Frederick Luis Aldama writes in his introduction to *Latinx Ciné*:

> While today Latinxs make up over 18 percent of the US population, in the media taken as a whole (film, TV, video games, literature, you name it) Latinxs appear in less than 3 percent. More often than not, when Latinxs do appear on mainstream screens, it's as if we've been cast forever in a stock set of stereotypical molds: drug kingpins, petty criminals, buffoons, hypersexualized lovers or prostitutes, or white-aspiring virginal maids, among other.[24]

Aldama points toward a stark disparity in Latinx representation in cultural production as well as an overabundance of misrepresentation in mainstream film and television. Guerrero inserts her film into this dynamic, presenting a coming-of-age story about two girls and their relatable adolescent explorations of gender and sexuality. During the planning and filming of *Mosquita y Mari*, the filmmaker made it clear that representation was important to her; she ensured that the cast was mainly local to Huntington Park and that the cast members spoke Spanish. The level of commitment on the part of Guerrero ensured that the film would fill a specific gap in Latinx film representation. Moreover, Guerrero avoided the clichéd images of the Latinx community on screen, portraying the daily life of families like those of Yolanda and Mari, working and striving for a better life.

Karavanta's discussion considers intersectional demarcations—ethnicity, race, religion, class, language, sexuality, and gender—as directly related to community. *Mosquita y Mari* represents each of these identity factors in the protagonists, their families, and their community. Moreover, as previously discussed, Yolanda's and Mari's adolescent experiences and their coming-of-age story are deeply influenced by their community. More specifically, the accepted mores of their Latinx community influence the young characters' adolescent sexuality as much as generalized heteronormative bias. However, Guerrero presents the story as one full of hope and possibility in the end, rather than restriction. The final scene unites the two in their favorite spot and offers a new path for gender and sexuality within the Latinx community, calling on what Karavanta terms the possibility of fluidity of intersectional lines.

There is a scene in the film related to gender, sexuality, and fluidity in which Yolanda is looking in her parents' bedroom and finds her father's cowboy hat. She tries the hat on while listening to music on headphones.[25] This scene portrays Yolanda's gender experimentation, as she tries on her father's male identity and takes on the male lead role when dancing with her mother, who discovers her in the room with the hat. At first, her mother enjoys the playful moment; however, she interrupts their fun and chastises Yolanda after she asks about her parents' love story. Once again, Yolanda's mother reminds her that her parents sacrificed many things to come to the United States and work tirelessly so that Yolanda can have a different life. She tells Yolanda that she should not think about such things and should only focus on schoolwork in order to be more

FIGURE 2.2. Yolanda in her father's hat. *Mosquita y Mari* (2012).

successful in life. It is not clear that Yolanda's mother captures the idea that her daughter is playing with gender roles; however, it is very clear that her mother is considering her daughter's socioeconomic status. She wishes her daughter to forgo any romantic involvements to avoid what she sees in her own past. The weight of this sacrifice is then shared with her child, who feels the pressure to sacrifice her teen years with their gender and sexual explorations for the sake of socioeconomic stability.

Considering Yolanda and Mari's relationship, they use their parents' and society's acceptance of girlhood friendship to explore their developing sexual curiosity for each other. Catrióna Rueda Esquibel contends: "In my research of Chicana literature, I have found a series of stories in which girlhood provides a space, however restrictive, for lesbian desire. Within the socially sanctioned system of *comadrazgo*, young Chicanas are encouraged to form lifelong female friendships, and it is the intimacy of these relationships that often provides the context for lesbian desire."[26] Later: "All of these fictions represent same-sex love and desire at approximately that moment at which girls are expected to set aside female friendships in favor of heterosexual relations."[27] First, Rueda Esquibel identifies girlhood friendship in Chicana literature as a space for sexual identity exploration. More precisely, the critic examines the idea of *comadrazgo*—stemming from *comadre*, which is a slang word used for a close friend. *Comadrazgo* then is the institution of close friendship and solidarity in the Latinx community, specifically referring to close connections between women. This might be a tradition of youth but can extend to adulthood, as well. For the protagonists in Guerrero's film, community and family acceptance of girlhood friendship provides the necessary space for their adolescent explorations of gender and sexuality. The *comadrazgo* to which Rueda Esquibel refers is clearly highlighted by the filmmaker; girlhood friendships abound in the film. Mari and Yolanda's friendship is at the center; however, many other same-sex friendships are highlighted, including those of the *cuatas*. The very idea of girlhood friendship is visually and narratively at the epicenter of *Mosquita y Mari*. Within the realm of these friendships, Guerrero examines the most important themes of the film: loyalty, adolescent experimentation, racial and ethnic binds, budding independence, and significantly, gender and sexuality.

Aldama specifically references Guerrero's depiction of gender and sexuality: "Twenty-first-century Latinx filmmakers such as Miguel Arteta, Cecilia Aldarondo, Peter Bratt, Aurora Guerrero, León Ichaso, and Cristina Ibarra have created films (documentary and feature) that enrich greatly the complex ways Latinxs exist in terms of gender and sexuality."[28] While there is not a chapter dedicated to Guerrero in the anthology, Aldama does address Guerrero's work briefly: "And we see Aurora Guerrero's masterful use of close-ups, assembly shots, and mise-en-scenes to subtly convey a natural and innocent exploration of same-sex teen love in contrast with objects and a world that make difficult this natural way of existing."[29] Indeed, in the scenes depicting the two protagonists alone together—in the abandoned garage, in Yolanda's living room, riding a bike together—the lighting is softer and creates a more intimate atmosphere. On the other hand, when the characters are dealing with other people—in the classroom, at work, with parents—the lighting is harsher, and the atmosphere is less supportive. In fact, the mutual support that the two girls find in each other, especially in the intimate moments where the lighting is softer, is a motif in the film. It is within this space that Yolanda and Mari explore their gender and sexuality without fear of repercussions.

Guerrero's exploration of same-sex desire is a subtle challenge to patriarchal conceptions of romance, both within US society at large and Latinx communities. Early fights for recognition among Latinx activists, writers, and creators tended to focus more on race and ethnicity than on gender. This was a clear example of not considering the intersectional nature of identity; the question of gender was sacrificed for the overall issue of Latino representation. In the late twentieth century, women and

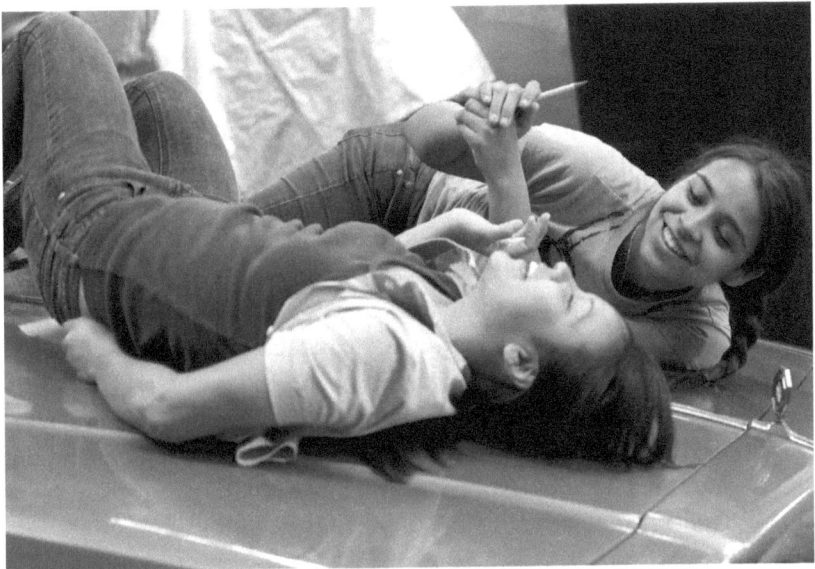

FIGURE 2.3. Mari and Yolanda on the hood of a car. *Mosquita y Mari* (2012).

LGBTQ Latinx activists and artists argued that gender and sexuality must be considered alongside race and ethnicity when discussing representation. Guerrero's *Mosquita y Mari* is part of a growing number of Latinx film directors exploring questions of sexuality in the late twentieth- and early twenty-first centuries.[30] Yolanda and Mari's relationship depicted on screen challenges the concept of compulsory heterosexuality.[31] Cheryl Clarke states: "For a woman to be a lesbian in a male-supremacist, capitalist, misogynist, racist, homophobic, imperialist culture, such as that of North America, is an act of resistance."[32] Likewise, for a director to make a film about same-sex desire is an act of resistance.[33]

Mariana Ortega discusses resistance in queer *latinidad* and photography:

> As a Latin queer lesbian, I wonder about loss, not the loss of an official visual archive or history of Latin women whose desire for women leads them to loves of which many still dare not speak their names—but about a loss that I feel in my day-to-day being in the world, a world in which women who love and desire women experience violence, especially if they are women of color; a world in which I need the company of a past that represents me; a world in which an image written with light of those like me can bring comfort. Piercingly, it is about a loss of something that perhaps never was and is in need of construction.[34]

Ortega wants representation; her remarks on the missing archive of Latinx lesbian desire refer to photography but the same can be said of film. Race and ethnicity—issues of belonging to a Latino community—have generally overshadowed intersectional questions of gender, sexuality, and race in literature, film, and photography. Traditionally, early Latino/Chicano literature and film assumed a homogenous Latino/Chicano experience within the United States and did not consider how women's experiences might have differed from men's within these same communities. The next step in these critical examinations was to consider women's experiences within Latino and Chicano communities. Finally, writers such as Moraga and Anzaldúa began to consider LGBTQ realities within Latinx communities. Referring to the latter, Ortega says: "Anzaldúa . . . reminds us that race, ethnicity, class, nationality, religion, ability, and other social locations cannot be neatly separated from sexuality."[35] Guerrero's film begins to answer this need for a more intersectional approach to Latinx experiences.

Although not squarely within the field of performance studies, *Mosquita y Mari* presents certain characteristics in line with what has been termed Borderlands consciousness and de-colonizing performatics. Sandoval et al. describe United States Latin@ Borderland Performance Studies as a field that "challenges the colonialist power that artificially disconnects and pulls apart race from gender and from sexuality."[36] Intersectionality theory inherently questions this separation of gender and sexuality along with other identity factors, recognizing the complicated junctions of identity. For Sandoval and the other editors, Borderland Performance Studies focuses also on the recovery of the body as central to decolonization theory: "its voice, its sensations, its perceptions, its connections to mind and feeling."[37] Returning to Borderland consciousness, the authors further define the concept as "a type of vital insurgency that inscribes alter-Native cultural vocabularies, musical times, and communal emotionalities."[38] The ideas presented here—decolonization, colonialist power, and the affective experiences of the body—relate to Guerrero's presentation in *Mosquita y Mari*. More specifically, the filmmaker highlights the Huntington Park community's position within systems of power, which directly affect the protagonists' lived experiences. Furthermore, Guerrero presents an affective, bodily approach to explorations of identity, community, gender, and sexuality. The affective nature of this examination comes from elements related to the cultural vocabulary of the film—food, music, dress, dance—as well as the bodily experiences of Yolanda and Mari.

NO ROBARÁS . . . A MENOS QUE SEA NECESARIO

Ecuadorian director Cordero's film *No robarás* also explores intersectional questions of identity, highlighting the connections between class and gender. In Cordero's film, the first scene begins with an image of red boots in the front window of a shoe store. With the opening credits and a melodramatic piano piece in the background, the image of the shop window with the red boots appears on screen. The camera remains fixed on the boots and after a minute the protagonist Lucía enters on screen. The camera moves so that the protagonist and the boots share the center of the image, and she says, "Wow. ¡Qué botas más hijueputa!" (What bitchin' boots!) She looks at them intently and enters, presumably to inquire about their price. The music that accompanies this scene corresponds to the action; when the store employee asks her about the boots, the song reaches a crescendo, and when she leaves without them, the song pauses for a moment and then continues more tenuous than before. In this sense, the music reflects Lucía's emotions—first, with rising energy when she sees the boots and, later, with the climax and fall when she hears the price and knows that she cannot buy them. The boots, symbolically red, are outside the girl's reach and represent various themes that relate to Lucía—her youth, her desire for a better life, and her lack or resources for attaining a better life. When she conforms to the impossibility of having the boots, her shoulders droop and she walks away, leaving the shot. This scene is an introduction to the theme of conflict between social classes in *No robarás*, a theme that runs through the entire film along with gender.

These two themes—gender and social class—correspond with Lucía's family's situation as her mother is imprisoned for defending herself from an abusive man and her children are left to take care of themselves, leaving Lucía responsible. In the corrupt legal system, Marta is guilty, even though her boyfriend attacked her. Before the law, as a woman, Marta has no rights and her family, from the urban subproletariat, does not have any social support in such a crisis. Thus, Lucía looks for work and falls to stealing because there is no alternative. In this sense, Lucía's family is a victim of structural oppression because of gender (a single mother) and because of social class (urban subproletariat). As Grzanka says, these are institutional systems of domination and violence; the legal institution judges Marta and not the abusive man and the social institutions do not support the family. Cordero underscores the reality of a young girl like Lucía and resists the stereotype of young women from her social class. The director understands what Lené Hole and the other editors of the *Routledge Companion* emphasize—that film, along with representing and reiterating, constructs gender, social, and ethnic norms. The theoretical framework of intersectionality helps us to understand the relationship between gender and social class as much as the power systems that marginalize the characters of *No robarás*.[39] As Collins would contend, these different forms of oppression unite to produce injustices.

Another scene relating to the themes of gender and social class is when Lucía and her siblings leave their apartment at night after their mother is imprisoned. The scene that precedes this one is of a guard locking the doors of a women's prison. The camera follows the guard, and the most dominant sounds are of the doors closing with force and a baby crying behind one of the doors. What follows is the image of Lucía's two younger siblings, yawning and rubbing their eyes; one of them says "Yo no me quiero ir" (I don't want to go). They leave the apartment with their possessions in plastic bags and Lucía's friend arrives to help. Lucía looks inside the house one more time and then shuts the door. Perhaps the image most emblematic of the entire film is the following: the five children in the center of the screen, walking in the middle of the night on a deserted street. Lucía is carrying her younger brother and she and her friend flank the group. Their heads are down and there is a melancholic piano piece in the background while the camera focuses on them from the front, the back, and then directly on the youngest one. The light changes through these shots to show that they walk for a long time, until dawn when they arrive at a door and wait outside.

Significantly, there is not one adult in this scene. Lucía, with the help of her young friend, is left to shoulder the burden of taking care of the family. Just as Mari in Guerrero's film cares for her siblings and takes on adult responsibilities, Lucía is tasked with moving the family out of their apartment, finding somewhere else to live, and figuring out how they will survive. There is no social network and no government program aiding them. Thus, at a young age, the protagonist must sacrifice her own adolescence to ensure the survival of her family. Here, gender and socioeconomic status collide; as a girl of the subsistence-class, Lucía must forgo a traditional teenage life. Harkening back to the title of the film, the protagonist has no knowledge or resources to support a family and steals out of necessity as she has no other way to feed herself and her siblings.

FIGURE 2.4. Lucía out at night. *No robarás . . . a menos que sea necesario* (2013).

Furthermore, the family is in this situation because the mother is suffering an unjust system as a woman and from the subproletariat class, one step from financial ruin and the streets. The law punishes her rather than her abuser. The lack of social support also indicates that the government has abandoned citizens such as Lucía and her siblings.[40] Cordero's film exposes the gender inequities that still exist and are interrelated with questions of poverty and unprotected social classes. The concept of intersectionality juxtaposes the various elements of Lucía's identity to reveal her marginalization.

Brenda Cielaika Vanegas León examines the concepts of gender and criminology in Ecuador's economic system. She states: "La feminización de la pobreza produce ese estado de vulnerabilidad de la mujer, lo que le hace presa fácil para ingresar en la delincuencia" (The feminization of poverty produces that state of a woman's vulnerability, which makes her easy prey for becoming a delinquent).[41] Later: "Los estudios de género deben contribuir a la Criminología con innovaciones teóricas sobre control social y política criminal para demostrar que los factores económicos, políticos y culturales afectan de manera diferente a hombres y mujeres" (Gender studies should contribute to Criminology with theoretical innovations about social control and criminal politics to demonstrate that economic, political, and cultural factors affect men and women differently).[42] Discussing the feminization of poverty, Vanegas León details that, worldwide, women earn an average of just slightly more than 50 percent of what men earn and that they have less access to loans, land, and inheritance.[43] On a global scale, lack of access to education and social services and being lower on the scale of priorities for access to nutrition and health care also contribute to the cycle of poverty of which women and children suffer.[44]

For Lucía and her siblings, this means that they are left completely alone when their mother is imprisoned. Vanegas León presents the idea of the feminization of poverty, a concept that recognizes the interrelated nature of gender and socioeconomic class. In *No robarás*, the mother is the victim of a system that has abandoned her to an abusive partner. Furthermore, when she defends herself, she is the target of the justice system rather than being protected by it. In a patriarchal society, her partner's physical abuse is not punished but overlooked. Her gender coincides with her poverty, making her more vulnerable. Not only does the justice system punish her, but the government also ignores her as there are no programs available to support her and her children. She is essentially on her own and when she is imprisoned, this same fate awaits her eldest daughter, herself only a child. Moraga's comments on poverty parallel the Ecuadorian context of this film—poverty is being brown, a woman, or "just plain poor."[45] Combining this with Vanegas León's comments, it is clear that in Ecuador and elsewhere, gender and poverty merge in the marginalization of women. They earn less on average, they have less access to loans, land, education, social services, nutrition, and health care. In this global system, their children suffer the same lack of access, as we see clearly in Cordero's film.

Of the Andean region countries, when speaking of her definition of intersectionality, Viveros Vigoya asserts that, along with speaking of women not Woman, she also addresses race: "En el caso de Colombia, las regiones están muy racializadas, las costas son más negras, el interior es más andino, las selvas son más indígenas; imagino que eso sucede también en Ecuador y Perú. Por razones históricas, la geografía también corresponde a una distribución del orden sociorracial" (In the case of Colombia, the regions are very racialized, the coasts are more Black, the interior is more Andean, the rain forests are more Indigenous; I imagine that this occurs also in Ecuador and Peru. For historical reasons, the geography also corresponds to a distribution of socio-racial order).[46] Moreover, as mentioned previously, the theorist contends that oppression is a historically developed phenomenon. In the case of Latin America, the historical specificity of current systems of oppression dates back to the Conquest. As with the other countries in the region, in Ecuador, the Indigenous communities were decimated or subjugated by the Spaniards and the survivors eventually either integrated or isolated in the rainforests. Ecuador follows the same general pattern as Colombia in terms of its three regions, coastal, interior, and the Amazon jungle—Quito being in the mountainous interior but close to the rainforests. Thus, as Viveros Vigoya contends, issues of race in the region have historically but also geographically developed patterns. In Ecuador specifically, the *mestizo* population is comprised of European and Andean Indigenous ancestries. Again, as with other countries in the region, racial oppression intersects with gender and class in Ecuador's power systems. It is important to keep in mind that Ecuador is what is called a plurinational state—in 2008, when Ecuador re-drafted its constitution, the country became plurinational, meaning that there are multiple political communities and constitutional asymmetry. Ecuador officially recognizes different national groups within the nation-state as well as multiple official cultures.[47] While this denotes progress in terms of Indigenous representation on the one hand, on the other, it does not eliminate the existence of racial oppression. It is one step in the process of decolonization and the recognition of difference and historical as well as ongoing oppression. In Cordero's film, the protagonist is mestiza with discernible Indigenous physical traits although she is not presented as an Indigenous woman. There is an argument for seeing her oppression as racial as well as gender- and class-driven.

Age is another factor in this intersectional analysis of representation and repression in Cordero's film. As with Guerrero's film, Cordero's *No robarás* highlights youth culture. Even from the first lines—"Wow. ¡Qué botas más hijueputa!"—youth lingo and culture are front and center. The director combines youth language with pop culture, punk music, and punk attire.[48] Lucía sings and plays in a punk band with other young people and tries to live out typical teenage experiences such as a budding sexual curiosity. Music is an element that unites this film with Cordero's other projects. As in *Sensaciones* (Sensations; 1991), the music in *No robarás* becomes a fundamental aspect, since Lucía is the main singer in the band. In the two films, Cordero captures the dynamic of being together in a music band, focusing on the personal relationships between the members. In *No robarás*, Lucía is romantically involved with a singer in the band until she meets another boy who lives in the same apartment building.

The new friend is the one who helps her and her siblings to move to a new place when her mother goes to prison. The film presents the inevitable conflict between the two boys and other tensions between the group members, reminiscent of those between the musicians in *Sensaciones*. In *No robarás*, the youth culture that is so prevalent juxtaposes directly with the protagonist's harsh reality. Whereas Lucía could be experiencing the typical teenage drama of two love interests, she is forced to act as an adult to ensure her family's survival. Like Mari in Guerrero's film, Lucía even considers offering sex for money but does not follow through with the transaction. Instead, she steals to feed herself and her family. Again, in Lucía's case, the youth culture she so clearly represents at the beginning of the film is in stark contrast to the role she is forced to take on as the family caregiver and provider.

The youth culture and lingo underscored in Cordero's film relate to what Lorde reinforces: "the master's tools will never dismantle the master's house."[49] Cordero's use of youth language and the way she highlights her protagonist's youth culture is a challenge to traditional cinema, either focused on middle-aged protagonists or on mainstream, middle- and upper-class youth. Cordero's protagonist lives at the crossroads of gender, class, ethnicity, and youth and her oppression lies within these intersections. Just as Lucía's choice of language, dress, and music contest traditional, conservative culture, Cordero's choice as a director to highlight this particular youth culture also challenges traditional filmmaking techniques. In so doing, Cordero brings to attention the plight of young girls like Lucía who are marginalized for being young, female, ethnically diverse, and poor. The protagonist's words as well as Cordero's film language (use of punk music and youth lingo, among other techniques) are meant to exhibit Ecuador's patriarchal society and the tendency to oppress women; they are a call to dismantle the master's house.

For Laura Podalsky, punk music is directly associated with an affective approach to youth film: "Whether in the form of Rodrigo D's blaring punk sound track or *Amores perros*'s dazzling camera work and editing, these films attest to the affective charge of everyday life for young adults."[50] Podalsky shows that the "affective play" in films involves how they "articulate, evoke, and deploy emotion."[51] For Cordero in *No robarás*, punk music and its accoutrements are symbolic of youth and rebellion, as they have been for filmmakers around the world. The loud

FIGURE 2.5. Lucía and her punk bandmates. *No robarás . . . a menos que sea necesario* (2013).

music, in-your-face lyrics, exaggerated dress, and makeup are all part of an emotional rebellious response to older generations. As Podalsky rightly recognizes, filmmakers use punk music to harness this youthful discontent on film through images, editing, and sound. The affective nature of the discontent is clear on screen in these films that evoke anger, elation, despair, jealousy, and even disgust. In Cordero's film, Lucía is the embodiment of this punk aesthetic and her emotions as well as her youth are never more present than when she is singing with the punk band. Thus, her involvement in punk music and culture is the antithesis of her eventual responsibilities as the caregiver of her family. Cordero juxtaposes these two realities for the young woman as a way of underscoring for the audience the dramatic shift in the protagonist's life. Even her affective presence on screen is altered when she is taken from the youthful scenes of punk music to the scenes where she must move herself and her younger siblings out of their family's apartment in the middle of the night. Whereas before, the music allowed her to display strong emotions associated with youth, her demeanor later in the film is much more subdued; Lucía has even been robbed of the youthful experience of affect.

FIGURE 2.6. Lucía sings with her punk band. *No robarás . . . a menos que sea necesario* (2013).

Geovanny Narváez analyzes *No robarás* alongside other contemporary Ecuadorian films that feature punk and rock music. Narváez places Cordero's film in the category that addresses marginality: "De forma general, por discurso de la marginalidad, entendemos ciertas películas de estética realista que ponen en escena a jóvenes personajes de la clase baja y que son víctimas de un sistema social del que tratan de escapar o buscar soluciones. Esta apreciación corresponde plenamente a *No robarás*." (Generally, for discourse of marginality, we understand certain movies of realist aesthetic that feature young, lower-class characters who are victims of a social system from which they try to escape or find solutions. This appreciation corresponds clearly to *No robarás*.)[52] The critic underscores the realist elements of Cordero's film as well as its emphasis on a protagonist confronting an oppressive social system. Specifically referring to Cordero's film, Narváez contends: "*No robarás* puede entenderse como una denuncia social o incluso, junto con *Mejor no hablar*, como una cartografía de lugares y gentes en circunstancias difíciles o mejor dramáticas (violencia familiar y social, adicción, homicidios)" (*No robarás* can be understood as a social denouncement and even, along with *Mejor no hablar*, as a cartography of places and peoples in difficult or, even better, dramatic circumstances [familial and social violence, addiction, homicides]).[53] Significantly, Narváez uses the term *cartography*, referring to a specific geographical location; in the case of Cordero's film, this is the urban environment of Quito. Just as Viveros Vigoya recognizes the geographical as well as the historical aspects of oppression, Narváez also sees Lucía's urban surroundings as important. The critic connects the ideas of urban youth, punk, and social protest in *No robarás*. In fact, when analyzing the specific lyrics of the punk rock song in *No robarás*, Narváez recognizes "un canto nihilista, relativo al estereotipo punk, que refleja la condición marginal, pero recae en la autonomía subjetiva" (a Nihilist song, related to the punk stereotype, that reflects the marginal condition, but relies on subjective autonomy).[54] First, Narváez focuses on the nihilistic aspect of the lyrics of Lucía's punk band—the teens are declaiming the meaninglessness of life, especially poignant when we learn of Lucía's difficulties. On the other hand, the critic notices in the lyrics a nod to subjectivity, which is highly significant in the current analysis of the film as a depiction of an adolescent who experiences traumatic events and must assume adult responsibilities while at the same time lamenting the loss of youthful experiences. These experiences include individualistic questions of autonomy and selfhood, truncated in the film when the protagonist becomes the sole caregiver for her family.

Narváez further highlights gender and class in his analysis of *No robarás*. In terms of gender, the critic emphasizes the female protagonist and the themes of social and domestic violence.[55] Significantly, he separates domestic and social violence in his examination of Lucía's situation; her mother and subsequently the whole family is victim of domestic violence. In addition, the legal injustice the mother suffers and the social oppression and neglect the family experiences are a form of social violence. In terms of class, Narváez describes a scene in the film in which a young, upper-class girl plays classical piano music, which contrasts with the protagonist's punk music: "los cruces de mundos diferentes contiene un binarismo básico: punk y música popular en la clase baja (marginales) y música culta en la clase alta" (the crossing of different worlds contains a basic binarism: punk and popular music in the lower-class [marginal] and cultured music in the upper-class).[56] Narváez views punk music in the film as a metaphor for working-class resistance. Cordero's use of punk music and its relationship to the protagonist's story is intentional and it places Lucía squarely within the context of class struggle. In addition, punk music is the link between age and class in *No robarás*; Cordero emphasizes punk's connections to youth culture as well as its tendencies to challenge the status quo promoted by older generations. An intersectional analysis reveals the web of power systems and oppression evident in Lucía's situation, where gender, age, and class intersect.

Within this intersection, Cordero depicts how young women like Lucía are subjugated and victimized both by individuals and socio-political institutions meant to protect them.

Comparing Cordero's *No robarás* to Guerrero's *Mosquita y Mari*, it is evident that the female body is central to a discussion of both films. Just as Viveros Vigoya stresses the corporeal nature of lived experiences, so do the two filmmakers in question. In fact, their filmic depictions of oppression, violence, and institutional neglect center around the young, female, working-class body. Moreover, the protagonists belong to an ethnically marginalized community, which intersects with their age, gender, and class. Moraga challenges the use and abuse of specific female bodies, asking how they can avoid using their "bodies to be thrown over a river of tormented history to bridge the gap."[57] The theorist calls out the use of the Latina body as an object, employed as a crutch for others. Likewise, Moraga decries the abuse of the Latina body within a system of social and political oppression. This relates directly to Cordero's and Guerrero's protagonists whose bodies are used and abused by others who oppress them due to their age, gender, class, and ethnicity. In *Mosquita y Mari*, Mari offers her body to a man for money to help pay rent; the man sees her body as a commodity. In *No robarás*, Lucía comes close to prostituting herself with a female client but does not follow through. However, the message is still clear that the protagonist was left with little recourse to support herself and her siblings—either offer her body for money or steal to survive. Both Mari's and Lucía's bodies, as depicted by Guerrero and Cordero, represent their intersecting identities as young, working-class women with Indigenous descent. The representation of intersecting power relations in both films underscores the young women's vulnerability and loss of agency when faced with dire economic situations. Thus, the female body is at the center of the protagonists' lived experiences and how others view their bodies impacts the young women's disadvantaged positions in systems of power.

Another comparison between the two films is the emphasis on music and youth culture. Guerrero's characters are high-school students in Huntington Park whose lingo, music, and dress reflect their age and bicultural identities. Cordero's protagonist is a high school student in Quito whose lingo, music, and dress reflect her youth and class. In both instances, youth and music culture intersect. Mosquita, Mari, and the other young people in Guerrero's film listen to a mix of music that reflects their parents' Mexican origins as well as their current reality in the

United States, emphasizing their unique experiences as young people connected to a specific community and yet branching out to create their own youth culture. For Lucía in Cordero's film, music is an affective outlet and a symbol of class struggle and youth confrontation with established norms. In each film, the young characters use their lingo, music, and dress to distinguish themselves from older generations but also to identify themselves as part of a particular community of young people.

In both Guerrero's and Cordero's films examined in this chapter, the protagonists struggle with the process of self-identification typical in adolescence; however, their experiences are heavily influenced by their economic difficulties. In other words, the experiences and experimentation characteristic of adolescence are hindered by lack of resources and the added adult responsibility of supporting their families. Specific lived experiences affect the teen years of the three young protagonists in *Mosquita y Mari* and *No robarás*—Yolanda sacrifices to live up to the expectations of her immigrant parents; Mari prostitutes herself to support her family financially; and Lucía steals to feed herself and her siblings. Gender, age, socioeconomic class, and ethnicity intersect for these young women. It is not enough to examine their gender in order to perceive the systems of oppression that influence their lives; it is necessary to see how their gender as women intersects with their youth, class, and ethnicity. Their bodies are "marked" (Alsultany) and read a certain way by society that represses them according to these demarcations. Moreover, these systems of oppression are historically based (Viveros Vigoya); for Yolanda and Mari, this is the socio-politico-cultural history of Huntington Park, and for Lucía, this is the socio-geographical history of Quito. As directors, Guerrero and Cordero challenge these systems of sexism, racism, classism, and heteronormativity by exposing the experiences of young women like Yolanda, Mari, and Lucía. In other words, the filmmakers use their films to challenge the status quo and bring to the forefront the struggles of young women in similar circumstances. In terms of technique, the films reflect the challenge; Guerrero uses language and cultural markers (dress, food, music) specific to youth culture in Huntington Park and Cordero uses language and music (punk, youth lingo) specific to youth culture in Quito in order to confront conventional film technique, as well. Just as Guerrero and Cordero emphasize gender, age, and ethnicity in their films, the following chapter shows how filmmaker Gabriela David depicts the intersections of these along with class, rural identity, and cognitive ability.

CHAPTER 3

INTERSECTIONAL SUBJECTIVITY
Gabriela David's *La mosca en la ceniza*

GABRIELA DAVID'S FILM *La mosca en la ceniza* (2010) presents two characters at the intersections of gender, adolescence, working-class socioeconomic status, rural otherness, and cognitive ability.[1] The film explores how these two young women from rural Northwestern Argentina become victims of a sex trafficking scheme that takes them to Buenos Aires. In so doing, David illustrates how the various aspects of the protagonists' identities converge to make them targets of this plot. This chapter focuses on specific scenes from *La mosca* that represent gender and age as well as rural and socioeconomic status. More specifically, this chapter argues that an intersectional approach to analyzing David's film reveals the extent to which the protagonists are victims of structural oppression and the degree of impunity surrounding these aggressions. As Collins and Bilge write: "[I]n a given society at a given time, power relations of race, class, and gender, for example, are not discrete and mutually exclusive entities, but rather build on each other and work together; and that, often invisible, these intersecting power relations affect all aspects of the social world."[2] Thus, we can better understand David's characters by recognizing that the diverse facets of their identities are interrelated and that those who victimize them take advantage of specific institutional and societal power structures to do so. Along with theories on intersectionality by Collins, Bilge, and Hurtado, this chapter calls upon recent analyses of Argentine film such as Daniel Omar de Lucía's study of the subaltern, Liliana Hendel's pop culture gender theory, and Traci Brynne Voyles's theory of "wastelanding." This chapter is in conversation with the groundbreaking work done by Ana Corbalán, Ana Forcinito, and Marta Boris Tarré on Gabriela David's oeuvre. Finally, the chapter calls upon concepts of subjectivity and agency to better understand the protagonists' relative ability or inability to act within their positions in structural power relations, and rural studies and theories of space to understand how their identities as rural citizens affect their place within these power structures.

In *La mosca en la ceniza*, Nancy (María Laura Caccamo) and Pato (Paloma Contreras) are recruited by an older woman to work in Buenos Aires. She visits them in their village in Northwestern Argentina and pressures them to quickly decide whether to move to the capital for supposed house cleaning jobs. It is clear that, of the two young women, Pato is driving this initiative while Nancy is reticent to leave. However, her mother tells her that they will be better off in their home with fewer people, implying that it is difficult to feed the children as it is. On the way to the capital, escorted by a young man on the bus, the young women watch out the window as the landscape changes, and become nervous when they enter the city and see the lights and people. When they arrive, Nancy says to Pato, "Vos me va a ayudar? A hacer bien las cosas, para no equivocarme" (You're going to help me? To do things the right way, to not get it wrong), and Pato sees a sign that reads "Agüero" (omen) and starts to suspect something is wrong. Here, David places a panning shot of the outside of the buildings. Reminiscent of films dealing with the Argentine Dirty War and the use of nondescript buildings as places of detention and torture, it is unclear from the outside that there is anything sinister about this place.[3] Afterward, we see inside one apartment with a mother and her young children, which contrasts with the inside of the building where Nancy and Pato are taken. It becomes clear that they are in a brothel and will be exploited to sleep with men for money, which they will not receive.[4] Pato fights against the betrayal and is subsequently handcuffed to a bathroom wall and beaten while Nancy quickly conforms. There are many shots of the young women in the house sitting in a cramped room and continuously being asked to put on high-heeled boots along with their dresses and makeup: "Ponete las botas. No te las saques más" (Put the boots on. Don't ever take them off). Pato temporarily escapes but has nowhere to go but the courtyard inside the adjoining buildings. For her part, Nancy befriends a client who is a waiter across the street and confides in him about their situation, hoping that he will come back and save her, like Hipólito in Federico Gamboa's *Santa* (1903).[5] Ultimately, the waiter does nothing and it is not until Nancy escapes and knocks on another man's door that the police come and arrest all those involved in the situation and ambulances come to take the young women. The film ends with Pato remaining in the capital and studying while Nancy returns to their village. The ending credits, just as with the opening ones, are set to the sound of birds, a symbol of freedom.

Critics see gender as one of the key factors in the situation depicted in David's film; as Boris Tarré contends: "El hecho que sean aun más las mujeres—y adolescentes—las que son engañadas o coaccionadas más que los varones hace que no se pueda entender este problema de trata sin vincularlo a un modelo social que tiene su base en el patriarcado" (The fact that it is even more women—and adolescents—that are deceived or coerced more than men makes it impossible to understand the problem of trafficking without linking it to a social model that has patriarchy as its base).[6] Thus Boris Tarré argues that gender is a fundamental part of the equation when questioning the situation of young women trapped in human trafficking. Forcinito, in an article on New Argentine Cinema, analyzes the characteristics of women directors in the movement: "Quiero sí remarcar que las nuevas cineastas se enfocan en visiones culturales marcadas por el género sexual y exploran mundos domésticos, íntimos y sexuales a través de la experiencia de mujeres, niñas y adolescentes (... la violencia de género desde el abuso doméstico hasta la trata de mujeres y la prostitución forzada)" (I do want to emphasize that the new filmmakers focus on cultural visions marked by sexual gender and explore domestic, intimate, and sexual worlds through the experiences of women, girls, and adolescents [... gender violence from domestic abuse to sex trafficking and forced prostitution]).[7] Forcinito emphasizes the centrality of gender in recent Argentine film. Moreover, the critic insists that the visual depiction of sex trafficking, for example, revolves around gender and sexuality.

GENDER AND AGE

Gender is central to the analysis of contemporary Argentine films, including David's *La mosca en la ceniza*. The focus of this chapter, however, is how gender intersects with other identity factors such as age, socioeconomic status, rural otherness, and cognitive ability. Feminist film theory's evolution—from considering gender in isolation to examining film from multiple perspectives—occurred alongside feminist film theory's incorporation of postmodern and postcolonial concepts. As Janet McCabe argues in *Feminist Film Studies: Writing the Women into Cinema*: "Orthodox feminist application of psychoanalytic models based on a rigid binary understanding of subject formation increasingly came under scrutiny from *within* the feminist academy."[8] McCabe also elucidates: "Interrogating the historical invisibility and theoretical elision of women of colour took on a new emphasis within the context of a postmodern discourse—questioning the hegemonic nature of dominant narrative and who had the right to speak."[9] In fact, theorist and filmmaker Minh-ha, in *D-Passage: The Digital Way*, specifically discusses the inability to speak for the other and the necessity, rather, of *listening* to the other. This feminist film theory turn encompasses a new perspective of film and gender that includes other intersectional considerations by necessity, as it became clear to theorists that a sole focus on Western, binary gender was lacking. Returning to McCabe, the author concludes: "What these theoretical interventions teach us is that we must analyse representation as a site of struggle, and as part of a complex web of competing knowledge."[10] Thus, representation is closely related to intersectionality.

Intersectional theory expounds on this idea; Hurtado underscores "intersections between identities in the modes of their oppression."[11] Later, the critic clarifies: "Like many feminist theoretical contributions, intersectionality was birthed from the necessity to address inequality based on sex, gender, sexuality, race, class, and ethnicity. Most recently, physical ableness has been added as another possible axis of inequality."[12] Collins and Bilge emphasize that as "an analytic tool, intersectionality views categories of race, class, gender, sexuality, . . . nation, ability, ethnicity, and age—among others—as interrelated and mutually shaping one another. Intersectionality is a way of understanding and explaining complexity in the world, in people, and in human experiences."[13] They continue with what they see as a core insight of the theory: "in a given society at a given time, power relations of race, class, and gender, for example, are not discreet and mutually exclusive entities, but rather build on each other and work together; and that, while often invisible, these intersecting power relations affect all aspects of the social world."[14] There are two elements here worthy of highlighting further: the ideas that different identity factors mutually shape one another and that power relations build on each other. As we will see, such an intersectional approach to *La mosca en la ceniza* better exposes the extent of the protagonists' subjugation and the impunity their aggressors enjoy. More precisely, the protagonists' varying identity factors (as young, rural, women, one with differing mental abilities) organically mold one another and, on the other side of that paradigm, those that enjoy institutional power do so from numerous standpoints, depending on their own identities within institutional structures (either as able-bodied men or as urban citizens).

In *Violencias de género: Las mentiras del patriarcado*, the journalist and feminist Liliana Hendel reminds us:

> Vivimos un espejismo de igualdades que, apoyándose en logros reales y avances inequívocos, desmienten que están vivas la cultura androcéntrica, la mirada machista y la valoración estereotipada de roles a los que se hace aparecer como determinados por la naturaleza. . . . El informe del Banco Mundial presentado en Washington en 2014 le pone cifras a estas cuestiones: más de setecientas millones de mujeres son víctimas de diferentes formas de violencias de género en el mundo.[15]

Later, speaking about Argentina specifically, Hendel shares another statistic from the World Bank: "[C]ada tres días una mujer es asesinada, en un altísimo porcentaje, por un varón que pertenece a su círculo de conocidos. . . . Si estos datos surgen de lo que se publica, no es arriesgado suponer que la cifra podría ascender a un feminicidio diario en el país" (Every three days a woman is assassinated, at a high rate, by a man who belongs to her circle of acquaintences. . . . If these figures come from what is publicized, it is not a stretch to suppose that the figure could rise to one feminicide a day in the country).[16] Finally, Hendel asserts: "No desciende el número de feminicidios a pesar de las leyes, por el contrario, aumentan los ataques con ácidos en algunos países como Colombia y se extiende, en el mundo, el no castigo para los abusadores sexuales al mismo tiempo que crecen las represalias hacia las mujeres que los denuncian" (The number of feminicides does not go down despite laws, on the contrary, attacks increase with acid in some countries like Colombia and impunity for sexual abusers, in the world, is extended at the same time that retaliation against women who accuse them grows).[17] David's film is a direct challenge to the impunity expressed here, as it underscores the lack of consequences for those who attack women physically and sexually. Furthermore, the film challenges the latent complicity of what Hendel rightly recognizes as the ever-existent androcentric, *machista*, stereotypical gaze. In fact, Laura Mulvey's concept of the gaze is still relevant to Hendel's ideas and to any examination of David's film; the male gaze is dominant in the sexual violence perpetrated against the young protagonists. On the other hand, David's female gaze as director challenges the status quo that allows this violent, male gaze to persist with impunity. Moreover, following Mulvey's ideas about visual pleasure, David does not create a film meant for the visual pleasure of the male gaze; the hard reality of these young women is the over reigning visual aspect.

In *La mosca en la ceniza*, there are multiple scenes involving a trapped fly that symbolize the young protagonists' entrapment and relate directly to gender and age. Just as the fly is trapped either in jars or closed rooms, so are Nancy and Pato; they are trapped in a patriarchal system that makes them victims of predators as well as a socioeconomic system that forces them into prostitution. Their unfamiliarity with urban Buenos Aires and their rural trust in others allow the other characters, male and female, to take advantage of them. In this way, the other characters play into a system that marginalizes and abuses young, poor, rural women. The protagonists' intersecting identities are central to understanding their situation. One final element essential in grasping the significance of the fly metaphor in this film is in the theory that a fly can be revived with ashes, signifying Nancy and Pato's ultimate survival. In an article comparing the politics of space and the relationship between women's bodies and cities in David's film to Beatriz Flores Silva's *En la puta vida* (In this tricky life; 2001), Corbalán asserts: "La película está plagada de simbolismo, ya que desde la primera mise-en-scène, hay una mosca que simboliza el ave fénix que resucita de entre las cenizas para representar el binomio muerte-renacimiento y las posibilidades de esperanza que se pueden presentar ante cualquier situación opresiva" (The film is plagued with symbolism, since from the first mis-en-scene, there is a fly that symbolizes the phoenix that rises from the ashes to represent the binomial death-rebirth and the possibilities of hope that can be presented before any oppressive situation).[18] Corbalán also emphasizes the parallels between the two protagonists of David's film and the trapped flies.

The film opens with birds chirping, insects buzzing, and a shot of flies overhead, with the sky in the background. In the first scene with flies, we see Nancy catching one of the insects on a table, putting it in a jar of water, and shaking the jar. The film shows her looking into the jar from different perspectives and then the fly swimming around on the surface, after which, Nancy pushes it down into the water with a stick and then her finger. She smiles to herself as the fly remains underwater at the end of the stick. The sound of her friend Pato interrupts her concentration. First, the character's surroundings are indicative of the material status of Nancy's family; there are bottles, cups, used forks, and rusted jars on the outside table, the house seems to be patched or stained with mud, and there are several items belonging to children strewn about the ground. There is the sound of a crying baby in the background and the sound of nature; it is clear that the house is in a rural area, set among many trees. There is a disconcerting pleasure that Nancy takes in drowning the fly in the jar. Although Nancy is five years older than Pato, there are indications that she is cognitively less mature than her friend, and she later reveals that she barely finished fifth grade. She follows Pato and grins, is unconcerned about her dirty feet and shoes, and enjoys watching the fly drown. Here in this first part of the film, we already see the intersectional identity factors that affect the young women's trajectories. Specifically, the two protagonists are young, female, working-class or poor, rural, and, in Nancy's case, cognitively impaired in some way. These intersectional identity factors make them easy targets and trap them in an abusive situation, just as the fly is trapped in the jar.

The second scene with a fly involves Nancy drowning one in another glass of water later in the film following the moment she sees the waiter through the window on the other side of the street, laughing with a police officer but not reporting what she had told him about their situation. She returns to a room with Pato, who has visible wounds, and shows her the jar, which she shakes more frantically and pushes the fly down. Pato tells her, "Te falta la ceniza. Tenés que buscar ceniza por allí" (You're missing the ash. You have to look for the ash somewhere). A few scenes later she finds cigarette ashes in a room she is forced to clean and saves them in an empty carton. When she returns to the room where the girls are held, she places the seemingly dead fly from the jar on the pile of ashes and covers it with more ashes. The fly starts to move and suddenly flies away; the camera captures the wings flapping rapidly and shaking off the ashes. At this moment, the film gives hope to the young women's situation; they will rise and escape just as the fly does. These scenes also represent the trapped young women, trapped in a system that oppresses them for their gender, age, socioeconomic status, rural origins, and cognitive ability.

A third scene involving a fly begins with a high angle shot, leaving Nancy looking vulnerable. In the foreground, we see one bright light bulb hanging uncovered from the ceiling and Nancy in the middle ground while in the background we see a thin, dirty blanket on the floor, a plate of food, and plain cement walls. The only sound we hear is a fly buzzing while the camera moves from focusing on Nancy to a point-of-view shot of the small, round window she is studying high up on the wall. The next sound is coughing and, through Nancy's point of view again, we see that there is another young woman in the room, sleeping on a small cot on the floor. Briefly returning to the idea of the gaze, these images are the opposite of traditional film from the perspective of the male gaze that seeks visual, sexual pleasure. During these shots, Nancy pulls down on the short dress she has been forced to wear and seems dazed. This scene follows ones in which the two protagonists realize they have been tricked and held against their will to be prostitutes. Those in charge beat Pato when she tries to resist and tie her up in a bathroom and leave Nancy in the aforementioned room. The images with the fly buzzing around the room and bumping up against the window mirror the two young women's reality, trapped against their will and with little chance of escape. The sound of the fly buzzing is also significant; Forcinito describes one of the tendencies in films by women directors of the New Argentine Cinema movement as a strategic use of sound in alluding to what is not seen: "Estos mundos, muchas veces invisibles e invivibles, son registrados a través de lo acústico, ya sea como susurros, como repetición de voces distorsionadas, como superposición de voces, como gritos, ruidos, explosiones o sonidos que señalan algún encuentro violento a la memoria del mismo" (These worlds, many times invisible and unlivable, are registered by way of the acoustic, either as whispers, as a repetition of distorted voices, as a superposition of voices, as screams, noises, explosions, or sounds that indicate a violent encounter to the memory of the self).[19] David uses the sound of a buzzing fly repeatedly in *La mosca* as an acoustic representation of the young protagonists' entrapment. Generally, this involves the sound of the fly butting up against a window and recurrently rediscovering the boundaries of its limited space. The fly is a symbolic stand-in for the trapped young women, and the buzzing sound is a constant reminder of the futility of Pato's attempts to escape.

Later in the film, there is a scene that depicts young women in the same room furtively eating fruit and looking out the door like caged animals. These images of the young women, in a closed room with one harsh light and the camera looking at them from above, call to mind the concept

FIGURE 3.1. Nancy with a trapped fly. *La mosca en la ceniza* (2010).

of the gaze. Parvati Nair and Julián Daniel Gutiérrez-Albilla discuss the concurrence of greater numbers of women directors and the use of the gaze by women: "no longer in any singular or fetishizing sense, but as an affirmation of plurality and alterity on- and off-screen. Indeed, the very foregrounding of the female gaze explodes any assumption that the gaze was ever the prerogative of the masculine."[20] In *La mosca*, David uses the idea of the gaze to do just that; the director positions the camera in such a way to foreground the young protagonists' victimhood at the hands of others. In so doing, she reveals how female directors highlight the dire situation of young women like Nancy and Pato through the use of the camera's gaze. Furthermore, David highlights the gaze that exists between the characters themselves. In so doing, she focuses on possibilities of solidarity between the young women.

IMPUNITY

Subsequently in David's film, Nancy escapes and eventually finds the back door of a man who will help, and the following scenes depict Pato in an ambulance and Nancy witnessing the other girls leaving with the police, hair disheveled and wrapped in blankets, looking confused and struck by the number of people on the sidewalk watching and by the bright sun. Nancy then witnesses the police removing the kidnappers, with their shirts over their heads. These last scenes are significant not only as a way of showing the beginning of justice but for two other reasons. They show the waiter looking at the scene from across the street and behind a crowd of people; when he sees Nancy looking at him from the ambulance, he walks away. This man represents all those who suspect or even know what is happening to the young women but say nothing. The second significant element of these scenes is the spectacle of removing the young women in contrast to the perpetrators. On the one hand, the criminals leave with shirts covering their faces and identities. On the other hand, the young women are removed fully visible and clearly identifiable to the large crowd; they are not afforded any privacy and are made a spectacle. These young women's bodies are used by others for pleasure; in this moment, to please the onlookers' curiosity. Forcinito examines sex trafficking in Argentina, specifically in the documentary *Vidas privadas* (2007, Chaya Comunicación Cooperativa); the television series *Vidas robadas* (2008, Miguel Colom); and David's film *La mosca en la ceniza*. In her article, Forcinito also focuses in on this last section of the film in which the victims are taken out onto the street without the option of hiding their identities, noticing how the other victims are separate from Nancy and Pato as they are taken in an ambulance: "En ese juego de miradas también comienza a verse el reconocimiento de sí y de los otros: una de las víctimas mira, y reconoce a un cliente en el policía que está presente en la multitud, al que mira y que la mira, aunque luego ya no puede sostener esa mirada" (In this game of glances, you can also start to see the recognition of the self and others: one of the victims looks, and recognizes a client in the police officer present among the crowd, at whom she looks and who looks at her, even though later he is unable to hold the look).[21] This directly relates to the concept of impunity mentioned above in which the male aggressors are afforded rights not given to the young victims. Likewise, it is only through an intersectional approach that we see the many identity dynamics that shape this situation. For example, the men can hide from any judgmental gaze whereas the women are fully exposed. Similarly, examining the men's intersectional power positions reveals the different ways in which they enjoy power and impunity.

FIGURE 3.2. Young women from a brothel are led away by police. *La mosca en la ceniza* (2010).

In an article on memory and the post-dictatorship era in Argentina, Forcinito analyzes a documentary (*Lesa humanidad*, 2018, Luis Ponce) from the perspectives of sexual violence and impunity. Of significant interest here is Forcinito's discussion on impunity, more specifically, impunity within the context of a post-dictatorship Argentina that swung between a clear focus on uncovering past atrocities to ignoring individuals' pleas for justice. While the contexts are not the same—Forcinito discusses sexual violence committed by government and military agents against victims of the Dirty War and David presents the situation of young women caught in a sex trafficking web—the idea of impunity is similar in both, especially when we consider David's connection to films that reference the Dirty War, such as Luis Puenzo's *Historia oficial*.[22] Forcinito explains: "En el marco de una injuria doble (primero la de la violencia y luego la de la complicidad silenciosa con la violencia) el documental . . . da cuenta de un nuevo momento en la construcción de memorias que se asocian a la lucha contra la impunidad en Argentina" (Within a double insult [first that of the violence and then that of the silent complicity with the violence] the documentary . . . gives an account of the new moment in the construction of memories that are associated with the fight against impunity in Argentina).[23] This concept of the double insult is relevant to the current discussion on David's film, as the young women not only experience the violence of being victims of a sex trafficking ring, but they also essentially must save themselves as the other characters who could help look the other way. Furthermore, authority figures in the film either look away or are, in fact, perpetrators of the violence. Relating to intersectional theory, the authority figures enjoy a special position within the power structures depicted; namely, those who trick the young women, those who trap them, and those who use them sexually are able to do so because of intersectional identity factors that place them in a position of power—male, urban, professionals with power status. Thus, an intersectional approach even to the idea of impunity allows us to see the interlocking mechanisms in the story David tells on screen.

Legal and social stances toward prostitution itself have evolved over time. It was once the case that sex workers were automatically prosecuted, regardless of whether they chose the work or were forced into it by a sex trafficking ring. In Argentina the legal code changed in 2016 to include sex work as a licit activity always provided that there is no exploitation or trafficking involved and that the work is performed voluntarily (Articles 125 and 127). However, a person who economically exploits the profession can receive four to six years in prison. In this way, those organizing the sex trafficking rings, particularly the procurers (those who seek out and ensnare victims) are found legally liable. This legal evolution is paralleled and undoubtedly spurred on by a progression in social thinking on the subject; sex work is considered more acceptable if by choice and public sentiment has shifted focus from the worker as a negative figure to those who are involved in human trafficking and sex rings as the perpetrators. Thus, in the legal realm, prosecutors have shifted their attention toward those who exploit sex workers and in the social and cultural realms the representation of sex work has changed as well. Film and television, for example, have depicted more examples of forced prostitution from the perspective of the victims, the women and men forced to perform sex acts for paying customers where the money goes to someone else. This is clearly the case in David's film, although it predates the new legal policies in Argentina. This is perhaps the reason for the other young women being taken away rather than taken in the ambulance along with Nancy and Pato.

Sex trafficking has a very specific history in Argentina. Daniela Goldfine examines one aspect of this history in the article "Sex Trafficking in Argentina Now and Then: Keepers of Memory in *The Impure*." The documentary in question is Daniel Najenson's *The Impure* (2017), which juxtaposes letters from the filmmaker's great-aunt, who was part of the group of Eastern European women sex trafficked to Argentina in the early twentieth century, with a contemporary survivor of forced prostitution who was taken from northern Argentina to Buenos Aires. The organized crime syndicate that trafficked young Jewish women from Central and Eastern Europe was called the Zwi Migdal; originating in Poland but mainly based in Argentina, the group trafficked Jewish women and forced them into prostitution. Goldfine focuses on the representations of memory from the periphery, sources of history that have not been traditionally centered. At the time of the Zwi Migdal (the last part of the nineteenth century and the first four decades of the twentieth century), prostitution was legal in Argentina and groups such as this one exploited the laws to take advantage of vulnerable young women. David explores these same concepts in her film; she focuses on the peripheral victims of sex trafficking, namely young women from the provinces who are typically overlooked and exploited due to their geographic and economic vulnerability. While Nancy and Pato are not taken from their home countries, as the young Jewish women were with the Zwi Migdal, they are removed from anyone who knows them and, thus, taken away from social support systems. In both cases, the perpetrators rely on a murky legal system and impunity as well as the gender, age, and ethnic or geographic vulnerability of the young women.[24]

Returning to the visual representation of impunity in David's film, sex trafficking rings rely on the complicity of other citizens, as Corbalán notes about *La mosca*:

> El espectador observa en numerosas escenas la vida cotidiana en la calle, donde se muestra hasta un policía controlando el orden y el espectador intuye que la gente que pasa por ahí sabe lo que está ocurriendo tras esas puertas cerradas, pero nadie hace nada al respecto. Incluso al final del filme, cuando se desarticula la red de prostitución, la cámara enfoca una serie de miradas que se desvían para evitar afrontar la realidad.[25]

There are multiple panning shots of the building façade, representing a superficial glimpse at what is happening inside the buildings. Clearly, there is much more happening inside than meets the eyes of the passersby. In fact, the superficial, panning shots are a key element in David's portrayal of the sex trafficking theme as they contrast starkly with the sequences that take place inside the building. This contrast between shallow glances versus profound gazes into the lives of the young women in the building is central to one of David's messages in this film: Argentine society condones sex trafficking by looking the other way. Moreover, the authority figures, as is evident in Corbalán's words, are complicit with this arrangement; some of them even take advantage of it themselves. Their impunity is also part of the director's condemnation; while the young women are outed publicly, the men who frequent the establishment, including the police officer, remain anonymous. Unambiguously, their power comes from their privileged positions within societal structures and institutions. The young protagonists experience the double abuse of sexual violence and impunity. Additionally, as Forcinito contends of the documentary she analyzes, it is part of a new era of creating memory and fighting impunity in Argentina. David's film is also part of a movement to contest impunity at the structural level and force a national reckoning of sex trafficking in the country.[26]

In this vein, it is clear that David places herself within an Argentine cinematic tradition dating back to the films that criticized the Dirty War (namely films such as Luis Puenzo's *La historia oficial*, as mentioned earlier). The buildings are symbolic in these films and the panning shots taken of them are central to their criticism of the military dictatorship's hidden violence. The same can be said of the unseen aggressions in David's film. Jens Andermann discusses architecture in documentary filmmaking and posits that: "a critical archeology of architectural place-making emerges, either as a form of memory-work that uncovers in built space a sedimentation of layers of meaning and affect."[27] Later, Andermann adds: "[T]he combination of static long takes and different kinds of panning shots exploring the dimensions of buildings' exteriors or the experience of immersion into them is already a kind of elementary grammar of this critical interrogation of architecture through film."[28] While Andermann is discussing documentaries, something similar occurs in David's film where the director peels the layers of the architecture to reveal the hidden suffering of the protagonists juxtaposed to the seemingly normal exterior of the building. In this way, David visually demonstrates how gender violence is made invisible, which permits the impunity of the perpetrators; we the viewers are only able to witness it because we have been given access through the film.[29]

Age is another major factor in David's film that intersects with gender violence. Carolina Rocha and Georgia Seminet affirm: "It is crucial to note that the use of children and adolescents in film is imbued with an ideological subtext that transcends the interest of a youth audience. The reason lies in the fact that the 'myth of childhood' is constantly evolving to accommodate the changing boundaries of social mores and political realities, within both the local and global contexts."[30] In *La mosca*, the youth of the protagonists serves to underline the dire conditions for women in sex trafficking rings. The director's choice of young, female protagonists destroys the idyllic myth of girlhood by placing the characters in a situation of forced prostitution. This commands a different reaction from the audience, a response that considers Nancy and Pato's youth. Thus, not only is their gender central to their identity and an understanding of the film, but their age is also of utmost importance. Once again, an intersectional approach is vital; if we were to only examine the protagonists' gender here, we would lose the significance of their young age, which intertwines with their gender to force the audience to come to terms with sex trafficking in a more shocking way.

One other aspect of gender and intersectionality relevant here is the idea of David's protagonists' subjectivity. Namely, this film presents the young women's struggles to form and maintain their subjectivity. In their introduction to *Violence and Subjectivity*, Veena Das and Arthur Kleinman define subjectivity as: "the felt interior experience of the person that includes his or her position in a field of relational power."[31] Correlated to this, agency is not simply the capacity to act, as Amy Hinterberger explains, but "the ability of the subject to resist, negotiate and transform certain forms of power that work on the subject both internally and externally."[32] These two concepts, namely subjectivity and agency, directly relate to the concept of intersectionality as well. As Das and Kleinman explain, subjectivity relates to an individual's position in power dynamics and Collins and Bilge see intersectionality as a way of better understanding the many identity factors that position a person within those structures of power. Intersectional theory also fosters a better understanding of the idea of agency and the relative ability/inability of the individual to act in certain situations with any amount of power. In David's film, Nancy and Pato are traded and sold as objects throughout, and it is important to understand the director's intentions in providing this representation. Not only is this the story of two young, Argentine women; it is also a symbol of women's subjugation in Argentina. More specifically, it is the tale of poor, rural, young women who have little recourse and fall victim to a system that tries to take away any possibility of subjectivity. As Collins and Bilge explain: "Using intersectionality as an analytic tool fosters more expansive understandings of collective identities and political action."[33] We must consider that one of David's motives in making

FIGURE 3.3. Nancy and other young women in brothel. *La mosca en la ceniza* (2010).

this film is to raise awareness of sex trafficking in Argentina. In this way, the director provides a tool for understanding the victims as part of a collective identity with more political power—at least, that is the goal, whether it is successful or not. Films such as *La mosca* create empathy in the viewer, who can then take this new knowledge into their daily political life, thus providing real young women similar to Nancy and Pato a network of support. When this film is taken into consideration along with Flores Silva's Uruguayan film *En la puta vida*, for example, we begin to see a collective film movement to confront this dehumanizing issue. As these directors are aware, many times it is visual representation that brings a problem to the public eye.

RURAL OTHERNESS AND LACK OF SOCIAL AND STRUCTURAL NETWORKS

David's protagonists' gender and adolescence intersect with their socioeconomic status and rural otherness. They are not only victims of a system that oppresses them for being young women, but also for being poor and rural. At the beginning of the film, we see the two characters in rural

Northwestern Argentina. In particular, we see Nancy's home, with children's items scattered throughout the yard. When we see Nancy and Pato in the restaurant with the woman from the capital, it has already been made clear that a job in the capital would be highly beneficial for the young protagonists' economic prospects. As mentioned earlier, Nancy's mother explicitly says that it would be better for her to go to the capital, as there would be fewer people at home, presumably fewer mouths to feed. The film's background work on the two young women explains why they might readily fall victim to the woman's scheme and believe her tale about giving them legitimate jobs in Buenos Aires. Nancy and Pato represent a sector of the rural populations in Argentina that is forced to find work in the capital in order to support themselves and their families at home. For Pato, this is also a way to continue her education and consider new possibilities for her future. However, David's protagonists represent rural Argentines who have few labor and educational prospects and suffer economically. In this way, the young women in *La mosca* are primed to believe the woman in the restaurant who offers them jobs. Furthermore, there is no social network—friends or family members—who can give the young women advice or who even have experience in the capital, so they are completely unaware that the woman might be lying to them. Thus, the woman, who the film reveals to be a type of *alcahueta*, or the procurer of young women for the prostitution ring, specifically relies on the young women's gender and age as well as their rural and socioeconomic status and their lack of a social network knowledgeable about the city.[34]

Rurality is also significant in Collins' and Bilge's discussion of global economic inequality: "By focusing on race, gender, age, and citizenship status, intersectionality shifts how we think about jobs, income, and wealth, all major indicators of economic inequality.... Black people, women, young people, rural residents, undocumented people, and differently abled people face barriers to finding well-paying, secure jobs with benefits."[35] It is significant that Collins and Bilge include rural residents and differently abled people in their conception of income inequality. It is impossible to comprehend Nancy and Pato's condition in *La mosca* solely from the standpoint of gender; on the contrary, this must be considered alongside their rural origins, Nancy's differently abled status, as well as their economic reality. Their socioeconomic status is also generational, another aspect of income inequality that Collins and Bilge address. Other characters in the film take advantage of the protagonists' vulnerability stemming from the social implications of their intersecting identity factors. Thus, the young women are more willing to take the risk of going to the capital based on the word of someone they do not know personally and the procurers who organize these sex trafficking rings rely on this vulnerability. They are very aware that these young women do not have options; for Pato, she wants to finish high school and keep studying and for Nancy, her family already has difficulties feeding and supporting everyone. Furthermore, when they are taken to the capital, they are far removed from family or anyone who knows them personally, essentially eliminating any social web they may have previously had. There are few people on whom they can rely in Buenos Aires; those who suspect or know do nothing, with the exception of the sole man who reports the ring to the police.

When Nancy and Pato take the bus to Buenos Aires, they watch out the window, visibly nervous when they reach Buenos Aires and all the lights. Many of those who take advantage of rural citizens in the capital exploit this initial surprise at the city's hustle and bustle. When they arrive, Nancy says to Pato: "Vos me va a ayudar? A hacer bien las cosas, Para no equivocarme." Along with showing Nancy's understanding that she must rely on Pato's cognitive abilities, this line also reveals that the young women have an idea that things work differently in the city than in their rural area. Moreover, Nancy's words expose the typical fear that somehow rural citizens do not know how to act in the city. Paradoxically, in the end, it is Nancy who devises a way to save the young women in the brothel. However, it is the young protagonists' rural status that makes them targets for the sex trafficking ring that brings them to the capital. This rural status, in conjunction with their age, gender, socioeconomic status, and Nancy's cognitive otherness intersect in David's film to represent how sex trafficking relies on young, rural women's lack of opportunities at home, the scarcity of resources in rural areas, and a missing social network that would support the young women both at home and in the capital.

Nancy's filmic and literary cousin is Macabea, the protagonist of Suzana Amaral's film, based on Clarice Lispector's novel *A hora da estrela*. Both Nancy and Macabea are rural citizens living in the city; others take advantage of them, for their rural otherness and their alternative cognitive abilities. Macabea comes from the Brazilian *nordeste* and arrives in the city (São Paulo or Rio, depending on novel or film) not understanding the intricate codes associated with city life. The same can be said for Nancy, who relies on Pato to instruct her in metropolitan ways. Both Nancy and Macabea fall prey to abusive men or men who take advantage of them because they are trusting, a typical and preconceived notion about rural people. It seems that Nancy, like Macabea, is slow to understanding others' expectations and consents to situations that others might not accept. For example, Nancy decides to cooperate at the brothel, presumably assuming that this was the easiest path to survival. On the other hand, Pato continues to rebel against their situation and is punished at every step. In a similar way to Macabea, Nancy adopts the makeup and dress, including the high heel boots, that the other girls wear; similarly, Macabea tries to imitate the models in magazines with the mismatching makeup she wears.[36]

Exploring further the idea of "ruralness" in the characters, it is useful to use the concept of "wastelanding" as described by Traci Brynne Voyles in her book *Wastelanding: Legacies of Uranium Mining in Navajo Country* (2015). In this book, the author examines the exploitation of Diné (Navajo) lands for minerals, dating the destruction of Southwest native lands to the first Europeans who destroyed the peach trees, corn stalks, and bean plants previously prevalent in the region. As Brynne Voyles contends, the soldiers and settlers likely had a vision of these deserts as dry and baron and some of the extreme violence enacted against the environment that accompanied the physical violence stemmed from frustrations that the native lands were so fertile.[37] For Brynne Voyles, it is not only the desert landscape that is rendered "pollutable" and thus irrelevant, but also the people and their history.[38] Reducing a land and a people to such insignificance paves the way for exploiting not only the environment but also the bodies of the inhabitants. It is certainly the case that Argentina has been capital-centric since the arrival of the European conquerors and the campaigns of colonizing the provinces, the so-called "conquest of the desert" discussed by many, including Domingo Faustino Sarmiento and the theory of civilization versus barbarism. Since the Conquest, Latin American cities were seen as the civilized center of vast barbaric regions, which in turn, have been viewed as exploitable territories for national and foreign profit. In David's film, the countryside and the provinces are the barbaric contrast to the civilized capital and the rural bodies therein are rendered exploitable, or as Brynne Voyles would affirm, they are made 'pollutable' for the benefit of the inhabitants of the capital. More specifically, Nancy and Pato's bodies are entrapped and consumed as expendable products of a rural wasteland.

In *Entre cabezas y trash: Cine y clases subalternas en la Argentina: 1990–2016*, Daniel Omar de Lucía examines David's short film *Tren Gaucho* (1989), about a group of scavengers that work in the garbage dumps in the outskirts of Buenos Aires. This is part of a group of films about garbage scavengers in Argentina, including Nahuel García and Sheila Pérez's *Tren blanco* (2003) and Verónica Souto's *Días de cartón* (2003). De Lucía includes an extensive list of Argentine films dealing specifically with this topic dating back to 1949.[39] Although de Lucía examines alternative visions of the subaltern from the perspective of workers and the unemployed, his insights into the changes in recent Argentine cinema are relevant to the current discussion. In his conclusions, he writes: "A nuestro juicio en el cine argentino de los últimos años puede identificarse un sistema de imágenes que refleja cambios en la percepción social de la marginalidad y sus relaciones con el universo de las clases subalternas urbanas" (In our view in Argentine cinema of recent years a system of images can be identified that reflects changes in the social perception of marginality and its relationship with the universe of subaltern, urban classes).[40] While de Lucía refers specifically to suburban working-class and transitional neighborhoods, he mentions images similar to those that appear in *La mosca*, such as the bus ride into the capital, representing the passage from suburban or, in David's case, rural zones to the urban zone for work. However, in David's film, this passage is not temporary; there is no return to home at the end of the working day and this is what differentiates her focus from the films that de Lucía examines. On the other hand, de Lucía's approach to Argentine film is through the ideas of class and ethnicity, specifically looking at new representations of the subaltern in Argentine cinema—characters who are from the unemployed and working class along with those who are racially and ethnically more diverse. In this way, his theory touches on the intersectionality this chapter addresses in David's film, particularly the intersections between class, ethnicity, and non-urban origins.

Carrie N. Baker examines the rescue narrative in US Hollywood depictions of sex trafficking: "The rescue narrative in the context of sex trafficking begins with an innocent and naïve young woman or girl who is tricked or abducted by a villainous trafficker, who imprisons her and controls her with brutal violence until the heroic rescuer, who often understands the female's victimization better than she does, overcomes tremendous adversity in order to save the female."[41] The critic questions the role and veracity of the heroic rescuer and clarifies that trafficking must be understood as a result of systemic failures that call for systemic solutions: "solutions to the problem of sex trafficking require attention to these broader systemic factors that make women and girls vulnerable to trafficking—economic conditions created by globalization and trade policy as well as migration policies."[42] Clearly, Baker sees intersectional factors involved in the victimization of these young women, which is directly related to David's film. As Baker contends, the existing conditions that allow sex trafficking to persist are systemic; they are rooted in structures of power which can only be understood from an intersectional approach. Namely, there are economic factors involved along with issues of gender, age, and ability.

Economic and labor issues in Argentina can be traced to the 2001 Argentine economic crisis. The country had been in a recession in the years leading up to this for many reasons. The twentieth century military dictatorships, foreign debt, periods of inflation in the 1980s, and corruption, among other factors, led the country to this point. Cuts to civil servant pay and pensions as well as government-instated austerity plans followed. Worry over the national economy caused many to withdraw large amounts of money and convert their pesos to dollars, known as a bank run. What followed was known as the *corralito*, in which bank accounts were frozen and only small amounts of money could be withdrawn. Large-scale demonstrations, *cacerolazos* (known for banging pots and pans), revealed widespread discontent.[43] One film that highlights this situation is Fabián Bielinsky's *Nueve reinas* (2000); at one point, one of the main characters goes to the bank to draw out a large sum of money but finds a crowd yelling and trying to get through the gaited entrance. While some years passed between the 2001 crisis and the making of David's 2009 *La mosca*, the shadow stretched to those years and beyond. Rural areas of the country did not escape the effects and part of the protagonists' families' economic situations stem from the country's past financial difficulties. While Argentina's economy began to recover, especially after paying down the foreign debt, in general, rural regions tend to bear the brunt long after their urban counterparts.

Looking to rural studies in the field of sociology sheds some light on the rural/urban dynamic, as well. Thomas et al. posit that social structure is as intimately connected to space in rural settings as it is in urban settings: "Space . . . affects the culture generated by the people who live in a particular area: space is important in the kind of daily life one experiences, which in turn influences the nature and quality of social

FIGURE 3.4. Nancy and Pato stand on a dirt road before being taken to Buenos Aires. *La mosca en la ceniza* (2010).

interactions, which of course is the mechanism by which culture is generated and produced."[44] Within this context, the authors refer to the term *urbanormativity*: "the general view of urban as normal and real, and rural as abnormal and unreal, or deviant."[45] This study also highlights what the authors see as a neglect of "place-based identity": "the gross neglect of how place (rural and urban identities) intersects with the other dimensions of identity such as race, ethnicity, class, and gender."[46] The inclusion of identity tied to place is significant to a full intersectional understanding of identity. More specifically, it is critical to consider David's protagonists' rural identity as central to an appreciation of the complexity of their situation. This identity, tied to place, is a key factor in their marginalization and subsequent vulnerability. Returning to the original idea of critical rural theory, social structure is associated with place, or space; both the rural and urban spaces in the film are another key to fully grasping Nancy and Pato's story.

Recalling the rural space Nancy and Pato inhabit in the first scenes of *La mosca*, certain elements are clear: there is an abundance of vegetation and natural light that overtake the buildings, paths, and roads; the only people in these opening scenes are the protagonists and the woman from Buenos Aires; and the setting is far from the capital.[47] On the other hand, later scenes in Buenos Aires show the characters arriving in the urban setting with the following: very little vegetation; crowded buildings; and many people walking on the sidewalks, eating in the café, and living in the surrounding apartments. On a second level, the film depicts the city in the following way: closed, dark spaces; young women cramped in small rooms; and the protagonists always inside rather than outside. There are three planes of spatial depiction here: outside and rural; outside and urban; and inside and urban. Carefully comparing these various spaces underlines significant themes and techniques in David's film. First, the outside and rural, as seen in the above-described scenes of Nancy's house as well as the path the young women take to the café and bus stop, are filled with the overgrown natural world that continuously encroaches on the characters and their dwellings. Moreover, natural light floods these scenes as they occur in the outdoors. While not necessarily idyllic, the film does set forth this original backdrop as positive in certain senses; for example, the young women have freedom to do as they please and go where they want as well as a distinct lack of overbearing authority hindering their movements. Thus, the naturally lit, open, vegetative spaces in the first scenes in a way represent an original paradise that is later lost. Moving on to the outside and urban setting when the young women arrive in Buenos Aires, these scenes still show natural lighting; however, the many buildings surrounding the streets impede direct light. Furthermore, there is not much vegetation other than the occasional tree planted along the sidewalk or personal plants from apartment buildings. While the young protagonists are essentially free to roam the dirt paths and roads in the first scenes, they are constricted in the city by proximate streets and city dwellers as well as their captors. These scenes represent the gateway to the young women's captivity—a transition from rural/outside to urban/outside. In turn, the following scenes portray their captivity in the urban and inside settings. These scenes feature very low lighting and no vegetation along with crowded spaces—the urban/inside space has fewer people than the urban/outside setting but much more than the rural/outside location. This final stop in the spatial planes is the confinement to which the young women have been taken; their captors enclose them in a space of low light, little room to move, and no connection to the natural world. The filmic depiction of space has proceeded from paradise to purgatory to the underworld.

Of course, there are certain contradictions to using these terms; for example, the protagonists' lives are not entirely idyllic at the beginning of the film. However, the progression of isolation from one space to the next removes the young women from the original space of relative safety; once they are removed from the rural/outside, they have no control over their bodies and movements. Pato senses this when the two arrive to the city, in the urban/outside space just before entering the building; she intuitively knows that this is the gateway between freedom and captivity. Returning to the idea of contradictions within the three spatial levels, again at the end of the film both rural and urban outside settings are tinted with menace. Nancy returns to the village and the film shows her outside, surrounded by nature and smiling; nevertheless, her partner/husband never shows her the letter Pato sent her. For her part, Nancy remains in the capital to study but continues to feel threatened in both the urban/outside and urban/inside locations. Walking the streets and catching the bus, Nancy continuously looks over her shoulder and watches a young girl whom she sees as a vulnerable symbol of herself. In the classroom, she ignores subtle advances from a young man, seeing them as a threat to her autonomy but also as a real, physical threat to her body. Accordingly, the three spatial levels: outside/rural, outside/urban, and inside/urban all represent different stages of the young protagonists' isolation and victimization. While the first setting seems to be the safest, the film shows how even this space is problematic.

Much of this discussion has centered around the split between spaces. However, Bachelard, in *The Poetics of Space*, cautions against the absolutism of the dichotomy of inside/outside: "Outside and inside form a dialectic of division, the obvious geometry of which blinds us as soon as we bring it into play in metaphorical domains. It has the sharpness of the dialectics of *yes* and *no*, which decides everything. Unless one is careful, it is made into a basis of images that govern all thoughts positive and negative."[48] Considering David's film, the temptation is to deem the outside as positive and the inside as negative, an argument motivated by the prison-like inside spaces that populate the majority of the film. However, there are certain exceptions; namely, the solidarity of the two protagonists in the inside spaces and the lack of true freedom for both protagonists at the end of the film. As to the first, Nancy and Pato's solidarity is a positive defiance of the negativity of the inside/urban space. There are several instances where Pato, for example, brings Nancy food or tries to help her in some way. Ultimately, Nancy flees so that she can help Pato and the other young women escape. As for the second, both the outside/urban and outside/rural spaces take on negative connotations. As some of the closing scenes intimate, Pato never feels truly comfortable or free in Buenos Aires and Nancy's partner controls her connections with the outside world, including her correspondence with Pato. Thus, while the temptation is to denominate outside as good and inside as bad in David's film, the reality is more complicated.

Later in his discussion of space, Bachelard ideates the door: "The door schematizes two strong possibilities, which sharply classify two types of daydream. At times, it is closed, bolted, padlocked. At others, it is open, that is to say, wide open."[49] While still avoiding the absolutism of the dichotomy of inside and outside, as cautioned by Bachelard, a discussion of David's film benefits from an examination of the space of the door. Doors and the sound of closing doors are ever-present in *La mosca*; for example, in the rural restaurant bathroom stalls at the beginning of the film, the street-level door of the building in Buenos Aires, the doors to the rooms where the young women are held and where they meet with clients, and the back door of the man who eventually helps Nancy. Whereas Bachelard addresses the image of the door in a more positive light—an entryway or starting point of a daydream—the doors in David's film are more sinister. The first doors, in the bathroom, hide Nancy's initial escape when Pato tries to talk her into going to the capital with the woman promising jobs. The street-level door in Buenos Aires is the last turning point for the two young women between freedom and captivity; Pato senses this and hesitates before entering. The individual room doors inside the building either hold the young girls in a specific place or enclose them with the men paying for their services. Finally, Nancy reaches the back door of a man who can help them escape. This is the only threshold that represents hope in a series of images of doors that entrap, enclose, and imprison. If we consider the differences between the protagonists' rural origins and urban experience, there are certainly more doors in the second and these doors represent, for the most part, restrictions and barriers. Moreover, in the end, the clichéd 'doorway to freedom' is not so free for Nancy and Pato, as discussed earlier.

In conclusion, David's feature film *La mosca en la ceniza* provides an opportunity to examine the young protagonists' lives from the perspective of intersectionality theory. In so doing, it is clear that Nancy and Pato's experiences directly relate to the intersecting factors of gender, adolescence, rural otherness, and cognitive ability. Whereas looking at one or two of these factors gives us an idea of what leads to young women being trapped in sex trafficking schemes, it is only when we view their identities from multiple standpoints that we see the full extent of society's oppression exercised against them and the degree of impunity their oppressors enjoy. Nancy and Pato's gender and age as young women work in tandem with their rural otherness and Nancy's alternative cognitive abilities, which make them marked victims of men and women from the capital who manipulate young women from the provinces and entrap them in prostitution rings. With this film, David enters a genre of filmmaking that highlights the experiences of these young women and challenges contemporary perceptions of gender equality. It also remains relevant amid current debates in Argentina over women's rights and contemporary social movements, including Les Pibes, Las Pañuelos Verdes, and #NiUnaMenos.[50] While David's film focuses more on the rural/urban divide, the films in the following chapter depict indigeneity on a rural/urban continuum.

CHAPTER 4

INDIGENEITY AND THE RURAL/URBAN CONTINUUM

Claudia Llosa's *Madeinusa* and *La teta asustada* and Itandehui Jansen's *Tiempo de lluvia*

COMPARING CLAUDIA LLOSA'S FILMS *Madeinusa* and *La teta asustada* to Itandehui Jansen's film *Tiempo de lluvia* offers new insight into facets of intersectionality and indigeneity. More specifically, the films in question highlight the crossroads between ethnicity, gender, national identity, regional origins, linguistic difference, and socioeconomic class. Furthermore, they provide a nuanced look at the rural/urban continuum. In contrast to the previous chapter examining the rural and urban in Gabriela David's *La mosca en la ceniza*, the three films in this chapter depict Indigenous characters moving between rural and urban settings. Thus, this chapter analyzes internal migration as it relates to indigeneity, "the other," and intersectionality and underscores two different approaches to Indigenous filmic representation. On the one hand, Llosa's films rely on a mythical interpretation of indigeneity and, on the other, Jansen's film underscores a migration story based on the script writer's personal experiences. Significantly, both the director, Jansen, and the writer, Armando Bautista, are of Mixtec origin. This chapter calls on the ideas set forth by Julia A. Kroll, Maria Chiara D'Argenio, Trinh T. Minh-ha, Paul A. Schroeder Rodríguez, Pirjo Kristiina Virtanen, Angus McNelly, Nancy Postero, and Freya Schiwy, among others. This chapter explores how an intersectional interpretation of Llosa's and Jansen's films underlines the structural oppression the protagonists experience as well as any possibilities for agency.

Madeinusa, Llosa's first feature-length film, tells the story of the homonymous protagonist (played by Magaly Solier) and her relationship with Salvador (Carlos J. del Torre), a geographer who arrives from Lima and is detained in Manayaycuna.[1] With the arrival of "holy time," a fictional Holy Week (Semana Santa), the members of the village of Manayaycuna believe that God does not see their sins from Good Friday to Easter. Therefore, they trade spouses, women pursue men, and Madeinusa's father, Cayo (Juan Ubaldo Huamán), waits for this moment to sleep with his daughter. Instead, Madeinusa sleeps with Salvador and asks him to take her to Lima, which he first refuses to do and subsequently accepts. At the end of the film, when Madeinusa kills Cayo, she and her sister Chale (Yiliana Chong) accuse Salvador of the murder and the protagonist flees alone to Lima. Llosa's second feature-length film, *La teta asustada* (The milk of sorrow), follows the story of Fausta (Magaly Solier) and her experiences in Lima after her mother's death. The film could almost be seen as a narrative continuation of the first. Fausta tries to take her mother's body to her village but cannot find the money or a way to do so. Consequently, she takes work in the house of Aída (Susi Sánchez), a musician who asks Fausta to repeat a song she sings in Quechua. Eventually, the film reveals that Aída has stolen the song for one of her piano compositions. While Aída garners acclaim for the piano piece, Fausta is abandoned by the side of the highway in the night for simply remarking that the public liked the song. Throughout, the film underscores the socioeconomic differences between the mestizo population in central Lima and the Quechua communities on the outskirts of the city.

Llosa's *Madeinusa* and *La teta asustada* depict nonspecific, mythical Andean Indigenous populations.[2] However, the actress who portrays the protagonist in both films is Magaly Solier from Huanta, Ayacucho, Peru. She is from a Quechua family and speaks both Quechua and Spanish. Since starring in Llosa's films, Solier has appeared in several films and series throughout Latin America and Europe. She is also a singer who performs in Quechua, Aymara, Ashaninka, and Muchik. While Llosa's films do not name a specific Indigenous population, and the mythical village in the film is called Manayaycuna (*pueblo encerrado*, "a town no one can enter"), they are filmed in the Province of Huaraz in Canrey Chico, Peru and Lima, Peru. They specifically depict Andean Quechua culture, a society descended from the Incas. While there are Quechua communities throughout the Andean region—including in Bolivia, Ecuador, Colombia, and Peru—Llosa's films depict Quechuan culture specific to the Peruvian Andes and the Cordillera Blanca in west central Peru. The Quechuan communities in the central Andes are descendants of the Incas, whose empire ruled for a century before the Conquest. This civilization had advanced governing structures, food storage systems, and architecture and was the largest pre-Columbian empire. Most Indigenous Peruvians are Quechua or of Quechua descent and the language is one of the official languages of the country alongside Spanish.

Jansen's *Tiempo de lluvia* shows the experiences of two women and migration—Adela (Alejandra Herrera), who moves to Mexico City for work, and Soledad (Ángeles Cruz), her mother who stays behind in their village and cares for Adela's young son José (Nu Kahnu).[3] Soledad is a healer and teaches her grandson about the different plants and remedies she uses. Adela works as a maid in a hotel in Mexico City to save money to bring her son to live with her in the capital. She is in an abusive relationship and is saved from the streets by a woman who takes her into her home and helps her to regain her confidence. The woman speaks Spanish and Nahuatl and the two talk about speaking another language that is not the dominant Spanish, as Adela speaks Mixtec along with Spanish. The last section of the film shows Adela finding a new job in a gallery, returning to her village, bonding with José, and returning to the capital with him. Some of the key intersecting elements of this filmic depiction of migration include a sense of loss and recovery of culture, linguistic difference, gender roles, and socioeconomic class. Furthermore, there is a contrast between the representations of rural versus urban Mexico.[4] The figure of the young mother, Adela, is key to this intersectional approach to Jansen's film; whether physically present, or absent yet omnipresent in the conversations and thoughts of Soledad and José, the young woman represents the crossroads of identities underscored by the director.

Tiempo de lluvia depicts a Mixtec community in the mountains of Oaxaca, Mexico. The Mixtec peoples were in the region by 1500 BCE and had developed sophisticated societies with architecture, terrace farming, irrigation, a calendar, and glyphic writing by 750 CE. Mixtec kingdoms are referenced in tenth-century codexes, with some dynasties lasting hundreds of years. In 1350 CE, the Mixtec society took control of Monte Alban near the city today called Oaxaca and ruled there until the Aztecs began to conquer the region in the fifteenth century and forced tribute payments on the inhabitants. The Aztecs did not seek to take the land from the Mixtecs; however, many Spaniards with their arrival at the beginning of the Conquest chose to settle in the region and take over historical and religious sites. The term Mixtec means "rain people" or "cloud people," thus the title of Jansen's film. Today, the Mixtec peoples live mainly in Northwestern Oaxaca and also represent a large portion of the immigrant population in California as well as the internal migrant populations of Mexico City and Baja California Sur. Along with Jansen's film *Tiempo de lluvia*, other representations of Mixtec culture include Ángeles Cruz's *Nudo mixteco* (Mixtec knot; 2021); Alfonso Cuarón's *Roma* (2018)—in the figure of the protagonist and the Mixtec language spoken in the film—; and Jansen's current film project *Ciudad de pedernales* (Flint City; in production), about a twelfth-century Mixtec princess.

There are clear similarities and differences between Llosa's and Jansen's films. Namely, the parallels among the three films include a contrast between an Indigenous village and the capital; the idea of Indigenous migration to the capital; Indigenous representation in terms of characters, language, songs, and dress; and notions of "the other," intersectionality, and indigeneity. On the other hand, the variations between them include Llosa's treatment of a realm closer to the mythic or at least an imaginary that relies on mythical tropes of indigeneity while Jansen's film is more straightforward and realistic. Additionally, Jansen's film is based on her and the screenwriter's personal experiences as Mixtec individuals while Llosa's film is created from a mestizo perspective. Through scene analyses, the similarities and differences between the two directors' approaches to Indigenous representation become apparent. Llosa's *Madeinusa* and *La teta asustada*, the first to be examined in this chapter, explore issues of indigeneity, "the other," intersectional identities, and the contrasts between the rural and urban settings. In particular, there are three scenes that exemplify Llosa's approach: from the first film, an encounter between Madeinusa and Salvador and the final scene of the protagonist leaving in a truck and, from the second film, the moment when Aída abandons Fausta on the road.

MADEINUSA AND LA TETA ASUSTADA

There is a scene in *Madeinusa* that begins with the image of the Andes and sounds of nature in the background and represents an abrupt change from a scene preceding it, containing the strident music of a festival. The first shot is a wide shot of mountains; the characters enter one by one, Salvador first. We hear his footsteps as he crosses out of the frame and disappears from view, then Madeinusa arrives with the sound of her footsteps and her costume. In the next shot, Madeinusa slowly follows Salvador until she joins him on some stones where they sit. Salvador comments, "Es un pueblo extraño, éste" (It's a strange town, this one), to which she replies, "¿Vienes de Lima?" (Are you from Lima?) What follows is a discussion of Salvador's need to leave, Madeinusa's offer to help him, and the confession that her mother lives in Lima. Afterward, she sings him a song, half in Spanish and half in Quechua where she declares her interest in stealing his heart. This entire scene is a microcosm of the film itself where Madeinusa follows Salvador in a seemingly docile and passive position while he appears to be in control, at least in his relationship with her. The song ends as the film ends—Madeinusa abandons her submissive position to communicate her plans to steal his heart and, at the end of the film, she leaves in a truck, taking the trip to the capital originally intended for Salvador.[5]

Analyzing this scene, the background sound signals changes in tone; the spatial relationship of the characters is significant to the theme of the scene; the dialogue introduces the motif of the "other"; and the song and the entire scene are a representation of the film itself. First, considering the background sound, in the moments before this one, the music is very loud, and the characters accompany it with their shouts and whistles. The cut to the next take is abrupt; only the birds and the wind in the grass are heard until the characters arrive with their quiet steps. Until this point in the scene, only the jingle of Madeinusa's costume stands out. However, this artificial and seemingly innocent sound is significant because it is a premonition of Madeinusa's power; it is she who makes her presence known in the scene the most through these adornments. The next observation relates to the position of the characters in the frame. Again, in the earlier scene, there are multiple characters in the picture, they are all moving frantically, and it is hard to follow anyone's image because others always appear between them and the camera. In contrast, the scene in question begins without characters, and when they appear, they arrive one by one in the frame and very slowly. There is a moment when Salvador is in the center of the frame with his back to the camera and Madeinusa emerges from the lower left corner and follows him, almost

FIGURE 4.1. Madeinusa at the village ceremony. *Madeinusa* (2005).

covering him with her own image. This scene is very peaceful compared to the chaos of the previous scene. Furthermore, her position covering his image is prescient of the end of the film when she takes his place in the truck to Lima.

The next observation is that the dialogue introduces the theme of the "other." Analyzing this scene independently from the others, Madeinusa's dress is the first visual element that introduces her "otherness"—it is a dress with an ornamental cover that jingles when she walks and is notable for not being traditional Western dress. The dialogue that follows between the two characters also underscores the theme of otherness or the other. First, Salvador comments that it is a strange town and then states that he is from Lima. They talk about Madeinusa's mother who went to Lima and how the protagonist wants to go to the capital. Salvador establishes the line of questioning of the other when he says that it is a strange town; he does not understand the customs and designates the townspeople as strangers. Seemingly, Madeinusa and her community are the others, and he, from the city, comes from the normative world. In fact, this interpretation has given rise to critiques of the film in that Llosa orientalizes—exoticizes—the members of Manayaycuna just as Salvador does. The interesting aspect of this scene and the last one of the

FIGURE 4.2. Madeinusa and Salvador sit in a field as they converse and she sings. *Madeinusa* (2005).

film, which is also analyzed in this chapter, is that they show the flip side of the theme of otherness: Who really is the other? Still in this scene, it seems it is Madeinusa in her guise as the representative of the "strange" town. Later, he asks her for a miracle, given that she is the town's "virgin" for Holy Week and then says, "O a ti también se te secó la mollera?" (Or did your brain dry up too?), as if this were the condition of all the people in the community. Nevertheless, this very fact of not understanding the customs insinuates that Salvador is the other in this situation, which will become clearer in the analysis of the last scene.

The last observation regarding this moment in the film is that Madeinusa's song and the entire scene are a microcosm of the film. The song begins "¿Por qué me miras así? No sabes de dónde soy. Yo soy una provinciana, Manayaycuna de corazón" (Why are you looking at me like that? You don't know where I'm from. I am a provincial, Manayaycuna at heart). Throughout the song, Madeinusa keeps her gaze passive, looking down and quickly glancing at Salvador, not meeting his eyes. This passive manner parallels how Madeinusa is with Salvador in most of the film. Likewise, the words of the first part of her song represent this posture and reinforce the image of her as the other. On the other hand, the second part of the song, in Quechua, affirms a more dynamic attitude:

"Con esta canción, te voy a robar el corazón" (With this song, I am going to steal your heart). This last part of the song is like a premonition of what will happen at the end of the film and represents a change of perspective and power between Madeinusa and Salvador, first because they are no longer passive words and, second because he does not understand Quechua. Paradoxically, the protagonist's gaze and her voice are lower in this scene; thus, the outcome is even more surprising. Julia A. Kroll examines this song:

> The second song, which is bilingual, creates a tapestry of subtext as it both wonders at and protests the alterity reflected in the stranger's perception of her.... Madeinusa then asserts the power of the Indigenous identity through native language.... Made's wonder and passivity are expressed in Spanish, with Quechua entering the song as a powerful, private instrument imbued with the capacity to maintain secret her desire and also, to transform an Andean woman's wishes into future action.[6]

Kroll also underscores the theme of otherness, alterity, and draws attention to the perspective of Salvador toward Madeinusa in the first part of the song. Likewise, the critic points to the change of power in the second half, when the protagonist sings in Quechua and communicates her desire to steal the outsider's heart. With all this, it is evident that the song is a representation of the film itself in which the protagonist begins as a passive object—following Salvador, looking down, with her hands over her mouth at various times and speaking in a very low voice—and ends as an active subject, taking away his freedom by accusing him of the death of her father. In addition, the roles are reversed as she is the one who takes his place on the truck that travels to Lima; in effect, she entangles him in a trap that allows her to finally escape the village.

Kroll's observation also brings to light the particular intersectionality presented in Llosa's film. Questions of gender, indigeneity, and the rural/urban continuum arise as the conversation and song progress. Madeinusa's apparent passivity seems to fit with traditional gender roles; however, throughout the film, the protagonist finds ways to control outcomes. She thwarts her father's efforts to sleep with her, lays the blame for his murder on Salvador, and travels to the capital in his place.[7] These scenes present the protagonist's intersecting gender and Indigenous identities. Again, while she seems to conform to stereotypical roles assigned to her by her community and outsiders, she in fact resists these roles. Moreover, the Holy Week time in the film shows other women also resisting passivity. Like her mother before her, Madeinusa disrupts the rural/urban divide. When she leaves Salvador trapped in the village and escapes to the capital, she turns the tables on the division between rural and urban. Llosa explores new ways in which her protagonist's gender and indigeneity intersect with rural/urban identity.

The last scene in the film when the protagonist leaves embodies the themes of the other and the powerful transformation of the protagonist. The last image before cutting to the end is of a statue of the Virgin with her arms up, imploring. Then, as in the first scene analyzed, the film cuts back to the image of nature when the truck slowly enters the frame. As in the first scene, only the sounds of the birds and the wind in the grass are heard until the truck approaches. It enters the screen on the right side and reaches the middle; after following it, the camera cuts to an image inside the truck. The background sounds are of the old vehicle clanging from the effort and uneven road. The camera focuses on the windshield with the shoe and bag hanging from the rearview mirror. Behind these objects, you can see the road that extends ahead into the landscape. Right in front is a hood ornament that looks like an angel flying over the road. The film cuts to the image of Madeinusa in the back, establishing a connection between her and the ornament in her freedom. As she braids her clipped hair to that of her doll, the driver asks her what her name is, to which she replies "Madeinusa" and then he asks, "¿A dónde vamos?" (Where are we going?) Madeinusa touches her earrings—her mother's, thus closing the circle of migration to the city—and replies smiling, "A Lima" (To Lima). As the driver's voice fades and the sound of the music rises, the camera follows the gaze of the protagonist, who looks straight ahead—to the highway, the angel, the mountains, and toward Lima.

Of this last scene in *Madeinusa*, the following reflections are relevant: first, the objects that appear in the image—the statue of the virgin, the doll, and the hood ornament—are significant; second, the perspective of the camera is parallel to that of Madeinusa and third, the ending with her smile highlights the theme of the other, exposing the man from Lima as other and not her. Regarding the first observation, not only the statue of the virgin, but all the objects that appear in the image of Madeinusa's father's attic represent her captivity, an image of enclosure similar to that of the characters in David's *La mosca en la ceniza*. Just before the last scene in the truck, the camera pans to the room where her father keeps the statues, dolls and objects dedicated to the virgin. In their combination, they symbolize the protagonist's captivity, as if she were the father's property. This is reminiscent of an earlier scene in which Madeinusa is trapped in the attic and her father offers the man from Lima something from the room, which he rejects. The connection is clear between the relics in the attic and Madeinusa—they are property to be held or given away by the father. On the other hand, the last scene embodies the protagonist's freedom, particularly with the juxtaposition of the image in the attic with that of the open field and the road stretching endlessly into the distance. The cryptic sound of the attic, with the tinkling of bells, is contrasted with the murmur of the birds and the wind in the last scene that symbolize a transformation for Madeinusa. The doll in her lap now bears her hair and, metaphorically, she holds it in her own hands—not an heirloom in the attic of her father's house. Likewise, the hood ornament is a symbol of her independence as it faces forward in front of the truck, toward a new life.

The second observation is that the camera's perspective resembles that of Madeinusa. After filming the truck from the side, entering the scene, the camera cuts and the image comes from inside the truck, in fact, from the back seat. Thus, the camera takes her subjective perspective and shows us how Madeinusa's escape is perceived from her gaze. This is significant because up to this point, the camera has captured the protagonist from angles that show her lack of power, for example, shooting her from above. When she is with Salvador, she covers her mouth with her hands in a gesture of nervousness and submission. The last scene is a clear departure from the previous stance; the protagonist smiles when she answers that she is going to Lima. This smile is a transformation of her behavior up to this point in the film; when she answers the driver, she is sure of herself and meets his eyes through the mirror. This change in Madeinusa brings us to the theme of the other because it is where Llosa confirms that Salvador, the man from Lima, is the other, the one who does not know the rules. For most of the film, the assumption is that Madeinusa is othered for being Indigenous and having beliefs different from those of the capital, but by the end, it is clear that Salvador is the one who does not understand, and the conclusion reaffirms this. As Kroll says: "When the camera-toting geographer from Lima enters the picture, he, like the viewer, becomes trapped in his incomprehension of the world unfolding before him."[8] In fact, Kroll discusses the idea of Madeinusa as a siren who catches Salvador in her spell, starting with the first song she sings to him.⁹ Earlier, Kroll explains the town name: "Portrayed communities is evident in the town name: Manayaycuna—which in Quechua means 'the town that no one can enter.' That the town is impervious to non-Indigenous understanding is clear in its name and in its traditional, hierarchical social organization."¹⁰ So, Salvador enters the town but does not understand its way of living or thinking; he is the other in this context while Madeinusa represents the establishment. These ideas take shape in the transformation of the protagonist from an extremely shy and nervous person to the young woman who smiles on the truck to Lima.

The theme of the other as it relates to indigeneity and intersectionality is central in the film *Madeinusa* and centers around the relationship between the protagonist and Salvador. The scenes discussed here illustrate how Madeinusa appears to be the other but she converts Salvador into the other, the one who does not understand and is outside the norm. In this sense, the customs of the Manayaycuna people govern and not those of Lima; apparent Indigenous traditions prevail over mestizo ones and the protagonist also triumphs in the end. The denouement confirms this with Madeinusa's triumphant escape. However, some critics point to problems with the image of Indigenous people in Llosa's films; specifically, Maria Chiara D'Argenio points to Llosa's films and their tendency toward "a colonialist-style discourse on the difference between The West and the non-West. The films' cultural and aesthetic 'operations,' . . . despite being well articulated, fail in proposing a non-Eurocentric approach to the Andean, as well as in addressing the intricacies of a multifaceted and multicultural Peruvian society."¹¹ D'Argenio goes on to challenge Llosa's depiction of otherness: "Rather, Peru appears as an ethnically, culturally and socially two-sided country within which the placement of tradition and modernity, backwardness and progress is made clear."¹² According to critics such as D'Argenio, Llosa presents a colonialist juxtaposition between Western and non-Western characters. According to this line of criticism, Peru is represented to the international public as a country of dichotomies between the people of Lima and the Indigenous populations, the moderns and the pre-moderns, and progress and stagnation. Part of the censure comes from Peru's image abroad, as Llosa's films have received considerable international attention. These comments explicitly criticize Llosa for exoticizing the other. The previously mentioned scenes in *Madeinusa* problematize this idea and complicate who the other really is.

FIGURE 4.3. Aída and Fausta in a garden. *La teta asustada* (2009).

In *La teta asustada*, there is not the same flipping of roles, however there is an explicit criticism of the treatment of Indigenous communities in Lima. Above all, this is interpreted in the relationship between the protagonist Fausta and Aída. First, when Fausta arrives at the house to work, another servant inspects her mouth, teeth, and hands. The inspection reduces her to physical property of the owner of the house and recalls slavery when value was measured by bodily appearance and health. The employee starts with the ears and then the mouth, teeth, neck and hands. She finds one long fingernail and says, "¿Por qué no te la has cortado? . . . Porque tú sabes que por estas cosas así, la señora se puede desanimar" (Why haven't you cut it? . . . Because you know that because of things like this, the lady can change her mind). Afterward, she instructs her to shower every day, put on deodorant without fail, and stay in the kitchen if the owner does not need her. The entire scene recalls the idea of the human body as property. Furthermore, insisting on the need to bathe and use deodorant every day is symbolic condescension toward the Indigenous population and prejudice against their cleanliness and health. Finally, by telling her that "the lady" can change her mind because of a long uncut fingernail, she reminds viewers of the lack of rights that domestic employees have. In this scene, Fausta is put in an othered position of submission. In contrast to the first film, *Madeinusa*, here Llosa emphasizes the reduction of the protagonist to the other and criticizes this systemic oppression more directly.[13]

This is clear in the scene when Aída throws Fausta out of the car. When the protagonist had first started working in Aída's home, the older woman had asked her to sing her songs, and toward the end of the film, Fausta listens to one of Aída's concerts in which she plays the protagonist's own song. Fausta is surprised and disappointed but says nothing until she is in the car with the woman and her son. The conversation between the two is as follows:

> AÍDA: ¿Y tú, qué? ¿No me dices nada? (And what about you? You have nothing to say to me?)
> AÍDA'S son: Felicitaciones. Estaba muy bien. (Congratulations. It was very good.)
> AÍDA: Estaba todo Lima, ¿no? (All of Lima was there, right?)

All this happens between the two of them, smiling and calm, sitting in the front of the car; the camera captures the conversation from behind, as if from Fausta's perspective. It cuts to an image of Fausta in the backseat, smiling too, as if sharing their happiness, and she says, "Les gustó mucho, ¿no?" (They really liked it, didn't they?) Suddenly, the woman's expression changes to one of hostility and a silence follows, after which Aída says: "Isidra [Fausta] se queda aquí. Ella va caminando" (Isidra [Fausta] will stay here. She is walking). Apparently, she has interpreted Fausta's comment as a reference to her own song. They stop at the corner; it is night, and we already know that Fausta is terrified of being alone and much more so at night. The young woman slowly gets out of the car, and as the car drives away, the camera catches an image of Fausta walking quickly down the side of the road with a terrified expression. The scene takes advantage of the camera angle and the position of the characters in the shot. During the hostile interaction, the camera inside the car focuses on Fausta, from Aída's perspective. Then the car, with the camera inside, moves to the right and soon Fausta disappears to the left, screaming in Quechua.

Aída's cruelty is evident in this scene and highlights Llosa's explicit criticism of the way Indigenous people are treated. In a previous scene, there is a moment when Aída tells Fausta not to get up, that she can wash her own dishes. At this point, it is possible to think that the older woman is not typical, and that she respects the younger woman. In addition, she insists that Fausta sing a song in Quechua, making us think that she is interested in her. However, during the piano concert later in the film, we realize that Aída has stolen the melody without giving Fausta credit. In a sense, this is what critics have said about Llosa as a filmmaker. However,

FIGURE 4.4. Fausta smells a flower. *La teta asustada* (2009).

even more so in this second feature film, Llosa criticizes the system that values the mestizo community over the Indigenous one and that takes advantage of the latter. This criticism is evident in scenes such as when Aída leaves Fausta by the side of the road in the middle of the night. Other scenes further underscore this critique of a system that divides the mestizo and Indigenous people of Lima geographically, socially, and economically. For example, Fausta lives on the outskirts of Lima where inhabitants must climb a very steep tiled slope to reach a town of much less luxurious houses with several people living in each home. On the contrary, in the center of Lima, Aída lives alone in a colonial house, with a huge patio closed off from the street. The separation between Aída's and Fausta's worlds is clear, and the physical division is the slope that only those from the outskirts have to cross to work in the city. Other divisions are the fence of Aída's house that divides her property from the street and the car that she and her son have that separate them from Fausta physically but also symbolically in terms of social class. Thus, *La teta asustada* represents a more critical censorship of the treatment of Indigenous Quechua peoples in Peru than *Madeinusa*.

Another factor is the title of the film, *La teta asustada*, which refers to the idea that a baby inherits the mother's fear through her breast milk when she has been raped during or just after pregnancy. It refers to a prolonged period of violence toward the Indigenous populations of the Andes in Peru in the 1980s and 1990s when Andean villagers were abused by the military and Shining Path revolutionaries. Central to the abuse was the rape of women, and the first song heard in *La teta asustada* is that of Fausta's mother who was raped and forced to witness the murder of her husband. A dominant theme in this film is the fear that Fausta inherits from her mother that, according to Fausta and her mother's songs, comes directly from this rape and abuse.[14] Fausta's fear manifests itself in an enigmatic way—she inserts a potato in her vagina. Critics have read this in different ways; while Gastón Lillo sees this as a mechanism of maintaining the memory of her mother's rape, Patricia Varas interprets it as a form of exercising agency—literally blocking her body from the possible invasion of rape.[15] Additionally, for Varas, the potato creates a memory connection with her community, namely those who fell victim to the violence, and serves as a deterrence to any possible violators: "Ella es una portadora de la memoria de su comunidad y ha convertido su cuerpo en abyecto" (She is a bearer of her community's memory and has turned her body into the abject).[16] *La teta asustada* continuously refers to the concept of inherited memory and fear and, in so doing, makes it central to the critique of the system that oppresses the Indigenous populations in Peru. In other words, indirect references to the violence appear frequently enough in the film that they must be considered—from the first interaction with the film, which is the title itself. Thus, Llosa criticizes the oppression of Indigenous populations through the theory of inherited fear. Within the context of the film, Fausta's terror is palpable on screen, and this becomes a constant reminder of her story, that of her family, and of her mother's rape.[17]

Regarding theories of speaking for the other, Minh-ha develops an alternative theory of "speaking nearby." Part of the criticism against Llosa as a director arises from this concern of speaking for the other, above all because she is from Lima and mestiza, and the protagonists of her first two feature films are Indigenous. Minh-ha argues for speaking nearby, "a speaking that does not objectify, does not point to an object as if it is distant from the speaking subject or absent from the speaking place. A speaking that reflects on itself and can come very close to a subject without, however, seizing or claiming it. . . . It is an attitude in life, a way of positioning oneself in relation to the world."[18] This same concern is also examined by Gayatri Chakravorty Spivak in "Can the Subaltern Speak," where the theorist criticizes that the Western subject

FIGURE 4.5. Wedding ceremony on outskirts of Lima. *La teta asustada* (2009).

speaks for the other, the subaltern. Minh-ha, on the other hand, advocates a practice of speaking close to the subject to avoid turning them into a passive object. In this way, the speaker attempts to avoid objectifying or taking possession of the other, but rather tries to get closer. This approach is fundamental for Minh-ha, since it implies respecting the agency and subject position of the person who is the center of any discussion in cinema, literature, and other forms of art. For Minh-ha, this also means that what appears in a film has meaning inside and out. According to her, we must approach the subject without preconceived notions—not imposing our own word, image, or sound to arrive at an idea that already exists within the subject, but approaching them, letting them speak for themself. Minh-ha touches on the method of speaking nearby in *D-Passage* as well, "entering . . . with the self as an empty, experiential site of reference."[19] Accordingly, the creator of art made about another approaches the subject with as little preconception as possible. Indeed, as Spivak questions, can the subaltern speak? In this context and with Minh-ha's comments, the question is, can the subaltern speak in a film not made by this same individual? Minh-ha's theory suggests so, on the condition that the creator approaches the subject adjacently rather than trying to take the other's position.

Thus, the question is whether Llosa approaches the Indigenous subjects of her films or tries to take their place and speak for them. According to various critics, she does the second, asserting a voice for the Indigenous protagonists, Madeinusa and Fausta. However, it is possible to consider how she does both in her attempt to portray the 'other' in her films. In addition, as in the example of *Madeinusa*, she removes the Indigenous protagonist from the position of the 'other' and places the character from Lima in this position, a character who generally would be the central Western subject. In the second film, *La teta asustada*, Llosa openly criticizes the system that keeps the Indigenous protagonist in the subaltern position. In this way, she tries to approach Fausta instead of appropriating her voice, as Aída does when she steals her song. In addition, the film includes several scenes in which the protagonist speaks in Quechua, although the filmmaker provides subtitles for the Spanish-speaking public. Llosa's protagonists sing in Quechua, a mode of representation akin to Minh-ha's idea of positioning oneself alongside— Llosa allows her protagonists to express themselves "verbally, musically, visually," making use of Minh-ha's concept. While it can be recognized that the director comes from what would traditionally be considered a Western position of power, she endeavors to let the Indigenous subjects of her films speak for themselves, specifically in scenes such as the ones analyzed in this chapter. Likewise, she criticizes the system of power that victimizes the Indigenous subaltern.

On *La teta asustada*, Schroeder Rodríguez writes: "From the very beginning . . . this film calls attention to rape as both an individual and a collective experience: individual because it was this specific woman and her daughter Fausta . . . who suffered the rape, and collective because rape was a weapon of war used by both the Sendero Luminoso and the state armed forces to terrorize Indigenous communities into supporting their side of the conflict."[20] The critic goes on the say: "the narrative does not center so much on the systematic rape of Indigenous women per se, as on the ensuing trauma, and more specifically, on how the past could be remembered in ways that aid rather than hinder the victims' recovery. Broadly speaking, Fausta's traumatic memory evolves from something that thoroughly limits her to something she can overcome through resilience."[21] Schroeder Rodríguez recognizes the possibilities for agency that Fausta holds in *La teta asustada*. The critic also emphasizes that this second film avoids conventional fable as it is set in modern times with a specific setting in Lima rather than a mythical time and place and does not propose a moral choice.[22] He later suggests that the film focuses on the individual and collective, "as part of an actual system of social practices and cultural values with historical, political, racial, ethnic, and gender dimensions that together foster and justify rape as a socially acceptable form of violence and repression. [T]his view of rape necessitates an understanding of trauma as a social phenomenon."[23] Schroeder Rodríguez identifies an intersectional explanation for the systemic inequalities that allow for the oppression of Indigenous communities based on questions of gender, race, ethnicity, and socioeconomic class, among others. However, as in the earlier quote, he also sees Llosa's filmic depiction of rape as individual in the sense that it explores individual trauma and the possibilities for recovery.

TIEMPO DE LLUVIA

Llosa and Jansen both focus on Indigenous protagonists in their films. Furthermore, both directors examine intersectional issues of gender and indigeneity, rural/urban identity, Indigenous migration, and the other. While Llosa's films are told from the perspective of Indigenous characters, she herself is mestiza and from the capital. In contrast, Jansen is Mixtec and the screenwriter, Armando Bautista, relies heavily on his own experiences as a Mixtec boy migrating to Mexico City. Jansen's approach to Indigenous filmic representation is of a more realist style than Llosa's and focuses on indigeneity represented on the rural/urban continuum. In particular, there are three scenes in *Tiempo de lluvia* that exemplify the film's depiction of indigeneity, gender, language, the other, and the rural/urban continuum: Soledad and José together in the mountains, Adela with the woman who saves her from the streets, and Adela and José in their Mexico City apartment singing a Mixtec song. Adela, the young mother in the middle of this generational triad is central to Jansen's filmic exploration of structural oppression and cultural and community tension.

The juxtaposition of certain scenes in *Tiempo de lluvia* illustrates the stark physical and cultural differences between the village in Oaxaca and Mexico City. In this way, Jansen audio-visually depicts the rural/urban disparity; however, she also highlights the continuum that exists between these two spaces, as the characters move and travel back and forth between the two. Visually, the Oaxacan village in the film is high in the mountains and the grandmother travels frequently to a spot with a waterfall and pool as well as a place that overlooks the valleys and peaks of other mountains. In one of these scenes, Soledad and José sit

FIGURE 4.6. Soledad and José sit in mountains in Oaxaca. *Tiempo de lluvia* (2018).

close together on what appears to be the peak of a mountain, looking out at a valley and another mountain peak beyond, the summit covered in clouds. Soledad's basket of medicinal herbs is on one side of her, and José is on her other side as they lean into each other. In this scene, José asks his grandmother about her travels and if she has ever gone beyond the adjacent mountain, to which Soledad replies that she used to travel to villages in those mountains with her parents, learning about the plants and herbs and visiting people. In this way, she learned her trade of healing, a knowledge that she begins to share with her grandson. Soledad is directly connected to nature, as most of her scenes involve herbs, trees, mountains, natural water features, or clouds. Moreover, she learns from nature and uses natural elements in her healing practices. She seeks to pass this worldview on to José as he walks with her collecting plants and visiting patients.

Considering this scene, the following observations can be made: the spatial relationship of grandmother and grandson is elemental; their dialogue reminds the viewer of Soledad's deep connection to nature and the surrounding communities; and this scene is symbolic of the rural end of the continuum represented in Jansen's film. First, the centering of the two characters closely together on screen and surrounded by nature is noteworthy. Jansen underscores Soledad and José's special relationship and closeness. They both sit calmly on the outcropping, looking out, and seem to be at peace where they are and with each other. They speak softly and listen intently to what the other is saying as well as the sounds of nature around them. As with the first scene examined in Llosa's *Madeinusa*, here the characters are placed together on screen, in nature, and are the only ones in the scene. As with Llosa's scene, Soledad and José sit on a rock and have a conversation. The relationship between these two characters is one of the most significant in the film. First, José has been living with his grandmother and this life is all he knows. She represents security, stability, gentleness, and love. The physical proximity and low, calm tones of their conversation manifest these characteristics of their relationship. Second, in the narrative arc of the film, Soledad and José represent two ends of a continuum. Eventually, José will go to the capital with his mother and Soledad will stay in the village; thus, the two represent the ends of the rural/urban continuum. While the film implies they are not definitively separated by this move, it is clear that the grandmother's life is in Oaxaca and José's is in the capital. Considering this as a rural/urban continuum is important, however, since the film also creates a structure for José to remain connected to his Indigenous culture and return to visit his grandmother in their village, as Adela does during the course of the narrative.

A second observation on this scene is related to the characters' dialogue. Visually, Soledad and José appear in a natural setting surrounded by mountains, plants, and Soledad's medicinal herbs. Their dialogue evokes this same connection to nature as well as the surrounding Indigenous communities. Before reaching the rock, Soledad and José gather herbs that she uses in her healing practice, and she answers her grandson's questions about their names and uses. He says when he grows up, he will heal people like she does to which she replies, this is why he needs to know the purpose of each plant. When they reach the outcropping, José asks about a village across the canyon and then: "Y más lejos de ese pueblo, ¿qué hay?" (And farther than that village, what is there?) She replies that there are more mountains. This conversation and the previous one anchor Soledad in her community, history, and surroundings. At the same time, it cleaves José to this reality, as well. The film implies that the young boy shares a deep connection with his grandmother's community, history, and surroundings. This is significant because it emphasizes José's strong bond with Oaxaca and his Indigenous identity. Furthermore, Soledad's story about visiting the other mountain villages with her parents reminds us of José accompanying her on her visits to other community members to offer her healing abilities. José follows in his grandmother's footsteps, learning her healing and community practices. Jansen insinuates that this is a central part of his identity. Even after he is in the capital, he draws pictures of the waterfall and other natural spaces he frequented with his grandmother.

FIGURE 4.7. Soledad and José sitting at table. *Tiempo de lluvia* (2018).

A final observation about this scene in the mountains is that it is symbolic of the rural end of the continuum. At this point in the film, it is unclear whether José will stay with his grandmother in the village or go with his mother to Mexico City. In fact, part of their conversation centers around the fact that Mexico City is beyond the mountains they see and José's mother lives there. To José and Soledad, the capital seems far away and unknown; their world spans the village and surrounding peaks. Furthermore, José's mother Adela is there, and she represents the unknown for her son. Like many Indigenous parents in Oaxaca, she has moved to the capital looking for work and a way to support her child. The conversation on the outcropping continues after Soledad tells José that there are more mountains:

> JOSÉ: "Y, ¿detrás de las montañas?" (And, behind the mountains?)
> SOLEDAD: "Allí es México. Allí vive tu mamá. Algún día vas a tener que ir allí." (That is Mexico. That is where your mother lives. One day you will have to go there.)
> JOSÉ: "Pero yo no quiero ir a México." (But I don't want to go to Mexico.)[24]
> SOLEDAD: "Pero allí vive tu mamá. Algún día vas a tener que ir a vivir allí con ella." (But that is where your mother lives. One day you will have to go to live there with her.)
> JOSÉ: "Pero quiero estar contigo." (But I want to be with you.)

She puts her arm around him, rubs his shoulder, and they both look out toward Mexico City. Although José expresses his desire to stay with

Soledad, she recognizes that he will eventually go to the capital to live with his mother. Soledad is clearly settled and attached to the village and Oaxaca and symbolizes the rural end of the continuum. José is in between, although he wishes to stay, and Adela represents the urban end of this continuum to which José will eventually go. However, rather than a divide between village and capital, Jansen's film depicts a continuum between the two spaces.

RURAL/URBAN CONTINUUM AND INDIGENEITY

It is important not to fall into the false assumption that indigeneity necessarily relates to nature, as critics have contended; however, Jansen clearly connects the two in her film, specifically with the character of Soledad. In *Tiempo de lluvia*, Soledad represents tradition, history, nurturing, a connection with nature, healing, and tranquility. Adela, on the other hand, represents change, the future, self-fulfillment, self-discovery, and action. Yet, Soledad has a modern understanding of her fellow villagers' difficulties and Adela exhibits significant self-sacrifice to provide for her son. Furthermore, Soledad does not keep José from his mother or hide information from him, just as Adela does not sever her ties with her past or her indigeneity. In this way, Jansen avoids a dichotomous representation of her characters, allowing them to inhabit both urban and rural settings, speak Spanish and Mixtec and wear mestizo and Indigenous dress. Unlike in Llosa's *Madeinusa*, the characters are clearly in the present, not in a mythical past, including the inhabitants of the village in Oaxaca. This is significant, as many filmmakers such as Llosa place Indigenous characters in a nonexistent time or the indefinite past and then portray mestizo characters in the modern-day present. What is more, the youngest character José is not forced to choose between the two realities; he does move to Mexico City with his mother, but they continue their traditions in a new setting and the film makes it clear they will have opportunities to return to Soledad for visits. In this way, José represents the future of migrants within Mexico who move to urban settings and forge new ways of being Indigenous.

Of *Tiempo de lluvia*, Jansen has said: "We have tried to stay very close to the Mixtec experience. But at the same time, it is a film about migration and internal migration. The differences between the village and Mexico City are large and financial issues also play a role in moving from village to city."[25] Jansen's comments encapsulate the intersectional focus of the film—the Indigenous, migratory, rural/urban, and socioeconomic aspects of the characters' identities. She emphasizes the equally important factor of economics in the decision of many to move to the capital, as Adela does in *Tiempo de lluvia*. The film's writer, Bautista, moved to the capital far from his parents in their small village of Santa María Apazco, Nochixtlán in Oaxaca at the age of ten to live with his older siblings. In an interview with Cesar Hernandez in *L.A. Taco*, Bautista shares:

> All my brothers and sisters emigrated at a young age without our parents to Mexico City. Many Indigenous persons in Mexico City have a similar story to tell. Opportunities to study and work are extremely limited in rural communities, and people feel they need to leave in order to have access to education and a better life. This process of migration was difficult and often painful in many ways. And, as it continues to happen today, I wanted to incite a reflection on what people leave behind and what happens to community and cultural continuity in this process.[26]

Bautista's insights reflect Adela's and, later, José's experiences leaving the village and going to Mexico City; they recognize the rural reality of needing to seek education and economic welfare in the city while at the same time attempting to maintain cultural continuity. The last scene speaks to Adela and José's continued connection with their Mixtec culture even within the space of an urban apartment.

Pirjo Kristiina Virtanen, addressing the changing motives for Indigenous youth moving to urban centers in Brazil, explains that the central reason for this migration is no longer solely employment but rather education: "However, attempts to achieve better education are still attributed to economic and social motives: education is also perceived as a way of improving one's livelihood."[27] Other reasons given in the study include "accompanying parents working in an Indigenous movement, conflicts within the community, the search for employment, and military service."[28] Considering the back-and-forth nature of Adela's existence and the probability that José will accompany her on her trips back to the village, it is worth noting the permeability of the urban-rural in *Tiempo de lluvia*. Virtanen questions this binary: "Many native populations today share common 'traditions' and histories that extend beyond rural-urban cultural borders, since members of an ethnic group may be residents in

FIGURE 4.8. Adela on bus in Mexico City. *Tiempo de lluvia* (2018).

both the city and the reserve. Movements of people between urban and rural areas are continuous."[29] These perceptions on indigeneity underscore Jansen's depiction of Indigenous migration as well.[30] While Adela's move to the capital is financially motived, her hopes are for her to son to have access to a more formal education than in the village. On the other hand, the film lovingly depicts the significant education José receives from his grandmother in Oaxaca. Virtanen highlights the idea of a rural/urban continuum rather than divide. As the critic contends, many Indigenous groups lead lives in both their village and the city, moving and traveling back and forth for various reasons. Furthermore, Jansen illustrates the metaphoric continuum between village and city through the cultural connection Adela and José bring with them and nurture in the capital. Thus, the idea of continuum more accurately describes these discussions of the rural and urban as they relate to indigeneity and Indigenous migration.

Angus McNelly examines urban indigeneity, in this case in Bolivia, recognizing the persistent negative connection between Latin American indigeneity, rurality, and "backwardness": "On the one hand, Indigenous peoples were considered cultural anomalies outside the modern world, cultural relics that need to be studied and protected. . . . On the other hand, they were considered a problem, a barrier to the modernisation of the continent that had to be overcome."[31] McNelly then references the body of literature that began to question these assumptions in light of renewed attention to Indigenous political and social movements: "This literature definitively ruptured with the hackneyed assumptions about Indigenous peoples, stressing their heterogeneity and the new forms of both indigeneity and urbanity produced by the social impacts of this new Indigenous citizenship."[32] McNelly analyzes and questions the historical persistence of the connections between indigeneity and rurality, criticizing the assumption of rural and Indigenous as underdeveloped. Moreover, the critic recognizes the ways in which Indigenous groups reflect their rurality. These reflections relate to Jansen's characters in *Tiempo de lluvia* as they navigate their Indigenous identities in Mexico City.

Like McNelly, Nancy Postero analyzes indigeneity in the Bolivian context: "Defining and representing indigeneity is a subject of great debate in Bolivia, as elsewhere in the world. Who counts as 'Indigenous' is a fundamentally political question, since such representations emerge from struggles over particular social, cultural, and economic matters during particular moments."[33] Bolivia's new constitution and recognition of the country as a plurinational state has meant more emphasis and study on indigeneity particularly in this Andean country. The question of indigeneity takes on a new importance with the recognition of multiple states, including Indigenous territories, being considered as equal parts of the whole of the country. Yet, as Postero contends: "indigeneity is deeply contested, and ... Indigenous peoples continue to be at the center of disagreements over the national development model based on natural resource extraction, new forms of government, and relations between the central state and local communities."[34] Postero alludes to the multitude of studies on indigeneity that stem from movements in the 1980s and 1990s, which, in turn, focused on such issues as ethnicity, culture, territory, self-determination, as well as exclusion from political institutions and economies.[35]

Along with the political and socioeconomic issues subtly foregrounding Jansen's *Tiempo de lluvia*, language is paramount to her filmic depiction of indigeneity. There is a scene that shows Adela conversing with a woman who saved her from the streets and took her into her own home after she was physically abused by her partner. The woman reveals that she speaks Nahuatl and Adela shares that she speaks Mixtec. Adela's language is another intersectional factor in her identity; she is a rural, young, Indigenous woman who speaks a non-majority language in Mexico. She also shares this characteristic with the woman who saves her and takes her into her home. They confide in each other about the uniqueness of identifying as a speaker of another language aside from Spanish. Moreover, this scene exemplifies the centrality of gender in Jansen's intersectional approach to indigeneity and migration to the capital. Adela is a victim of gender-based violence and her lack of resources and support stem directly from her identity; governmental and societal support structures are not in place to defend young women such as Adela or give them the tools to defend themselves. However, the woman who saves her in the street recognizes her as a victim of violence and societal oppression. Along with gender, ethnicity, rural origin, and socioeconomic class, language is central to Jansen's exploration of Indigenous identity, indigeneity, and oppression in *Tiempo de lluvia*. Like Llosa in *Madeinusa* and *La teta asustada*, Jansen provides a central place in the narrative for Indigenous language.

Language plays a key role in Jansen's characters' continued connection with their Indigenous identities and communities. This is evidenced in a final scene when Adela and José are in their apartment in Mexico City singing a Mixtec song that Soledad had taught them both. This scene, as well as scenes juxtaposing Adela and her son walking in Mexico City and Soledad in the village singing and chanting in Mixtec, represent the continuum rather than the divide between their rural and urban identities and the link is their indigeneity they celebrate in their new urban life. In the scene in the apartment, Adela lovingly holds José on her lap and sings to him in Mixtec. Directly following is a scene of Soledad in Oaxaca climbing up into the mountain with water from the waterfall and flowers like those she gathered with José. As she chants in Mixtec, the film transposes the sound of her voice over an image of Adela and José walking hand in hand in the city. Audibly and visually, the Mixtec language unites the three characters—Adela and José singing the song in the capital and Soledad reciting in Oaxaca. Moreover, the film symbolically unites the characters through the Mixtec words. The camera slowly backs away and up and then cuts back to Soledad in a rock circle before returning to an image from the beginning of the film of the Oaxacan village.

Going back to Minh-ha's concept of "speaking nearby," the critic calls this "a speaking that does not objectify, does not point to an object as if it is distant from the speaking subject or absent from the speaking place. A speaking that reflects on itself and can come very close to a subject without, however, seizing or claiming it."[36] Just as Llosa films her characters singing in Quechua, Jansen also depicts Soledad, Adela, and José speaking and singing in Mixtec. In this way, both directors allow their characters to express themselves apart from a traditional narrative; they give the characters and, in fact, the actors, a space for communicating. In other words, they do not distance the protagonists from the speaking position, if we assume that this position of filmic creation and power is based on a non-Indigenous, capital-centric, Spanish-speaking identity. It could be argued that this is where the two directors differ. If the question is whether they approach Indigenous representation on film as "speaking for" or "speaking nearby," one argument is that all directors "speak for" in a sense. However, the identities and life experiences of the directors differ enough to question whether this makes a difference in their filming approaches. Namely, Jansen is of Mixtec origin and speaks the Mixtec language whereas Llosa is mestiza and does not speak Quechua.

Following this line of questioning, D'Argenio further develops her analysis of Llosa's *Madeinusa* and *La teta asustada*. D'Argenio distinguishes a trend in current Latin American filmmaking: "inter/cultural feature films made by non-Indigenous directors . . . —in varying degrees of collaboration with Indigenous actors—which tell Indigenous stories, played by Indigenous actors and spoken in Indigenous languages, and are made for global (mostly non-Indigenous) consumption."[37] Discussing Llosa's films specifically, according to D'Argenio, "the films construct an image of Peru which is, on the one hand, defined by essentialized dualities, and, on the other, by the reduction of complex cultural alterity to familiar categories of difference."[38] Later, looking at the reactions to the film, "the controversy is related to the ways in which *Madeinusa* and *La teta asustada* articulate well-established Eurocentric discourses at both a national and international level which thus produce a simplified, easily accessible and marketable portrayal of the country for audiences abroad."[39] Considering the ideas of rural and urban, D'Argenio criticizes Llosa's filmic depiction in *Madeinusa*: "The opposition is ethnic, geopolitical and economic. Manayaycuna is inhabited entirely by Indigenous Quechua-speaking people and is cut off from the rest of the world. . . . The urban and Westernized culture is represented by Salvador and Lima, the city where he lives. The latter is evoked throughout the film as the place of modern life and salvation."[40] In *La teta asustada*, D'Argenio sees the "same type of dualistic narrative and the same opposition between Andean and Western categories."[41] She continues later, "the division here is between rationality and progress, and irrationality and tradition."[42] Finally, the critic argues: "Dualities in terms of geography,

FIGURE 4.9. José looks at carving. *Tiempo de lluvia* (2018).

race, class, culture, symbolic universes, languages and systems of values recur throughout the two films. These dualities can be recapitulated, establishing certain patterns at a paradigmatic level: province/city, sierra/coast, Indigenous/white, peasant or lower class/upper class, non-Western/Western, primitive/civilized, irrational/rational, and traditional/modern."[43] According to D'Argenio, these dichotomies in Llosa's work represent a Eurocentric view of Indigenous communities.

For D'Argenio, Llosa would be "speaking for" rather than "speaking nearby" her Indigenous characters. Her films fit into what the critic terms "Indigenous plots" by non-Indigenous directors that rely on Eurocentric tropes concerning Indigenous life and culture. For D'Argenio, this criticism relates directly to the misconceptions contained in the dualities she presents that fall along the lines of rural versus urban and the subsequent categories that follow: Indigenous versus white, traditional versus modern, et cetera. While Llosa does rely heavily on these dichotomies to create her myth-based filmic depiction of indigeneity, she also allows her characters to control the narrative, especially when they sing in Quechua. Furthermore, in terms of gender-related issues, Llosa's protagonists are not passive subjects as D'Argenio suggests. For example, Madeinusa finds a way to control her own destiny and tricks Salvador into taking her place in her village. Though this confirms the critic's idea of Llosa's depiction of the capital as salvation, it does allow the character agency in her quest to regulate her own life. As mentioned earlier in this chapter, Llosa also makes clear her condemnation of the oppression her Indigenous characters face, especially in *La teta asustada*.[44]

Bautista, the writer for *Tiempo de lluvia*, also addresses filmic representation of Indigenous characters: "Of course there are many cases of explicit racist or just stereotypical representation. It is also very common that Indigenous characters are represented as mythical beings of the past, or at least on their way to become part of the past."[45] Bautista's comments mirror those of D'Argenio in terms of the tendency to equate Indigenous characters with metaphorical tropes and mythical pasts that are incongruent with the present or the future. Bautista also contends: "A different issue is that Indigenous writers, storytellers, and filmmakers have limited access to film production. So in Mexico, quite often films are made about Indigenous peoples but not necessarily by Indigenous filmmakers."[46] These comments are relevant to a comparison of Llosa's and Jansen's filmic representation of indigeneity. On the one hand, Llosa is a non-Indigenous filmmaker who has made films about Indigenous peoples. As Bautista's remarks contend, other Indigenous Peruvian filmmakers may not have had access to funding. On the other hand, Jansen is Indigenous and therefore has a different perspective.[47]

Cultural production is central to national imaginary and the idea of national identity. As Bautista recognizes the importance of access for Indigenous directors, Freya Schiwy likewise emphasizes cultural representation as central to the creation of Indigenous agency and inclusion: "I suggest that decolonization at the beginning of the twenty-first century focuses not only on the struggle over territory, legislation, and political representation but also, perhaps more important, on epistemes. In other words, Indigenous movements recognize that representation—audiovisual, literary, and scholarly—entails the power to shape lived reality."[48] Certainly, filmic representation affects world views; culture has the power to insert ideas into the popular imagination which, in turn, become part of a system of understanding. This is true for the development of national identity as well and Indigenous movements acknowledge this and work to develop cultural production that complements political action. Indigenous filmmakers create Indigenous representation and, as Schiwy asserts, this influences the lived reality of a nation. With respect to Llosa and Jansen, they both shape Indigenous representation in the national imaginary in different ways.

A fundamental question in this chapter's comparison of Llosa's and Jansen's work is the idea of indigeneity and the representation of Indigenous characters. Several critics have analyzed indigeneity in Latin America. Andrea Canessa takes an intersectional approach to examining

Andean indigeneity as she explores how "identities—racial, generational, ethnic, regional, national, gender, and sexual—are mutually informing, even as they may be contradictory, among subaltern people of the Andes, where national sensibilities are not only strong but multiplying."[49] Canessa contends: "If Indigenous people struggle to assert and celebrate their identity, it is also the case that dominant national imaginings may include much that is Indigenous. This inclusion of indian imagery in national ideology is, however, often at a far remove from the cultural practices of contemporary indians; it tends to be on the level of the folkloric rather than a lived culture."[50] Canessa explains her use of the term "indian" and acknowledges its controversial nature, explaining that the choice is conscious and "points precisely to the unequal power relation that [she] seek[s] to interrogate."[51] Canessa's edited volume analyzes how urban communities define what is national—through politics, media, and schooling—and these concepts "are produced, reproduced, and contested by those who, according to the dominant nationalist discourse, are on the geographical and social margins of the nation, namely, the people who populate the rural Andes and have long been regarded as ethnically and racially distinct from the more culturally European urban nationals."[52] Canessa encourages looking at the idea of the nation in relation to race and gender, as all three "flow in and out of each other at the level of meaning and practice."[53] Significantly, Canessa contends: "It is not simply that indians and indian women do not conform to the national ideal but, rather, that the national ideal of progress is constructed in contradistinction to the rural, indian, and feminine."[54] Thus, the critic underscores the theoretical impossibility of Indigenous populations being included in the national ideas of progress. Finally, she clarifies: "Given the short historical depth of the idea of mass national identity in the Andes, the internal borders of race, class, and gender around which this identity is constructed are open to multiple interpretations. . . . The borders between tradition and modernity, center and periphery, national and international are perforated and twisted at every turn."[55] These questions of gender, national identity, and the urban/rural directly relate to Llosa's and Jansen's films. Moreover, Canessa's ideas pertain to the earlier discussion of the rural/urban continuum and how it relates to other intersectional factors in the three films examined here. National identity is central to these discussions as it has been since the creation of Latin American nations. D'Argenio's criticism of Llosa's works as well as questions of indigeneity and filmic representation have at their heart the concept of national identity—who is considered a part of the official image of the nation and who is not. As Canessa contends, more often than not, Indigenous women are excluded from the national imaginary and seen as antithetical to national progress. Indigenous communities—as rural and excluded from national socioeconomic prosperity—are also not considered within the framework of the traditional national imaginary. Canessa does note, however, that the relative brevity of the concept of mass national identity has allowed for new imaginings on the idea of nationality. Postero's thoughts on Bolivian identity and the declaration of the country as plurinational are relevant here, as well. These critics underscore Andean nations and the possibilities of viewing nationhood and nationality from a new viewpoint.

Christian Elguera discusses race in Brazil and comments on racial democracy as a concept that "reflects the ways in which Brazilians (from hegemonic to popular classes) affirm that harmonious relations and mixtures between different ethnic and social groups characterize their country."[56] On the other hand, Elguera posits that: "Regarding native populations, the discourse of racial democracy imposes a false inclusion that admits certain historical values and exotic representations but refuses to accept political rights."[57] Elguera discusses the danger of mythologizing and stereotyping Indigenous peoples in the Brazilian context: "The damage done by these representations has been irredeemable to this day. For instance, the argument of primitivism has justified a plethora of invasions, dispossessions, and the environmental destruction of Indigenous territories as well as the subsequent racialization of their residents."[58] Elguera brings to the forefront the real dangers that exist in perpetuating stereotypes regarding Indigenous communities.

Indeed, there is a long racial history of Indigenous exclusion in Latin America. In *Poetics of Race in Latin America*, Arturo Arias asserts: "Although Spaniards brutally enslaved both Indigenous and African people in their colonial enterprise in the Americas, it was not until the second half of the twentieth century that the racialized nature of their efforts was truly recognized."[59] Arias continues: "Following the foundational social and political transformations that Latin America underwent in the 1960s, Indigenous subjects' participation in political organizations empowered them to renegotiate their relationships with Criollo/Mestizo hegemonic cultures, rendering them visible within their respective nations, as well as in international spheres."[60] Arias generalizes: "What connects heterogenous Indigenous subjects is, ultimately, their being enlisted to political relations that need to preserve them as subalternized to enable Mestizos' claim of being 'white' and Eurocentric, thus preserving their position of power and privilege in Mesoamerican countries."[61] For Arias, national identity in Latin America is tied to the exclusion of as well as the necessity of difference from Indigenous communities, mirroring Canessa's ideas. In other words, mestizo culture defined itself as progressive, white, modern, and in opposition to Indigenous culture as regressive, non-White, and part of the past. The critic's comments harken back to D'Argenio's questioning of Llosa's filmic depiction of the Indigenous characters as tied to a mythical, regressive past.[62]

Comparing Llosa's and Jansen's representations of indigeneity, certain aspects come to the forefront. For example, both directors focus on intersectional identity as it relates to their main characters; any discussion of the protagonists in *Madeinusa*, *La teta asustada*, and *Tiempo de lluvia* must include an analysis of gender, race, ethnicity, language, socioeconomic class, nationality, and rural/urban identity. Many of the ideas on indigeneity discussed by the aforementioned critics relate to the comparison of the films in question in this chapter. In fact, indigeneity is central to an understanding of all three films—as related to the identity of the characters as well as that of the directors themselves. In addition, who is considered "the other" is also key to an examination of these films. While Llosa relies on mythical tropes and metaphor to create an image of indigeneity in her films, she does allow for a space for agency and autonomy in her Indigenous characters. Likewise, Jansen depicts an image of indigeneity that spans the rural/urban continuum, therefore questioning previous notions of Indigenous and national identity. National identity and intersectionality are also the focus of the following chapter on Kaori Flores Yonekura's and Cecilia Kang's films.

CHAPTER 5

INTERSECTIONALITY AND INTER-NATIONALITY

Kaori Flores Yonekura's *Nikkei: Un viaje extraordinario* and Cecilia Kang's *Mi último fracaso*

NATIONAL IDENTITY IS CENTRAL to an intersectional study of both Venezuelan filmmaker Kaori Flores Yonekura's *Nikkei: Un viaje extraordinario* (Nikkei: An Extraordinary Trip; 2014) and Argentine filmmaker Cecilia Kang's *Mi último fracaso* (My Latest Failure; 2016). Both directors' filmic depictions of identity involve the concept of inter-nationality— in the sense of pertaining to two nationalities but also in the interstitial sense of existing between two cultures. The films analyzed in this chapter visually and audibly represent the interlocking influences of national identity, gender, age, race, ethnicity, socioeconomic class, and language as well as the power structures that exert pressure on the subjects of the two documentary films. Just as with Latin American literatures, cinema from the region has also focused on the all-encompassing but varied concept of national identity—dealing with questions of what it means to be Venezuelan or Argentine, for example. As has happened globally, cinema has taken a central role in the depiction of national identity both within Latin American countries and as an external representation. Thus, the ways in which films present nationality are important and, unquestionably, not homogenous. With the globalization of popular culture, the stakes are high for national identity representation and many debates about films arise from this phenomenon. This chapter argues that an intersectional examination of Flores Yonekura's and Kang's autobiographical documentary films exposes the structural and historical oppression affecting their subjects as well as opportunities for identity exploration and possibilities for agency within specific cultural frameworks.

In Venezuela and Argentina, questions of gender, race, ethnicity, class, and ancestry have all played key roles in the filmic depiction of Venezuelan and Argentine national identities.[1] In Venezuela, the contemporary focus on Indigenous populations as well as the inception of the concept of plurinationality have influenced the idea of national identity in the country. Filmmakers such as Flores Yonekura enter a field that has a long tradition of depicting various identities. Argentina's historical trajectory, including the destruction of Indigenous communities in the name of civilization and the influences of Italian and Spanish migration have made national identity a focal point for much of Argentine cultural production. The relatively recent arrival of Korean communities in Argentina makes the perspectives in Kang's documentary unique; Kang introduces a new viewpoint on the national imaginary by adding Korean-Argentine culture to the question of what it means to be Argentine. Moreover, both Flores Yonekura's and Kang's portrayals of cultural practices that span Japan and Venezuela or Korea and Argentina, respectively, introduce the ideas of transculturality and inter-nationality. They also show how transcultural representation is intersectional, overlapping with gender, age, ethnicity, language, class, and national origin.[2]

Argentina and Venezuela have differing film histories; whereas Argentina has a trajectory of sustained film production from the advent of the technology, Venezuelan cinema has been more intermittent. Much of the difference in film production between Latin American countries is due to varied national funding for film and cultural production. As Schroeder Rodríguez affirms, the advent of more economical cameras, the creation of regional film cycles, and the showing of local newsreels before films aided in supporting film production in the region. Of the last, Schroeder Rodríguez contends: "As a result, newsreel production provided the only schooling for many budding filmmakers and the only form of continuous practice for experienced ones. Given the important ideological role played by newsreels in promoting official versions of reality, it is not surprising that it alone received the kind of state support needed for stable and continuous output."[3] The nonfiction style of filmmaking was fundamental from the beginning of film production in Latin America and provides a historical basis for the documentary films analyzed in this chapter.[4] While Flores Yonekura's and Kang's films are not newsreels, they portray a glimpse of reality based on quotidian life. They also expose a specific reality and portray lived experiences of groups of people who have not been traditionally represented in the respective countries' films. Schroeder Rodríguez also recognizes precursors to New Latin American Cinema as moments of coalescence around the expository social documentary, which manifested in different ways; one example is the government-funded Instituto Boliviano Cinematográfico (Bolivian Institute of Cinematography) in 1953 "not to sing the praises of the nation's elite, but to produce expository social documentaries focused on the needs of the country's marginalized groups."[5] Another example in Argentina is the collaboration between Fernando Birri and students from the Universidad del Litoral's Film Institute that produced *Tire Dié* (Throw Me a Dime; 1958), which "begins in the expository mode and very quickly shifts to neorealist representational strategies such as on-location shooting, the use of direct sound and nonprofessional actors, and a sympathetic treatment of the plight of the poor."[6] Of the images of children begging for money from wealthy travelers, the author says: "Such powerfully denunciatory images of social inequality were unprecedented in Latin American cinema, and it is this new use of the medium to condemn social inequality that makes *Tire dié* an important precursor of the NLAC."[7] From these origins, it is possible to trace current documentary filmmaking trends, which also center social inequality. While the films prior to and during the New Latin American Cinema movement focused more on class, current documentaries, such as Flores Yonekura's and Kang's, observe the intersections of class with gender, age, race, ethnicity, language, as well as regional and national origin. Moreover, contemporary documentary films such as the ones examined here portray the intersectional power dynamics—evident and indirect—in contemporary Venezuelan and Argentine societies.

Flores Yonekura, a Venezuelan filmmaker and publicist of Japanese descent, wrote, directed, and produced the documentary *Nikkei: Un viaje extraordinario*. *Nikkei*, winner and nominee in various international film festivals—such as winner of Best Documentary at the Festival de Espiritualidad en el Cine Venezolano (Festival of Spirituality in Venezuelan Film) and at the International Human Rights Film Festival—follows the director as she traces her grandparents' path from Japan to Peru and then

Venezuela in the first half of the twentieth century. Flores Yonekura's documentary, in Spanish and Japanese with subtitles respectively, includes a collage of interviews, recordings, personal narrative, still photographs, conversations, poems, songs, and animated drawings. The director combines nonfiction documentary storytelling with introspective reflections that lend the film a philosophical tone. Flores Yonekura's testimonial-style film examines her own identity as a Venezuelan who descends from Japanese grandparents while also investigating the history of Japanese migration to Latin America, in particular Peru and Venezuela. By employing intertextuality—still photography, drawing, and animation in the film—the director examines the historical reality of her ancestors, their arrival in Latin America, their experiences during World War II and the internment camps, and the reality of contemporary Venezuelans of Japanese descent. The main themes of *Nikkei* are national identity, personal reflection through art, and historical influences on current lived experiences.

In an interview, Flores Yonekura talks about Japanese migration to Venezuela and Peru and these communities' experiences during World War II. She says that the first Japanese immigrants arrived in Peru in 1899 within the context of the symbolic emancipation of slaves; landowners were searching for other sources of indentured labor. Moreover, according to Flores Yonekura, Japan had recently "opened to the West" and Japanese citizens had passports only in Japanese and without photographs, which affected the way they were treated upon arrival in Latin America. As the director asserts, many of the community members became part of the Catholic Church, were baptized, and married; during these events, the Church registered them and they were generally given Hispanicized names, effectively erasing official documentation of their Japanese identities. Prior to this, Flores Yonekura confirms that they were given the names "japonés número uno, el número dos, el número setenta y ocho . . ." (Japanese Number One, Number Two, Number 78 . . .).[8] Eventually, the communities in Peru prospered with their own businesses and welcomed newer generations of immigrants from Japan, who generally worked in these businesses as well. With this prosperity came social strife, as rumors circulated of Japanese communities having weapons, promoting an attack from Japan, or even taking jobs away from Peruvians. Flores Yonekura also talks about how the number of remittances sent back to Japan from Peru was questioned and about the beginning of the internment camps for Japanese communities in Latin America. Specifically concerning Venezuela, the filmmaker explains that Venezuela has always been a country with open doors; "un país que ha sido mestizo desde hace muchísimo tiempo atrás. También ha sido un país de libertades. Ha sido un país libertario. En este sentido, también recordemos que Bolívar era caraqueño, era venezolano, y dentro de sus tropas había mucha gente de todas las razas" (a country that has been mestizo from a long time ago. Also it has been a country of liberty. It has been a libertarian country. In this sense, we should also remember that Bolívar was from Caracas, he was Venezuelan, and within his troops there were people from all races).[9] Within this framework, Flores Yonekura contrasts the reception of the Japanese immigrants in Peru and Venezuela.

Cecilia Kang is an Argentine filmmaker of Korean descent who directed, co-wrote, and co-produced the documentary *Mi último fracaso*. The film has been screened in several international film festivals across Latin America and Spain, including FEMCINE: Festival Cine de Mujeres (Women's Film Festival) in Chile; CineFem: Festival Internacional de Cine de la Mujer (International Festival of Women's Film) in Uruguay; and BAFICI: Buenos Aires Festival Internacional de Cine Independiente (Buenos Aires International Independent Film Festival) in Argentina. In an interview with "Hablando de cine" (Speaking of Film), Kang explains that the film is about women in the Korean community in Buenos Aires and their personal relationships. The director discusses her identity as a Korean-Argentine, underscoring the film's theme of women existing between two national identities; "cómo es esta dualidad que tienen . . . de ser coreana, de ser argentina. De no saber bien qué es una a veces afecta a la hora de tomar decisiones" (what is it like to have that duality . . . being Korean, being Argentine. Not knowing well what you are and sometimes this affects your decision-making process).[10] Kang includes herself in these reflections and answers the interviewers' questions about the relatively closed nature of the Korean community in Buenos Aires; she feels that the community has opened up, particularly with the birth of new community members in Argentina and the younger members of the community speaking Spanish as well as they speak Korean. As part of the film also takes place in South Korea, it provides a view of the contrasting cultures of the two countries, not only in terms of language but also with respect to public space, body language, volume modulations of the voice, food and food presentation, among other factors.[11] One of the major themes of the documentary is the question of marrying within or outside of the Korean-Argentine community. For her, the question directly relates to the limits of the community and its cultural influence; she highlights her belief that with time the second and third generations of Korean Argentines will marry more outside, and the cultural influences will not be quite the same.

In his study on Korean communities in Sao Paulo, Brazil, and Buenos Aires, Argentina, Won K. Yoon establishes a history and timeline for immigrants in both cities, dating from the first to arrive in the 1960s under government agricultural agreements. Yoon explains that the immigrants in Buenos Aires settled around three years after those in Sao Paulo; however, both communities shared a preference for the city rather than agricultural life mostly due to the fact that they were educated, middle-class citizens sent from Korea. Early Korean immigrants who remained in Buenos Aires lived in lower-income neighborhoods such as Barrio Rivadavia along with families from Paraguay, Bolivia, and Chile.[12] According to Yoon, this neighborhood was known as the 109 Village because the 109 bus route ended here and it eventually became known as "Korea Town" and the city named part of Avenue Cobo "Avenida Corea."[13] There is a moment in Kang's documentary where she shows images at her family home of the first Argentine Catholic Pope alongside Korean deities. As Yoon illuminates, Korean Catholics first started to assemble in 1968 and requested that a Korean priest be sent to Buenos Aires.[14] These families were shuffled around to different locations in the early years but united once more after another Korean priest was sent and in 2005 "the Korean Catholic church in Buenos Aires had 778 families with 2,450 individual members registered."[15] Of the Korean communities in South America, Yoon contends that they reveal the history of their country of origin: "In the beginning, the Korean communities were regarded as refuges for those who were seeking security and stability elsewhere. At the present time, however, the same communities are looked upon as international outposts of the global Korea, especially for trade and culture. The socioeconomic standing of Korea in the world has significantly affected the images of these overseas communities among Koreans at home and abroad as well.[16]" On the other hand, Yoon contends that the communities in South America are overlooked. A telling scene in Kang's documentary is when Ran's sisters express their initial surprise that she would go to Argentina rather than Europe or the United States. Yoon clarifies: "South America has been somewhat unfamiliar to most Koreans. It is not like other Western continents, such as Europe or North America. From the Korean perspective, South America is in the byway of the international human and communication traffic."[17] Ran's decision to go to Argentina did not adhere to the trajectory of most Koreans who left the country at the time.

Both Flores Yonekura and Kang address issues of inter-nationality through an intersectional lens as well as a personal, subjective perspective. Their films include analysis of the filmmakers' own cultures and how they experience and exist in an interstitial space between two cultures and nationalities. Both directors emphasize how cultural pressures from without and within their communities influence themselves and their other subjects. Furthermore, these filmmakers visually represent the uses of everyday activities such as artmaking and food preparation as a means of considering identity. Theories of intersectionality, national identity, and diaspora are key to examining both documentary films and understanding how intersecting identity factors and power structures influence the lives of the films' subjects. Specifically, this chapter calls upon the intersectional theoretical analyses of Crenshaw, Hurtado, Viveros Vigoya, as well as Collins and Bilge. Additionally, Avtar Brah's thoughts on diaspora as well as Pablo Piedras', Diana Paladino's, and Beatriz Sarlo's concepts of subjective cinema and documentary filmmaking are key to understanding Flores Yonekura's and Kang's filmic representations of identity. Finally, Minh-ha's theories of filmmaking and "speaking nearby" serve to underscore Flores Yonekura's and Kang's documentary styles.

As established earlier, much of the theory of intersectionality developed from a need to address feminism's tendencies of focusing solely on the average experiences of white, middle-class women. Women of color, from working-class backgrounds, of differing abilities, and from outside the United States and Europe understood the importance of examining gender in conjunction with race, ethnicity, class, national origin, and ability, among other factors. Theorists already sought to expand the concepts of feminism before the term intersectionality was coined by Crenshaw in the context of the law; their ideas reflect the same preoccupations with alternative modes of understanding lived experiences. Hurtado discusses intersectionality as a way of describing the "intersections of identities in the modes of their oppression."[18] Collins and Bilge relate intersectionality theory to "how intersecting power relations influence social relations across diverse societies as well as individual experiences in everyday life."[19] As we have seen, for Viveros Vigoya, who focuses on corporeally lived experiences, intersectionality "es una perspectiva donde ya no se habla de la mujer, sino de las mujeres porque somos conscientes de las diferencias de clase, etnicidad, raza, generación, sexualidad, entre otras" (is a perspective where you no longer speak of woman, but of women because we are conscious of the differences in class, ethnicity, race, generation, sexuality, among others).[20] Viveros Vigoya discusses the dangers of considering only one aspect of identity alone when examining oppression or reducing the issues to an arithmetic equation: "la dominación es una formación histórica y que las relaciones sociales están imbricadas en las experiencias concretas que pueden vivirse de muy variadas maneras. Los parámetros feministas universales son inadecuados para describir formas de dominación específicas en las cuales las relaciones se intrincan y se experimentan de diversas formas" (domination is a historical formation and that social relations are overlapping in the concrete experiences that can be lived in many different ways. Universal feminist parameters are inadequate to describe forms of specific domination in which relationships interlock and are experienced in distinct ways).[21] For Viveros Vigoya, it is essential to recognize how oppression has developed through time in a particular historical context. As discussed before, the Colombian theorist emphasizes the idea of lived experiences, challenging the precepts of a universal feminist approach. The power relations and oppression discussed by Hurtado, Collins, and Bilge are particular to each particular case according to Viveros Vigoya, who is speaking from an Andean post-colonial society.

Key to any discussion of intersectionality is not the mere existence of intersecting identities but the ways in which individuals experience marginalization and powerlessness as a consequence of those intersections; lived experiences are central to this concept. For Viveros Vigoya specifically, oppression is historical in that it is the result of specific historical and social realities. Of intersectional power structures, Collins and Bilge assert:

> *The intersectional domain of power* refers to how individuals experience the convergence of structural, cultural, and disciplinary power. Such power shapes intersecting identities of race, class, gender, sexuality, nation, and age that in turn organize social interactions. Intersectionality recognizes that perceived group membership can make people vulnerable to various forms of bias, yet because we are simultaneously members of many groups, our complex identities can shape the specific ways that we experience that bias.[22]

Collins and Bilge underscore the power structures that influence individuals' lives in varied ways, depending on their perceived and presented identities. For Viveros Vigoya the specific ways people experience oppression are influenced by historical factors particular to their multiple communities. The "convergence of structural, cultural, and disciplinary power" exerts pressure on individuals depending on their interlocking identities. Both Flores Yonekura and Kang explore the intersectional identities of their documentary film subjects and reflect on the power structures that influence their lives.

NIKKEI: UN VIAJE EXTRAORDINARIO

Flores Yonekura's film *Nikkei* is divided into three sections: Japan, Peru, and Venezuela. In the first section, the director travels to Japan and searches for her ancestral home, meeting family acquaintances and relatives while there, who remember when people left the country to look for work, marry, or study in places like Argentina and Brazil. The director ruminates: "Siento el Japón como un encuentro con lo impermanente. La casa ya no es. Mis abuelos ya no están. Y yo no pertenezco de todo a este lugar. Es algo como una belleza imperfecta" (I feel Japan like an encounter with that which is impermanent. The house is no longer there. My grandparents are no longer there. And I do not belong completely to this place. It is something like an imperfect beauty). The director's testimonial style allows for both an academic and philosophical reading of the film; we see the logistical consequences of diaspora, but we also sense the affectual significance. Moreover, we physically see the movement between the two countries with images of the director traveling to Japan and seeing Tokyo; we also view how the director affectively reacts to arriving and meeting family and family acquaintances. Flores Yonekura, identifying herself as Nikkei, explores the facts behind her grandparents' migration, yet she also delves into what must have been their emotional experience as well as her own while retracing it. For her, Japan is part of her identity yet not fully connected to her current reality; the encounter with the country of her grandparents is incomplete. While she still feels a connection to the place, as she says, she does not fully belong. She offers the idea of an imperfect beauty, an identification with a nationality that is not entirely hers, nonetheless, it holds a specific fascination. It also affects her contemporary daily life; she declares in an interview that being of Japanese descent and knowing about the experiences of family during World War II and the internment camps affects the daily reality of Latin Americans of Japanese descent.[23]

During the second section of the film, on Peru, Flores Yonekura interviews writer Doris Moromisato, who discusses the rejection of Peruvians of Asian descent in the national imaginary: "En el imaginario común del Perú, en este caso, no se incorpora el asiático, ya sea en su mensaje de país, de república" (In the common imaginary of Peru, in this case, the Asian person does not become a part of it, either in the country's message, the republic). This is a continuation of the oppression experienced by Japanese immigrants in Peru and other places in Latin America during the first part of the twentieth century. The director traces the history of Japanese immigrants specifically as they arrive in Peru, following her grandparents' path. She interviews individuals who made the same journey or came into contact with these groups. One man discusses the poor working conditions for the Japanese workers; Flores Yonekura's own grandfather escaped from the Hacienda San Agustín in Peru. One woman reminisces about leaving Japan to marry a man in Peru, remembering the many Japanese immigrants who died of malaria and typhoid. Another woman explains how the only documentation these groups had were their passports without pictures, so they were encouraged to convert to Catholicism in order to have a registry of their existence. Of the Japanese experience in Peru, Flores Yonekura explains that, while they started to develop an economic safety net in the form of businesses and personal wealth, Peruvian society rejected the immigrant communities.[24]

The third and final section of the film is set in Venezuela, Flores Yonekura's grandparents' final destination. After having been rejected from Colombia, they arrive in San Antonio del Táchira close to the border, as Venezuela had been more accepting of Japanese migrants than Peru; however, with the advent of WWII and outwardly neutral Venezuela's commercial relationship with the United States, the conditions deteriorate. During this time, several countries in Latin America sent people of Japanese descent to concentration camps in the United States and Panama. Whether they were fully recognized as citizens of these countries previously, upon arrival in the camps, they were labeled "illegal" and without papers. In Venezuela specifically, citizens like the director's grandparents were confined and spied on. Yet again, their national identity, along with race and ethnicity, are central to the oppression they experience. In addition, as Flores Yonekura mentions in the interview,

FIGURE 5.1. Kaori Flores Yonekura journaling and thinking. *Nikkei: Un viaje extraordinario* (2014)

these experiences affected not only the family members in the internment camps but also future generations of Latin Americans of Japanese descent. In the film, we learn this information from narration, personal interviews, news clips, drawings, and photographs. The affective element is vital in Flores Yonekura's portrayal of the Nikkei community. In other words, each mode of representation she uses involves affect, from sitting down with family members, friends, and new acquaintances to looking at old photographs and listening to them remember the past to going through her own family pictures and creating a scrapbook history of her ancestors. Moreover, by including herself as a representative of the descendants of Japanese migrants, the director enriches the affective element of her documentary film.

Perhaps the most compelling element of Flores Yonekura's documentary is that it is so personal. She includes herself and her own artistic creations throughout, animating her drawings and family pictures. There are moments in the documentary where the camera focuses on Flores Yonekura writing in her journal or simply sitting and thinking. In other moments, her drawings and reconfigured family portraits come to life, telling the story of her ancestors. Still photographs become animations, journal entries reveal the director's personal thoughts, and songs and poems accentuate the transitions in the film. The intertextual and affectual nature of this work are its most salient features. The film ends with Flores Yonekura's musings on identity: "Hay algo más allá de tu piel, de tus huesos, de lo que pasa por tu cabeza. Te hace ser quien eres. Quizás sea el árbol de donde desciendes" (There is something beyond your skin, your bones, what happens in your head. It makes you who you are. Perhaps it is the tree from where you descend). Moraga, in her most recent book *Native Country of the Heart: A Memoir*, speaks of the idea of body memory in much the same way when referring to her mother, whose body remembered when she forgot. Flores Yonekura intimates this idea in her film's closing words; there is a component of identity that is intangible and lies at the crossroads of all its individual elements.

The focus on sociopolitical identity and the use of intertextuality, particularly with still photography in film, is central to Latin American documentaries. David William Foster asserts that documentary filmmaking in the region is associated with the Cuban Revolution, Marxism, and sociopolitical activism: "Issues such as workers' movements, the struggle for the land, citizen rights, protection from oppression and persecution, the truth about political revolution and the repression of it from both without and within, important social projects, and the micropolitics of exemplary lives have served as the basis of Latin American filmmaking."[25] Clearly, Flores Yonekura's unwavering attention to the experiences of Japanese immigrants in Peru and Venezuela upon arrival, during World War II, and in the present, is part of the Latin American documentary filmmaking legacy of which Foster writes. Alejandra Kelly Hopfenblatt and Silvana Flores explain: "The social and political Latin American films of the 1960s and 1970s combined the specificity of photography and cinema, using still images for their testimonial value in which the link with the real (historical reality, landscapes, and characters with social markers) was the principal axis."[26] Discussing Fernando Birri's style of filmmaking in the New Latin American Cinema movement, the same authors state: "the still photograph allowed for a closer relationship to reality."[27] Both of these comments underscore still photography as vital to Latin American film for its testimonial power as well as its close relationship to reality. In effect, Flores Yonekura's film is replete with still photographs, not only for the purposes of giving testimony from those who are no longer present, but also for fostering an affective approach to the subject matter. Flores Yonekura, as a contemporary filmmaker, combines this focus on art, photography, and intertextuality to highlight the intersectional experiences of her ancestors and herself as a Venezuelan of Japanese descent.[28]

For Nikkei communities, descendants of Japanese citizens but not citizens of Japan themselves, the question of nationality and national origin is part of the matrix of intersecting factors that problematize interrogations of identity. As Collins and Bilge remind us "intersecting power relations" directly influence social interactions and everyday lived experiences. For Viveros Vigoya, these lived experiences are necessarily corporeal, they are experienced in a particular body with specific signifiers. Moreover, Viveros Vigoya emphasizes the historical aspect of oppression as it is related to intersectional identity factors. Working from this matrix, Flores Yonekura's documentary makes clear the power relations that resulted in the oppression of Japanese diaspora groups as well as the oppression of subsequent Nikkei communities in Latin America. Flores Yonekura combines interviews, historical knowledge, and family history to represent her grandparents' oppression. In the meantime, she presents personal narrative and reflections to acknowledge her own lived experiences as a Venezuelan woman of Japanese descent. Implied here is the generational trauma and continued exclusion felt by Nikkei communities in the project of the nation in various countries in Latin America due to the corporeal racial and ethnic reality of having Asian and specifically Japanese physical attributes.

Viveros Vigoya's emphasis on the historical aspect of intersectionality is imperative as it reminds us that modes of oppression in Latin America directly relate to historical processes and realities. For Nikkei communities, the exclusion they experience relates not only to racial and ethnic prejudice but also to questions of national origin and nationality. Their identities are still bound to Japan, whether they are from original diaspora groups or succeeding descendant communities. As Flores Yonekura comments in the documentary: "Ser Nikkei no es estático. Ser Nikkei es el resultado de una elaboración simbólica, social y política. Es la combinación de elementos culturales y de relaciones modernas largas y muy intensas" (Being Nikkei is not static. Being Nikkei is the result of a symbolic, social and political elaboration. It is the combination of cultural elements and long and very intense modern relations). The director recognizes what Viveros Vigoya sees as the centrality of historical developments in any question of identity. She also presents identity as an ongoing process, influenced by everchanging social and political realities. For example, in her film, she shows how her grandparents' identities were accepted in Venezuela up until World War II and Venezuela's trade relations with the US and clandestine diplomatic relations with the Allies.

Another example is writer Moromisato's words on Peruvian citizens of Asian descent; she illustrates their exclusion from the ongoing process of nation-building and the national imaginary. The examples in the documentary, whether visual material, oral interview, or personal reflections, underscore the centrality of nation of origin and national identity in an intersectional approach to marginalization and oppression.

The concept of diaspora is relevant to an examination of national identity, migration, and oppression, as well. On the notion of diaspora, Avtar Brah affirms the following: "Diasporic lives are lived through multiple modalities produced through the intersection of race, class, gender, sexuality, disability, religion, generation, and so on. Construction of a common 'we,' then, is not a straightforward process but involves complex cultural and political negotiation involving conflict and contestation as much as solidarity."[29] As Brah attests, individuals and groups experience diaspora in different ways, depending on many factors. Just as Viveros Vigoya highlights the historical nature of intersectionality and lived experience, Brah stresses the significance of historical specificity in the phenomenon of diaspora. Revisiting Flores Yonekura's documentary *Nikkei*, it is evident that the director's grandparents had a unique experience leaving Japan in search of work in Latin America. Their diasporic path led them through Peru, Colombia, and Venezuela and their lives in Venezuela were heavily influenced by historical factors related to WWII. Furthermore, the director's own lived experiences and her ideas on the notion of national identity are affected by these histories. Finally, Flores Yonekura makes it clear that, as Brah declares, the lives and identities of Japanese immigrants in Peru, Colombia, and Venezuela are developed "through multiple modalities" and are constructed in various ways.[30]

MI ÚLTIMO FRACASO

While Flores Yonekura's film focuses on Japanese communities in Venezuela, Kang's film highlights the experiences of Korean communities in Argentina. *Mi último fracaso* is divided into three general sections: the first focuses on Ran "Teresa" Kim and her life between Korea and Argentina; the second is a series of conversations with women in their twenties and thirties; and the third centers on the director's sister, Catalina "Cata" Kang. The documentary, in Spanish and Korean, presents a personal view of these women's lives, inside their homes, in their conversations with family and friends, and in conversations with the director. The film incorporates such themes as marriage, romantic relationships, friendship, the cultural significance of food and food preparation, nationality-based community, cultural differences, generational differences, and personal fulfillment. Intersectional issues of gender, race, ethnicity, class, language, and national origin are key to Kang's presentation, and they are the driving force behind the journey through which the director takes us in this film. Kang's style is relaxed in that the different sections are not structurally enforced, and the transitions are organic. Furthermore, Kang moves back and forth behind and in front of the camera, continuously breaking the invisible wall between the documentary filmmaker and the subjects, allowing herself to be scrutinized as well. This personal style allows for a subjective, affective exploration of what it means to Kang to be a young, Korean Argentine woman looking to other women both within and outside of her community for clues on how to live a fulfilling life. At the same time, Kang examines the impediments to finding meaning for young women such as herself who are encouraged by the previous generation to look to marriage as a forgone conclusion "despite" also having a profession. Gender is not the only focus in this enigma, as the director emphasizes; nationality, language, culture, and ethnicity intersect with gender in the decision-making process for these women.

The first section of *Mi último fracaso* focuses on Ran Kim, both in Korea and Argentina. Ran is an artist and youth art teacher who, in the course of the documentary, travels to Korea to visit friends and family. Specifically, she visits with her two younger sisters in Seoul and pays respects at the cemetery. Kang films Ran arriving at the airport, eating with her friends, visiting the cemetery with her sisters, and riding in the car with them on the way back to the airport to return to Buenos Aires. In the conversation with friends at the table, Ran declares that Kang is witnessing the get-together of the women who decided not to marry, and they all laugh. This scene introduces themes that will be central to the remainder of the documentary—the centrality of food in relationships, gender and marriage, as well as national identity. This is the first of many sit-down meals that the documentary's subjects share, and Kang is careful to capture not only the meal but the preparation of the food and the conversation at the table—the *sobremesa*. Marriage and the idea of not marrying comes up in the conversation, as Ran shares that she and the other women sitting around the table chose not to marry. Later, Ran shares with Kang the pressure she felt to get married after her father died and her mother was alone. The cultural indication was that, as the oldest sibling and as a woman, she would need to incorporate a male protective figure into the family. Finally, the women speak in Korean and discuss Ran's binational existence as well as another woman's desire to move from Seoul. In the scenes at the cemetery, Ran takes turns kneeling before a gravesite with her sisters and leaving offerings. On the car ride back to the airport the sisters talk about their relationships and discuss how it was for them when Ran left for Argentina—one of the sisters exclaims that she was surprised her sister moved to Argentina and not Europe or the United States. The depiction of the trip to Korea and the discussions surrounding Ran's move to Argentina underscore the topic of national identity and how it is complicated by the psychological, emotional, and physical bonds that hold a person to more than one nation. This inter-nationality is vital to Kang's representation of Korean Argentine identity.

The second section of the film is a series of conversations with women in their twenties and thirties discussing marriage, gender expectations, careers, and the joys and difficulties of living between two cultures. Kang begins this section with a mother of two young daughters who explains that, while her husband is relatively open-minded, many of her friends' husbands feel that if their wives work it is just to buy the things they like and the man is still the provider, "el hombre de la casa" (the man of the house). She says that a woman's career comes second to the needs of the family; for example, the man expects the food to be on the table when he arrives, a classic example of what Arlie Hochschild referred to as the "second shift."[31] Another woman jumps in to say this is changing; however, the first woman emphasizes that this is still the case for many women in her community: "En la colectividad pasa, todavía pasa" (In the community it happens, it still happens). Gender expectations within the Korean Argentine community are made clear in these statements; as with the filmmaker's mother who prioritizes marriage to a career for young women, the mother here presents the gender dynamics at play in Korean-Argentine families. Like the gender expectations set for other Argentine communities, the women interviewed by Kang describe a situation of passive male acceptance of women's careers but never at the expense of responsibilities to the family. This mirrors Ran's comments, as well, in which she expressed the pressure she felt to marry after her father's death; others tried to compel her to carry out traditional duties to the family rather than leave and pursue her career.

In this section, Kang also films groups of young people gathering, walking along storefronts, and singing at a karaoke bar. The young women discuss whether they feel they must marry a Korean man or can marry outside of the community; the opinions are divided with some feeling more comfortable than others marrying a man who was not Korean. One woman interjects: "Yo soy argentina también, pero a la vez, en el fondo soy mucho más coreana. Mis viejos son coreanos, la cultura de mis viejos es coreana" (I'm also Argentine, but at the same time, deep down I'm much more Korean. My parents are Korean, my parents' culture is Korean). To emphasize this point of view, when Kang shifts to the young people gathered at a karaoke bar, they take turns singing songs in Korean. It is clear from their emotional singing and the expressions on their faces that they are familiar with these songs sung in Korean and connect to them on an affective level. Thus, they alternate on screen between conversing in completely fluent and Argentine-accented Spanish to singing nostalgic songs in Korean. The linguistic fluidity mirrors the comments made by the young women about marriage options. However, as they express, there are still certain cultural influences that are hard to challenge. In the radio interview, Kang also expresses this idea when she affirms that the cultural pull within the community is shifting over time and that, possibly in a generation or two, it will be less imperative, for example, to marry within the community. One of the pieces of evidence she gives for the shifting culture is the fact that the younger generations speak fluent Spanish and are culturally immersed in Argentina as well as family-established Korean cultural practices.

The third and final section focuses on Cata (Catalina Kang), the filmmaker's older sister, beginning with her scrolling through the Facebook page of an ex-boyfriend and describing to Kang how they broke up. Cata says that he told her he was in an arranged marriage, and she told him to never call her again. Once again, the theme of marriage appears, here with the traditional practice of arranged marriages, and Cata finds herself caught between two cultures. Similar to scenes in Flores Yonekura's documentary, Kang films herself with her sister, looking through old photographs. She also films herself with her mother washing cabbage to make Korean kimchi. Returning to her conversations with her sister, Kang reveals her family's history through Cata—the family lived in Korea, the father left within a year of Cata's birth, she lived alone with her mother for nine years, then they moved to Argentina and Cecilia (the filmmaker) was born. In Kang's film, Cata represents the in-between

FIGURE 5.2. Cecilia Kang takes a photograph. *Mi último fracaso* (2016).

feeling of many immigrants, having lived a portion of their lives in their first country before moving to a new one. In fact, Kang accompanies the following images with a song performed by Chico Unicornio, a cover of a Jeanette song, "Si te vas" (If you leave): "Si te vas, te vas / para no volver, nunca, nunca. . . . Si te vas, te vas del todo, para no volver jamás" (If you leave, you leave / to not return, ever, ever. . . . If you leave, you leave for good, to never return). While the words are a reflection of Cata's relationship with her ex-boyfriend, they also embody her feelings as an immigrant who left her country and is finding her way in a new place.

In this section, Kang films a get-together with Cata's friends and interviews them about her sister's illness; she had a brain tumor ten years prior and they were not sure she would survive. While Cata's friends emotionally reminisce, they remember how their friend's mother and father struggled to understand what was happening to their daughter medically due to the linguistic challenges of not speaking fluent Spanish. This linguistic difference between the generations is driven home when Kang films the young children at the party sitting on the couch watching cartoons in Spanish. In another moment, the parents watch a Korean soap opera while one of the daughters watches a documentary in Spanish in the bedroom. Kang presents language as one of the main themes of *Mi último fracaso*; generational linguistic differences as well as language as a barrier or key to cultural acceptance and change. Along with gendered marriage expectations and everyday cultural practices, language plays a key role in both the intersectional manifestation of identity and what Collins and Bilge term the intersectional domain of power. Kang portrays cultural pressures from both within and without Korean Argentine culture that affect the films' subjects' lives.

At the end of her film, Kang returns to images of everyone interviewed accompanied by the song "Mi último fracaso," performed by Trío los Panchos. The lines of the first stanza are as follows: "Es mi destino vivir así / Triste agonía vivir sin ti / Me siento perdido en este mundo / Y mi último fracaso será tu amor" (It is my destiny to live like this / Sad agony living without you / I feel lost in this world / And my last failure will be your love). As with the previous song, "Si te vas," the music complements the themes Kang presents—love, loss, and belonging. Again, this relates to her sister's relationship; however, because the song accompanies images of all those included in the documentary, the message is overarching, encompassing the experiences of all the immigrants, their families, and later generations that Kang films. It is for the loss of Ran's father and Cata's love as well as the lost years spent with loved ones left behind, and the years spent adapting to a new country. Moreover, the lyrics reflect themes related to migration presented by Kang, such as fulfilling one's destiny in a new place while feeling a loss for the old. *Mi último fracaso* is a story of transnationality and the individual, communal, and generational challenges that come from immigration. The director's radio interview comments are relevant here; her film explores the dual nature of the women's identities as both Argentine and Korean, underscoring this duality as an added complication in such life decisions as marriage and profession. On the other hand, the documentary celebrates the richness of the subjects' identities, focusing on specific manifestations of their culture such as language, music, and food.

One of the main cultural themes of Kang's documentary is food and food preparation. There are multiple scenes that highlight the communal experience of preparing and sharing meals. In fact, in almost every major scene, the subjects are eating or preparing food and this is always depicted as a shared experience. One of these scenes depicts the director preparing the elements of the Korean dish kimchi with her mother; they copiously wash the cabbage and set it out to be added to the other ingredients. As with the other scenes involving food, this is a shared experience and a cultural practice passed down from one generation to the next. The images also serve to highlight an aspect of Kang's culture that might not be familiar to Argentine audiences. In other scenes, Kang shows herself and her subjects eating out at Korean restaurants and karaoke bars as well as preparing and eating Korean food at home. The act of sharing a meal is a universal element of culture; likewise, the conversations held around the table are revealing. Thus, Kang focuses on these settings when she interviews or converses with her subjects, knowing there is an element of comfort in the act of eating with someone else. In one sense, the idea of the *sobremesa* has existed for as long as there have been shared meals and linguistic communication. However, there is a particular inherited cultural element to this practice in countries such as Argentina, showing the influence of Spanish culture on Latin American countries. The practice of conversation at the table is also important to Korean culture, as evidenced in Kang's film, for example, in the images of the women eating together in Korea.

SUBJECTIVITY, AFFECT, AND THE EVERYDAY

Flores Yonekura's and Kang's films share certain key elements—they both include themselves in their documentaries and provide a subjective and affective perspective; they both focus on specific cultural practices that underscore their inter-national identities; and they both depict the act of traveling between the ancestral and adopted countries. Of the first, the two documentary filmmakers analyzed in this chapter share a singular focus on giving a personal, subjective, and affective account of their own and others' lives.[32] In the process, they cross the so-called fourth wall and subscribe to a documentary style that recognizes the existence of the documentarian and the filming apparatus itself. In this way, they avoid any artificial separation between themselves and their subjects while including their own stories in their films. According to Argentine theorist Pablo Piedras, "las narrativas en primera persona trastornan los modos habituales del documental para explicar el mundo, representar a sujetos sociales y establecer pactos comunicativos con el espectador" (first-person narratives destabilize the usual documentary modes of explaining the world, representing social subjects and establishing communicative pacts with the viewer).[33] Traditionally, the documentary filmmaker has chosen others as subjects of study, and it is not until more recent times that documentarians have begun including themselves and their own experiences. As Piedras contends, this shift changes the way documentary film examines and explains the world; by including themselves, the directors forge a

FIGURE 5.3. Cecilia Kang and her sister in café. *Mi último fracaso* (2016).

more direct path to the viewer and engage themselves as social subjects. For Flores Yonekura and Kang, this shift brings with it a more subjective and affective mode of representation; in other words, feelings and affect are an intrinsic part of the filmmaking process for these directors. The outcomes would be vastly different if they had chosen, not themselves, but rather subjects with whom they did not identify personally, subjects who merely fit the logical description of their case studies. By including themselves, they allow for a less scientific approach that incorporates their own lived experiences, feelings, and physical reactions.

Furthermore, the documentary voice is less authoritative and more exploratory in Flores Yonekura's and Kang's films. In a sense, *Nikkei* and *Mi último fracaso* allow the film to follow its course on screen and the subject matter unfolds as the filming happens. As viewers, we follow the subjects in their own personal journeys and make discoveries along with them instead of witnessing a pre-planned systematic study of case subjects. As discussed earlier, Minh-ha argues for a cinematography that places the director next to or nearby the subject; in this way, the filmmaker "speaks with" rather than speaking "for, about, and on behalf of."[34] She explains: "In the context of power relations, speaking for, about, and on behalf of is very different from speaking with and nearby.... Making a film that shows and speaks with the subject of your inquiry as if she is listening and looking next to you would shift subtly but radically your mode of address, of framing and contextualizing."[35] Flores Yonekura and

Kang place themselves literally inside the documentary as subjects of study and exploration rather than authoritative scientific voices, studying the subject matter as outsiders. What is more, they "speak with" the other subjects in their films through conversations, informal interviews, and spending time on screen with them. One clear example is Kang's revelation of her sister Cata's story—the story is revealed through Cata's own words, emotions, and gestures. While the director appears and we can hear her voice occasionally, she is experiencing the feelings with her subjects rather than analytically studying them. In the same way, Flores Yonekura looks at old family pictures in Japan and waits for the other people on screen to explain what they see and how it connects to the film's subject matter. The moments when Kang prepares food with her mother, for example, also illustrate this way of filmmaking that entails "speaking with or nearby"; these events can even be silent and represent the act of experiencing togetherness.

Cultural practices are central to both Flores Yonekura's and Kang's films; these include art, music, food, pop culture, marriage, religion, and photography. Minh-ha explains: "there is always the possibility of the everyman turning into a suspect and of everyday activities turning into political activities, as exemplified by the struggles of women and marginalized peoples around the world. The everyday, punctuated by the ritualistic and the ceremonial, is what I often translate onto film and video media."[36] Both Flores Yonekura and Kang underscore the everyday as well as the ritualistic in their films. For instance, riding public transportation and sitting by the water become sites of meaning in Flores Yonekura's *Nikkei*—they signify moments of pause and contemplation. In Kang's *Mi último fracaso*, riding in a car and walking down the sidewalk are instances of the everyday and expressions of aloneness and gathering whereas making food is an illustration of the ritualistic. Of this last, the rituals surrounding food are the central visual metaphor in Kang's documentary. In this fashion, the director places her culture, family life, and friendships at the center of her personal exploration, since preparing, sharing, and eating food are some of the most frequent and important parts of our daily lives. Kang continuously returns to these ritualistic images as a metaphor for love, loss, and belonging—the food is lovingly prepared and shared, the meals remind the subjects and the viewers of those present and those no longer there, and the act of sharing food creates a strong sense of belonging to a community. Rather than approaching her subject matter as a traditional documentary filmmaker who is an outsider, Kang places herself in the ritual experiences and affectively portrays what it is like to live in the Korean Argentine community in Buenos Aires.

In her *Respuesta a Sor Filotea*, Sor Juana explains her intrigue in philosophizing about everyday objects and actions. Following a mathematical and physics quandary she makes about the trajectory of a spinning toy top, Sor Juana ruminates on the ways she practices thinking and mental experimentation even through cooking, "de los secretos naturales que he descubierto estando guisando" (of the natural secrets I have discovered while cooking).[37] She later ruminates: "Bien dijo Lupercio Leonardo, que bien se puede filosofar y aderezar la cena. Y yo suelo decir viendo estas cosillas: Si Aristóteles huberia guisado, mucho más hubiera escrito" (As Lupercio Leonardo said well, that one can just as well philosophize and get dinner ready. And I often say seeing these things: If Aristotle would have cooked, he would have written a lot more).[38] All this to say that Sor Juana understood the vital role food and food preparation have in our daily lives and in our thinking process. For her part, Kang shows how preparing food is an act of thinking, loving, and sharing. Just as Sor Juana places value on cooking as a way to philosophy, Kang also places worth on food and food preparation as a process of meaning-making. In so doing, the Korean Argentine filmmaker visually represents the cultural act, in this case, the cultural act of preparing, sharing, and eating food. Kang's documentary philosophy parallels Sor Juana's in that it takes into account the everyday and teases meaning out of it.

In *Nikkei*, Flores Yonekura explores other aspects of the everyday and the ritualistic. Whereas food and food preparation are the central metaphor in Kang's documentary, Flores Yonekura uses the image of art and art-making to visually and affectively communicate her message about culture and identity. Throughout her film, she returns to images of herself drawing and creating collages with family photographs, in a sense, representing the act of living and making culture. As with Kang, Flores Yonekura physically and emotionally places herself within this visual metaphor. Moreover, she silently interacts with the subjects in these scenes, namely her ancestors in the photographs; she "speaks nearby" these subjects by presenting them on screen in the photographs, allowing the pictures to tell their own stories. Minh-ha describes a filmmaking process that requires the director to enter "fieldwork with the self as an empty, experiential site of reference."[39] Like Kang, Flores Yonekura enters the field herself and offers her own life as a subject of examination.

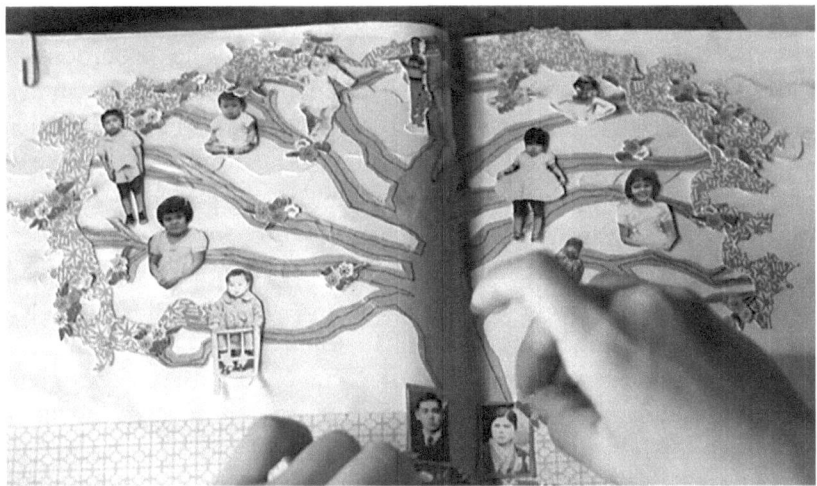

FIGURE 5.4. Kaori Flores Yonekura's family tree with photos. *Nikkei: Un viaje extraordinario* (2014).

The subjective documentary film has been central to the development of documentary filmmaking in Latin America from its inception. Contemporary filmmakers such as Flores Yonekura and Kang explore their own identities through this cinematic mode. In Argentina, for example, the history of the country impacted the development and uses of documentary films. Within the context of her discussions on memory and post-dictatorship Argentina, Beatriz Sarlo asserts: "Del pasado no se prescinde por el ejercicio de la decisión ni de la inteligencia; tampoco se lo convoca simplemente por un acto de la voluntad. El regreso del pasado no es siempre un momento liberador del recuerdo, sino un advenimiento, una captura del presente" (You cannot dispense with the past by force of decision or intelligence; neither is it invoked simply as an act of self will. The return of the past is not always a liberating moment of memory, but an advent, a capturing of the present).[40] The significance of this train of thought for the current discussion of Kang's as well as Flores Yonekura's work lies in the idea that the act of calling up and communicating the past is not only looking back but also looking to the present moment—the subject necessarily brings the past to the current context and many times judges or comments on the present moment through their observations on the past. For example, Kang's *Mi último fracaso* features subjects such as Ran and Cata talking about their past experiences in Korea in ways that harken to the present moment they are living in Argentina. Ran's decision-making process regarding marriage when she was young offers glimpses of her current way of living and the decision-making processes the other women share in the film. Additionally, Cata's dialogue on her family and personal memories about the move from Korea to Argentina are at once personal and collective, serving to memorialize her own past but also to give narrative to the past and present experiences of many others in the Korean Argentine community in Buenos Aires. Furthermore, Cata's comments capture the present, using Sarlo's wording, as they encapsulate a feeling of being in between, not fully pertaining to either country or culture but also pertaining to both.[41]

Pablo Piedras recognizes the close connection between documentary filmmaking and the cultural and socioeconomic contexts in which it flourishes. Piedras reflects on the trend toward subjective documentary filmmaking: "El surgimiento de narrativas en primera persona en el documental argentino de la última década expresa, en el terreno de lo audiovisual, nuevas identidades políticas, sociales, culturales y de género que, si bien habían sido representadas en el documental precedente, no constituían la fuente y el eje de validación de la enunciación" (The emergence of first-person narratives in the Argentine documentary of the last decade expresses, in the field of the audiovisual, new political, social, cultural and gender identities that, while they had been represented in documentary previously, they did not constitute the source and axis of the validation of the enunciation).[42] Flores Yonekura and Kang are part of a contemporary documentary filmmaking movement that sees first-person narrative and subjective perspective as the "source and axis" of the meaning of the films they produce.[43]

Examining subjective documentary, Argentine theorist Diana Paladino sustains: "la voz que adopta el documental subjetivo es la primera persona del singular; en ella se condensan la perspectiva del cineasta y la del narrador. Su lugar no es periférico sino que, por el contrario, se entroniza como el narrador principal del relato, y, en la mayoría de los casos, asume el rol de personaje que se interpreta a sí mismo" [the voice that the subjective documentary adopts is first-person singular; in it the filmmaker's and the narrator's perspectives condense. Their place is not peripheral but rather, on the contrary, they become entrenched as the principal narrator of the story, and, in the majority of cases, assume the role of the character that plays themselves].[44] Paladino describes two examples of typical contemporary Argentine documentaries in first person—one that begins with a life event as the principal motivating factor in the narrative

FIGURE 5.5. Kaori Flores Yonekura's family album. *Nikkei: Un viaje extraordinario* (2014).

and another that depicts life in a family as the narrative impulse. For Flores Yonekura and Kang, both the life event of returning to their families' home countries as well as the depiction of family life and everyday cultural and ritual practices are the narrative motivators in their films.[45]

Flores Yonekura and Kang both highlight the life event of returning to their families' countries of origin—Japan and Korea, respectively. In so doing, the filmmakers further underscore their transnational identities and again provide a physical, affective representation of what it means to have a familial, cultural, historical, and emotional attachment to more than one country. It is striking that both directors chose to film their journeys and feature them so prominently in their films, including the flights, the ground travel, and meetings with family and friends. The scenes in *Nikkei* and *Mi último fracaso* that focus on the trips include visiting with people and going to specific homes; while Flores Yonekura concentrates more on photographs and spaces such as buildings and neighborhoods related to her family, Kang emphasizes food and gathering at the table and cemetery. Once again, both filmmakers underline the everyday and ritual cultural practices that compose their trips and their connections in Japan and Korea. The act of returning to the "mother" country clarifies both women's proximity to and distance from these cultures as well; just as the depiction of cultural practices in their families' adopted countries clarifies their lived experiences as citizens who are both similar and different from other Venezuelans and Argentines. The interstitial space between feeling a sense of belonging or not, between intuitively knowing what to do in a certain instance or not, and between feeling comfortable in a given situation or not are central to both filmmakers' explorations of their inter-national identities. What is more, as Brah asserts on diaspora, both filmmakers depict the complex individual and social negotiations that shape a person's identity, particularly an individual who forms part of a diasporic community.[46]

Furthermore, for Flores Yonekura and Kang, their inter-nationality intersects with their gender, age, ethnicity, class, and language, as is apparent in both films. Examples of this include specific cultural expectations surrounding young women in Korean and Korean Argentine cultures, the socioeconomic class of their families and communities when they moved to Latin America, and the language they choose to speak in any given instance. More specifically, Kang explores the narrow gender expectations of young Korean and Korean Argentine women, highlighting the pressures to marry and focus on family rather than a career. Even if there is a passive acceptance of a woman's career, it comes second to marrying and keeping house. Moreover, while some of these pressures are generational—the mother and older relatives focus more on marriage expectations—even the younger women in their twenties and thirties understand the cultural weight of the institution of marriage. Marriage is also a theme in Flores Yonekura's film, as seen in the scenes with the woman who married and moved from Japan to rural Peru, where she witnessed the devastating effects of malaria and typhoid outbreaks. Age is a factor in how cultural and gender identity intersect; Kang, for example, portrays the specific burden of feeling the need to find a partner and marry in the scenes with her sister, her friends, and even with Ran. Class is another significant element that intersects with national origin in both films as they represent the experiences of family and ancestors and the reasons for their migration as well as the specific circumstances of their arrivals. Flores Yonekura traces her family's journey from Japan at a time of great poverty to Peru and then Venezuela, examining the poor living conditions and mistreatment they suffered along the way, especially as agricultural workers in Peru. Their experiences as sub-working-class migrants intersect with religion, as well; the Japanese community that migrated to Peru was encouraged to convert to Catholicism just to be registered in Church documents as a way of documenting their very existence. In Kang's case, the Korean community that migrated to Latin America was generally middle-class, according to Yoon, and did not have the farming skills needed for the agricultural jobs awaiting them in rural Argentina. These families tended to move to urban centers such as Buenos Aires and Sao Paulo, Brazil, and develop culturally specific communities and neighborhoods. Finally, even medical access is intersectional, as seen in Kang's film where her sister Cata's friends discuss the parents having difficulties understanding medical procedures and outcomes due to linguistic differences.

Inter-nationality as a theme highlights how these filmmakers portray their intersectional identities both in individual and communal terms. The films examined in this chapter are personal, subjective accounts of young women experiencing life between two cultural and national identities. Nevertheless, each filmmaker highlights the history of their respective communities and the communal cultural practices that differentiate them from mainstream culture in their adopted countries. Intersectionality studies have recently questioned the fixedness of identity and identity politics; as Collins and Bilge contend, the danger lies in believing that identity is always fixed rather than "differentially performed from one social context to the next."[47] The theorists contend: "The extensive body of scholarship within intersectionality that engages themes of individual identities as intersecting and performative has changed the meaning of identity from something one *has* to something one *does*."[48] This line of thought parallels feminist debates surrounding body politics and identity and the question of postmodern understandings of identity in opposition to physical lived experiences in particular bodies. In terms of Collins and Bilge's comments here, culture can be seen as something intrinsic but also changing, depending on the socio-cultural context. For example, viewing identity as a process and action in Kang's film and radio interview allows for a deeper understanding of the shifts in language and communication depending on the situation and the interlocutors. When Kang speaks with the interviewers, she speaks fluent Spanish with a marked Argentine pronunciation, and the conversations within the film move fluidly between Korean and Spanish, depending on the context as well as the subject matter. The context-driven aspect of intersectional identity is also evident in the conversations about marriage; whereas the young women in a group of young people express doubts about whether they will marry Korean or Argentine men, Kang limits herself to a small smile when she is conversing alone with her mother who emphasizes marriage as an important journey even if a woman has a career. Caution is necessary here, though, in not interpreting identity as entirely malleable; the lived experiences of both filmmakers are heavily influenced by their physical attributes as Latin Americans with Japanese and Korean characteristics. As theorized by Viveros Vigoya, lived experiences are denominated as necessarily corporeal as well as historical.

Theorist Trinh T. Minh-ha describes the transcultural aspect in her film *Night Passage*: "Here trans- is not merely a movement across separate entities and rigid boundaries but one in which the traveling is the very place of dwelling (and vice versa), and leaving is a way of returning home—to one's most intimate self. Cultural difference is not a matter of accumulating or juxtaposing several cultures whose boundaries remain intact."[49] She goes on to affirm: "The crossroads are where the dynamics of the film lie. They are empty centers thanks to which an indefinite number of paths can converge and part in a new direction. Inter-, multi-, post-, and trans-: these are the prefixes of our times. They define the before, after, during, and between of social and ethical consciousness."[50] First, Minh-ha recognizes the movement between as essential to any depiction of transculturality; this is evident in Flores Yonekura's and Kang's films through their physical trips to Japan and Korea. Second, both filmmakers use their travels to reflect on the most intimate of their own and others' cultural identities. Furthermore, as with Minh-ha, these two filmmakers focus on the in-between spaces in the middle of two cultures, where cultural and everyday practices flow. Finally, Flores Yonekura and Kang explore the interstices of identity and in so doing, examine their own and their communities' "social and ethical consciousness."

Through a subjective and affective filmic representation of identity, Flores Yonekura and Kang explore the intersections of national identity, gender, age, race, ethnicity, socioeconomic class, and language. Flores Yonekura focuses on art and photography and Kang highlights food and food preparation as everyday cultural practices that shed light on their lived experiences as transcultural and inter-national individuals. Moreover, both filmmakers portray the historicity of lived experiences as well as intersectional power structures that influence their decision-making processes and the ways in which their subjects (including themselves) are influenced and pressured by these power domains. In *Nikkei* and *Mi último fracaso* the interstitial space between two cultures and nationalities provides a space for personal reflection as well as sociopolitical commentary.

CONCLUSIONS

THE LATIN AMERICAN AND Latinx films and series analyzed in this book visually represent female adolescence and young adulthood as a symbolic site for questions of identity, power, oppression, and agency. Specifically, the directors—Patricia Arriaga-Jordán (Mexico), Aurora Guerrero (United States), Viviana Cordero (Ecuador), Gabriela David (Argentina), Claudia Llosa (Peru), Itandehui Jansen (Mexico), Kaori Flores Yonekura (Venezuela), and Cecilia Kang (Argentina)—highlight the multifaceted realities of young women in Latin America and US Latinx communities. The films included in this study represent the experiences of young women in locations and contexts across the region, including Huntington Park, California, the Andean regions of Ecuador and Peru, rural and urban Argentina, and the crossroads between Japan and Venezuela and South Korea and Argentina. In addition, the streaming series by Arriaga-Jordán illustrates the lived experience of a young woman in colonial New Spain. The directors herein embody various perspectives, including Latinx, Mixtec, Venezuelan of Japanese descent, and Argentine of Korean descent, and their films represent differing genres such as streaming series, fictional films, and documentaries. An intersectional understanding of these films recognizes that women's lives are not, in fact, universal but determined by factors such as geography, economics, and numerous social influences. More specifically, the identities and experiences of the film's protagonists are marked by the intersections of gender, sexuality, race, ethnicity, class, age, language, ability, region, and national origin. Within this nexus of identities, these female directors capture the unique struggles of young Latin American and Latinx women as they navigate issues of identity, structural suppression, and the possibilities of agency.

Intersectionality theory and its precursors are central to this analysis of Latin American and Latinx films made by women. Moreover, feminist theories in Latin America, such as decolonial feminism, concurrent with intersectionality theory, underscore the particularity of lived experiences in the various countries represented in this study. For example, María Lugones's decolonial feminist theory highlights the colonial view of gender as it intersects with race and class. She contends that gender and sexuality must be viewed through the lens of historical specificity in Latin America. For her part, Mara Viveros Vigoya challenges the view of woman as a universal concept; like Lugones, she argues for a historical approach that considers the many facets of identity with an additional emphasis on corporeality. Aída Hurtado also addresses intersectionality directly, emphasizing that oppression is context-dependent. Considering these three theorists together, a picture of intersectional theory unique to Latin America emerges. This vision focuses on the historical, corporeal, and contextual lived experiences of women in the region. The same can be said for theories developed within the US Latinx context that are precursors to intersectionality. Cherríe Moraga's and Gloria Anzaldúa's groundbreaking work in *This Bridge Called My Back*, which led to subsequent work by these authors and others, encompasses the precepts of intersectionality before the term was established. Notably, Moraga and Anzaldúa questioned the supremacy of Anglo-American feminism and introduced the importance of race, ethnicity, class, language, and sexuality to the conversation on gender. Like their Latin American counterparts, they also stressed the singularity of lived experiences for Latinx and other marginalized individuals.

Many theorists have addressed intersectionality directly, accentuating the course feminist studies have taken. Several recent books have focused solely on this theory and its current and future directions. These formulations lead back to Patricia Hill Collins and her original discussion of intersectionality, namely, the impossibility of understanding the complexities of identity through one lens alone. Collins's theory of structural oppression is based on intersecting identity factors; it encompasses the concept of a matrix of domination, a thread that runs throughout contemporary intersectionality theory and decolonial feminism. Rather than an outside theoretical framework imposed on Latin American and Latinx cultural production, intersectionality theory merges with Latin

American decolonial feminism and US Latinx border and gender theory. Moreover, Latin American and Latinx theorists and cultural critics continue to produce gender and intersectional theories specific to the region. On the other hand, theorists such as Moraga and Anzaldúa have transcended the region with their influence on theories of gender, body, and sexuality. Likewise, theorists like Lugones move seamlessly between the Latin American and Latinx dialogues on gender, race, and colonialism. Appraising Latin American and Latinx gender theories together reveals how they were integral to the development of intersectionality and contribute enduring intricacies to this theoretical framework.

The Latin American and Latinx cinema analyzed in this book grew out of the same context of gender theory. These women filmmakers developed their cinematic craft within a cultural milieu consistent with that of theorists such as Lugones, Viveros Vigoya, Hurtado, Moraga, and Anzaldúa. This fact is significant, as cultural production analysis must consider the creators' geographical, historical, creative, and intellectual contexts. Gender representations in the films and series of Arriaga-Jordán, Guerrero, Cordero, David, Llosa, Jansen, Flores Yonekura, and Kang echo an intersectional approach. For instance, the crossroads of gender and age are central to a comprehensive understanding of the young female protagonists in *Juana Inés, Mosquita y Mari, No robarás . . .* , and *La mosca en la ceniza*. In the first, Juana Inés is dismissed in part because of her young age, which intersects with her gender in creating a situation of dismissive and calculating persecution and subjugation. Yolanda and Mari in Guerrero's film and Lucía in Cordero's film are forced into adult situations despite their youth. Their age and socioeconomic circumstances traverse their gender within a vacuum of societal and governmental support, making them victims of a system in which they have little recourse. The same is true of Nancy and Pato in David's film; the young, female, rural protagonists become victims of a sex trafficking ring due to a lack of resources and social safety net. Regional origin is critical in interpreting the characters in *La mosca en la ceniza, Mosquita y Mari, Madeinusa, La teta asustada, Tiempo de lluvia, Nikkei: Un viaje extraordinario*, and *Mi último fracaso*. Nancy and Pato represent a rural identity—infrequent in contemporary Argentine film—whereas Yolanda and Mari correspond to a specific cultural and socioeconomic region of southern California. Likewise, Llosa's Madeinusa and Fausta and Jansen's Adela navigate the boundaries between Indigenous rural Peru and Mexico and urban Lima and Mexico City. The imbricated identities of these characters underscore the varied yet, at times, similar lived experiences of young women from such vast geographical locations. The interconnected nature of gender, class, and region is noteworthy in these films.

National identity and language are also common threads for the protagonists of Arriaga-Jordán's series and the films of Guerrero, Llosa, Jansen, Flores Yonekura, and Kang. Some of these characters navigate between two national identities and languages, like the latter two in their autobiographical documentaries. For Madeinua, Fausta, and Adela, the divide is between rural/urban and Indigenous/non-Indigenous. While Jansen's film represents more of a continuum between rural and urban, Llosa's film presents a cultural dichotomy between the two. At the same time, all three films along with the streaming series explore Indigenous identities as they intersect with gender, class, and national identity. Looking at Llosa's and Jansen's films in tandem allows for the interpretation of trends in cinematic Indigenous representations. For Flores Yonekura and Kang, their identity explorations span different continents, nations, and languages. Thus, these filmmakers question the solidity of national identity and what it means to be Venezuelan and Argentine, respectively. Significantly, the visual depiction of young women on screen in all the films in this book is intersectional; gender interweaves with age, sexuality, race, ethnicity, class, ability, language, and regional and national origin to portray the multilayered circumstances of young women in Latin American and Latinx communities.

Many intersecting depictions of young women remain to be examined and included in these dialogues on Latin American and Latinx cinema. For example, it is essential to consider the connections between cinematic production by female filmmakers in the Global South, Latin America, and US Latinx communities. In addition, the questions raised by directors like Flores Yonekura and Kang regarding national identity must be considered in other Latin American countries with communities connected to the regions of Asia. Similarly, it is imperative to consider the hundreds of Indigenous identities across the region and how they are depicted on screen by Indigenous women filmmakers. In each of these endeavors, it will be crucial to reflect on Trinh T. Minh-ha's words concerning "speaking nearby" and listening rather than 'speaking for' the subject of study; cultural critics must strive to highlight the voices of Latin American and Latinx women's films from this perspective. Examining these cinemas accordingly allows for a critical representational space for the many lived experiences of young women in the region that encompasses, in Moraga's words, the possibility of young people "walking in the world" with knowledge of their origins and a counter-narrative to hegemonic identity norms. Film and television can be powerful tools for social change and with the rights and safety of women in jeopardy across the region and in the world at large, Latin American and Latinx cinematographic representations of female adolescence and youth are catalysts for greater understanding and empowerment.

NOTES

INTRODUCTION

1. Cherríe Moraga, "Cherríe Moraga, Author—*Native Country of the Heart: A Memoir*," interview by Sheryl McCarthy, *One to One*, CUNY TV, April 15, 2019, https://www.youtube.com/watch?v=X8AY9xPlSaU.
2. Moraga, "Cherríe Moraga" interview.
3. The term *Latinx* has recently been contested; however, many cultural critics and activists in both the United States and Latin America use the term. The Merriam-Webster dictionary adopted the term in 2018. In the 1980s and 1990s, there was a shift from using Hispanic to Latino, yet many were uncomfortable with the masculine ending. In *Latin American and Latinx Philosophy*, the editor Robert Eli Sanchez Jr. addresses this issue in the introduction: "In the same spirit, we decided to adopt the term 'Latinx' (as opposed to 'Latino/a' or 'Latino'), even though none of the contributors is fully satisfied with the terms. Some of us are worried that it will prove to be a fad; others, that it is an Anglicization of the Spanish language imposed on Spanish-speakers, largely by academics. Others still are bothered by its inelegance and awkward pronunciation, especially in its plural form. In the end, however, we came to the consensus that despite our reservations, and until something better comes along, 'Latinx' best represents our desire to raise awareness about hierarchies and other forms of exclusion that are concealed by language, often in the name of tradition. In the contest between linguistic conservatism and being more inclusive, we chose the latter." Sanchez Jr., *Latin American and Latinx Philosophy*, 8.

4. In their introduction to gender and cinema, the editors of *The Routledge Companion to Cinema and Gender* outline the relationship between these two concepts: "Cinema and gender are concepts with a long and complicated relationship that extends to every aspect of filmmaking—production, representation, exhibition, spectatorship, reception, and distribution." Lené Hole et al., introduction to *Routledge Companion*. We know that, historically, women filmmakers have experienced more difficulties securing funding to produce their films and more obstacles in exhibiting their films on the big screen. Moreover, public composition and reception is typically different for films made by women. Finally, distributors traditionally do not commit the same resources to distributing their films. And, as the editors of the volume on gender and film assert, cinema tends to create an identity-based reality: "Over the course of the twentieth century, cinema has not only reiterated raced and classed gender norms, but *constructed* them as well." Lené Hole et al., introduction. It is important to underline this last point, given that film is one of the most significant contemporary influences on popular perceptions of identity. Furthermore, in this statement, the editors anticipate an intersectionality that exists between gender, race, ethnicity, and social class, concepts that cannot be examined disjointedly. At the same time, as critics examine film, they have the responsibility to recognize and problematize the fact that films construct identity norms.
5. Shaw, "Latin American," np.
6. Shaw, "Latin American," np.
7. *Latin American Women Filmmakers: Production, Politics, Poetics*, edited by Deborah Martin and Deborah Shaw; *Latin American Women Filmmakers: Social and Cultural Perspectives*, by Roberts-Camps; *Hispanic and Lusophone Women Filmmakers: Theory, Practice and Difference*, edited by Parvati Nair and Julián Daniel Gutiérrez-Albilla; and *Cine y mujer en América Latina: Directoras de largometrajes de ficción* (Film and woman in Latin America: Directors of feature-length ficitional films) by Luis Trelles Plazaola.
8. *Palabra de mujer: Historia oral de las directoras de cine mexicanas (1988–1994)* (Woman's word: Oral history of Mexican women directors), by Isabel Arredondo; *Lita Stantic: El cine es automóvil y poema* (Lita Stantic: Film is automobile and poem), by Máximo Eseverri and Fernando Martín Peña; *Mexico's Cinema: A Century of Film and Filmmakers*, edited by Joanne Hershfield and David R. Maciel; Leslie L. Marsh's *Brazilian Women's Filmmaking: From Dictatorship to Democracy*; and *Women*

Filmmakers in Mexico: The Country of Which We Dream, by Elissa J. Rashkin.

9. For childhood and adolescence: *New Visions of Adolescence in Contemporary Latin American Cinema*, Geoffrey MacGuire and Rachel Randall, editors; *The Child in Contemporary Latin American Cinema*, by Deborah Martin; *Representing History, Class and Gender in Spain and Latin America: Children and Adolescents in Film*, edited by Carolina Rocha and Georgia Seminet; and *Screening Minors in Latin American Cinema*, edited by Rocha and Seminet. For childhood and agency: *Growing Up in Latin America: Child and Youth Agency in Contemporary Popular Culture*, by Marco Ramírez Rojas and Pilar Osorio Lora; and *Children on the Threshold in Contemporary Latin American Cinema: Nature, Gender, and Agency*, by Rachel Randall. For childhood and affect: *The Feeling Child: Affect and Politics in Latin American Literature and Film*, edited by Philippa Page and Inela Selimović; *The Politics of Affect and Emotion in Contemporary Latin American Cinema: Argentina, Brazil, Cuba, and Mexico*, by Laura Podalsky; and *Affective Moments in the Films of Martel, Carri, and Puenzo*, by Inela Selimović. ·

10. *The Child in Film: Tears, Fears and Fairy Tales*, by Karen Lury; Debbie Olson's *The Child in World Cinema*; and *Youth Culture in Global Cinema*, edited by Timothy Shary and Alexandra Seibel.

11. Trelles Plazaola's *Cine y mujer en América Latina: Directoras de largometrajes de ficción* is a foundational precursor to these studies. Trelles Plazaola includes introductions, filmographies, and interviews in his study. He writes about the following directors: Suzana Amaral, Ana Carolina, María Luisa Bemberg, Busi Cortés, Marcela Fernández Violante, Solveig Hoogesteijn, Eva Landeck, Matilde Landeta, Teresa Trautman, Matilda Vera, and Tizuka Yamasaki.

12. Deborah Martin and Deborah Shaw's anthology *Latin American Women Filmmakers* includes an introduction to the history of women filmmakers and filmmaking in general in Latin America. They identify a series of pivotal moments in this history: first women's films in the first two decades of the twentieth century; women's rights in the 1920s; hierarchical shift in filmmaking in the 1920s; foundational filmic narratives; 1950s Italian neorealist influences; relative absence of women filmmakers in the 1950s and 1960s; academic training and women's film collectives in the 1970s and 1980s; 1975 UN Conference on Women that took place in Mexico City; video production and grassroots organizations in the 1980s and 1990s; digital technology and Indigenous filmmaking;

increase in commercial success of women filmmakers in the 1980s; and different production conditions and transnational productions in the 1990s and 2000s.
13. Rocha and Seminet, eds., *Screening Minors*, xi.
14. Rocha and Seminet, *Screening Minors*, xii.
15. Ramírez Rojas and Osorio Lora, eds., *Growing Up in Latin America*, xviii.
16. In an interview with CNN's Chris Wallace, Tarantino expresses his quandaries about his future in filmmaking: "Right now I don't even know what a movie is. Is that something that plays on Netflix? Is that something that plays on Amazon . . . and people watch it on their couch with their wife or husband? Is that a movie? Because my last movie opened up in 3,000 theaters and played all over the world for, you know, for a couple of months." O'Rourke, "Quentin Tarantino Explains."
17. In Cacilda Rêgo and Carolina Rocha's anthology *New Trends in Argentine and Brazilian Cinema*, the authors discuss the relationship between cinema and television in these two countries. For example, Courtney Brannon Donoghue analyzes Brazil's "star system": "One of Globo Filmes' strongest advantages are the telenovela stars under contract with its sister organization, TV Globo. In Brazil, the star system is associated more with the television industry, and particularly with the Globo network and its major product, telenovelas, than with cinema. . . . In order to put together viable film projects, Globo's film production branch has found an efficient way to utilize a major asset of the television network—the brand name stars." Brannon Donoghue, "Globo Films," 57.
18. Thornton, "Online Distribution and Access," 370.
19. The first chapter in this book focuses on Arriaga Jordán's series *Juana Inés*. The series was created and produced in Mexico and shown on television in Mexico, as discussed in Chapter 1. However, when Netflix acquired the rights to the series, it deemed it a "Netflix Original" and had complete control over access. Furthermore, continued access to other films in this study was an issue as well, underscoring the diminishing access to Latin American film.
20. Barker and Wiatrowski, introduction to *The Age of Netflix*.
21. Lobato, *Netflix Nations*, 13.
22. Lobato, *Netflix Nations*, 13.
23. In recent years, viewers have criticized Netflix's selection of US Latinx content. The Spanish-language content on the platform skews toward shows from Spain, Mexico, and some content from countries such as Colombia. However, US Latinx culture has narrower selections. One

exception was Gloria Calderón Kellett and Mike Royce's *One Day at a Time*, based on the 1975 original of the same name. The newer series (2017–2019 on Netflix, with a one-year extension in 2020 on Pop) focused on a Cuban-American family; however, Latinx audiences with origins in many different Latin American countries identified with the show and protested when it was canceled. Other similar Netflix series include *Mr. Iglesias*, based on the stand-up comedian "Fluffy" Gabriel Iglesias, and *Selena*, based on the Tejana singer of the same name. Each of these shows deals with intersecting issues including race, ethnicity, national origin, language, and sexuality. For example, these series examine youth and sexuality (*One Day at a Time*); the use of the term Latinx (*Mr. Iglesias*); and the intersections of Latinx and mainstream pop culture (*Selena*), among many other themes.
24. The term *intersectionality* is from legal theorist Kimberlé Williams Crenshaw. Carastathis, *Intersectionality*, 3.
25. Collins, *Black Feminist Thought*, 18.
26. Collins, *Black Feminist Thought*, 246.
27. Grzanka, introduction to *Intersectionality*, xv.
28. Grzanka, introduction to *Intersectionality*, xv.
29. Hancock, *Intersectionality*, 23.
30. Hancock contends: "From the middle of the nineteenth century, activists have offered important insights into the twin intellectual projects of intersectionality—the visibility project and the project of reconceptualizing categorial relationship." *Intersectionality*, 38. Hancock underscores intersectionality's multicultural epistemology and highlights theorists such as Gloria Anzaldúa, Cherríe Moraga, and Elena García (72). She also emphasizes the importance within the field of an examination of the relationships between intersectionality and women of color feminisms; a citation of "the early intellectual bonds between intersectionality-like thought and social constructivism" (163); and the assertion that "intersectionality-like thinking about how power is relationally constituted predates and anticipates Michel Foucault's well-known arguments about power" (164).
31. Carastathis, *Intersectionality*, xvi.
32. Carastathis, 2.
33. Carastathis, 13. Carastathis writes, "Animated by concerns stemming from women-of-color feminisms and decolonial feminisms, I problematize the institutionalization, mainstreaming, or neocolonization of intersectionality, tracing these developments to particular occlusions

of Crenshaw's argument—provisionality (the footnote); hierarchy (the basement metaphor); coalitional identity (the normative conclusion)" (13).
34. Carastathis, 15, 17.
35. Carastathis, 106.
36. Collins and Bilge define intersectionality: "Intersectionality investigates how intersecting power relations influence social relations across diverse societies as well as individual experiences in everyday life. As an analytic tool, intersectionality views categories of race, class, gender, sexuality, class, nation, ability, ethnicity, and age—among others—as interrelated and mutually shaping one another. Intersectionality is a way of understanding and explaining complexity in the world, in people, and in human experiences" *Intersectionality*, 2.
37. Collins and Bilge, *Intersectionality*, x.
38. Collins and Bilge, *Intersectionality*, 2.
39. Eguchi, Calafell, and Abdi, eds., *De-Whitening Intersectionality*, xix.
40. Holling, "Intersectionalities in the Fields," 17–18.
41. Rafia Zakaria turns a reflexive eye on intersectionality studies, as well, in *Against White Feminism: Notes on Disruption*. Zakaria denounces "white feminism," referring to those who refuse to "consider the role that whiteness and the racial privilege attached to it have played and continue to play in universalizing white feminist concerns, agendas, and beliefs as being those of all of feminism and all of feminists" (xv). Zakaria defines a white feminist not by skin color, but rather as someone who "earnestly salutes the precepts of 'intersectionality' . . . but fails to cede space to the feminists of color who have been ignored, erased, or excluded from the feminist movement" (xv). This argument is central to criticism of Eurocentric feminist and gender studies that privilege European and Anglo-American theorists. Like *De-Whitening Intersectionality*, Zakaria's *Against White Feminism* seeks to expand intersectionality beyond the perspectives that center white, middle-class, European, Anglo-American, able-bodied, heterosexual individuals and give space to feminists of color.
42. See Stephanie Rivera Berruz's "Latin American and Latinx Feminisms" for another review of the history of the feminisms in Latin America and the US Latinx context in Sanchez Jr.'s *Latin American and Latinx Philosophy*.
43. Lugones, "Revisiting Gender," 34.
44. Lugones, *Theories of the Flesh*, 35–36.

45. Lugones, "Toward a Decolonial Feminism."
46. Within this framework, the "European, bourgeois, colonial, modern man became a subject/agent, fit for rule, for public life and ruling. . . . The European bourgeois woman was understood as his complement, but as someone who reproduced race and capital through her sexual purity, passivity, and being homebound in the service of the white, European, bourgeois man." Lugones, "Toward a Decolonial Feminism," 743.
47. Lugones, "Toward a Decolonial Feminism," 743.
48. Lugones, "Toward a Decolonial Feminism," 743.
49. Argentine philosopher María Luisa Femenías's contribution to *Theories of the Flesh*, "From Women's Movements to Feminist Theories (and Vice Versa)," adds to the histories of feminism in Latin America. Specifically, Femenías looks at the decolonial turn, highlighting the work of Argentine essayist Zulma Palermo. The author calls "for a genuinely 'polyphonic' presence of the plural voices of women in positions of political representation and in national and transnational public spaces" (49).
50. Viveros Vigoya and Lesmes Espinel, "Cuestiones raciales," 16. All translations mine unless otherwise noted.
51. Fournier-Pereira, "Feminismos e interseccionalidad," 71.
52. Fournier-Pereira, 74.
53. Fournier-Pereira, 76.
54. It is not the same to self-identify as a lesbian feminist in Matagalpa, Nicaragua, as in Montevideo, Uruguay, to be a lesbian feminist field worker in the Aguan, or to be a Nicaraguan feminist lesbian migrant in Upala, Costa Rica; just as it is not the same being trans in Tegucigalpa as in Buenos Aires, in the neighborhoods in the south of San Jose of Costa Rica, or in Sao Paulo, Brazil. Fournier-Pereira, "Feminismos e interseccionalidad," 81. Fournier-Pereira contends that the oppressions may share certain characteristics or circumstances, yet they manifest themselves differently and require varying tools to challenge them (81).
55. Moraga and Anzaldúa, eds., *This Bridge Called My Back*, xvi.
56. Elizabeth Martínez's *De Colores Means All of Us: Latina Views for a Multi-Colored Century* addresses the place of Latinos in the "Black and White" discussions of race in the United States; immigration and national borders; the link between Latino communities and environmental justice; gender in Latino communities; and new movements leading up to the turn of the century.
57. Anzaldúa, *Borderlands/La Frontera*, n.p.
58. Anzaldúa, n.p.

59. Anzaldúa, 195.
60. Carla Trujillo's edited volume *Living Chicana Theory* must be added to the work that was already addressing these concepts in the eighties and nineties.
61. *This Bridge We Call Home: Radical Visions for Transformation*, edited by Gloria E. Anzaldúa and AnaLouise Keating, echoes some of the same concepts found in *This Bridge Called My Back*—the bridge as metaphor, identity labels, Lorde's ideas on the master's house, identity, and academe, among others. In her preface, Anzaldúa relates: "Today categories of race and gender are more permeable and flexible than they were for those of us growing up prior to the 1980s. *This Bridge We Call Home* invites us to move beyond separate and easy identifications, creating bridges that cross race and other classifications among different groups via intergenerational dialogue." Anzaldúa and Keating, preface, 2. As AnaLouise Keating says in her introduction, "Our goal is not simply to commemorate *This Bridge* but to examine the current status of multicultural feminist theorizing and to reinvigorate *Bridge*'s call for new forms of community, identity, and activism." "Charting Pathways," 17. The contributions include such entries as Rebecca Aanerud's "Thinking Again: *This Bridge Called My Back* and the Challenge to Whiteness"; Amy Sara Carroll's "Interracial"; Evelyn Alsultany's "Los Intersticios: Recasting Moving Selves"; Mary Loving Blanchard's "Poets, Lovers, and the Master's Tools: A Conversation with Audre Lorde"; and Migdalia Reyes's "The Latin American and Caribbean Feminist/Lesbian Encuentros: Crossing the Bridge of Our Diverse Identities"; among others. In the title and essays included, the editors make a case for looking forward and creating a vision for future reflections and actions on race, ethnicity, gender, and class. Hence, the anthology also focuses on an aspect that is central to contemporary intersectionality studies—the need for strategies of resistance to the matrix of domination.
62. Hurtado, "Intersectionality," 164–65.
63. Hurtado, "Intersectionality," 167.
64. Foundational film director Lourdes Portillo (born in Mexico, raised in Los Angeles, and Chicana-identified) is a precursor to many Latinx directors. She explores themes related to gender, adolescence, class, and violence in films such as *Señorita extraviada* (Missing young woman; 2001).
65. Along with the directors included in this study, there are many other Latin American and Latinx filmmakers who explore female adolescence

in their films. For example, Argentine director Lucía Puenzo portrays gender, sexuality, class, and adolescence in *XXY* (2007), *El niño pez* (The fish child; 2009), and *El médico alemán* (The German doctor; 2013), as well as her latest film *La caída* (Dive; 2022), out on Netflix. Ecuadorian director Tania Hermida explores girlhood and gender in *En el nombre de la hija* (In the name of the girl; 2011); Uruguayan director Virginia Martínez looks at gender, adolescence, young adulthood, and state-sponsored violence in *Por esos ojos* (For those eyes; 1997); Uruguayan director Beatriz Flores Silva also explores gender and state-sponsored violence in *Polvo nuestro que estás en los cielos* (literally, "Our dust that art in heaven," but released in English under the title *Masangeles*; 2008); Colombian director Laura Mora Ortega also examines gender, youth, and violence in *Matar a Jesús* (Killing Jesús; 2017); and Costa Rican director Laura Astorga Carrera looks at gender, race, and adolescence in *Princesas rojas* (Red princesses; 2013); among many other films and directors.

CHAPTER 1

1. Castellanos, *Mujer que sabe latín . . .*, 9.
2. Castellanos, *Mujer que sabe latín . . .*, 9.
3. Castellanos's 1973 collection refers to this phrase, much-used in Spanish: "Mujer que sabe latín, no tiene buen fin" (A woman who knows Latin does not end well). There are some variations, including, "Mujer que sabe latín, no tiene marido ni buen fin" (A woman who knows Latin, neither does she have a husband nor does she end well).
4. While Arriaga-Jordán's historical biopic includes conventional aspects of the genre (period dress and historical figures, among others), it also provides a space to analyze contemporary issues of identity.
5. An entry in *De series*, "Juana Inés, estreno Canal Once," provides specific information on the series. According to the entry, there were 54 actors involved; filming time was 532 hours; filming format was high definition (2K); the film debuted on Saturday, March 26, at 9:30 p.m.; the program was transmitted on Saturdays at 9:30 p.m. and repeated on Tuesdays at 10 p.m.; and the filming locations included the Ex-Hacienda de Santa Mónica, Catedral Metropolitana, Ex-Convento de San Agustín, Capilla gótica del Centro Cultural Helénico, and the Antiguo Colegio de las Vizcaínas.

6. Other awards include several awards for Crystal Screens Festival Mexico City: Production Values, Photography (Luis Ávila), Screenplay, Editing-TV Series, Casting (Luis Maya), Art (Marisa Pecanins), Investigation (Arriaga-Jordán), Actress (Arantza Ruiz), and Actor (Hernán del Riego). It was also nominated for Best Postproduction, Soundtrack (Michael Nyman and Nicolas Engel), and Audio (Javier Umpierrez). IMDB, "Juana Inés," accessed Oct. 15, 2024, https://www.imdb.com/title/tt5593998.
7. See Roberts-Camps, chapter 1 of *Latin American Women Filmmakers*, on Bemberg's depiction of Sor Juana.
8. A Colombian series acquired by Netflix called *La Niña* (directed by Rodrigo Triana and Juana Uribe, 2016) that came out the same year shares similar themes of gender and adolescence. The Colombian series, produced by CMO Producciones for the open Colombian channel Caracol, also examines the themes of violence and reintegration into society.
9. Baudot, "La trova náhuatl," 849.
10. Bravo Arriaga, "Sor Juana Inés de la Cruz," 21.
11. Bravo Arriaga, "Sor Juana Inés de la Cruz," 23.
12. Anzaldúa, "Speaking in Tongues," 170.
13. Considering the death of Sor Juana, see Sara Poot Herrera's essay "Sor Juana 325 (1695–2020)" and Guillermo Schmidhuber de la Mora's essay "1695: Crónica verdadera de la muerte de Sor Juana Inés de la Cruz."
14. Episode 1: "Miradme al menos" (At least look unto me); episode directed and written by Patricia Arriaga-Jordán, release date March 26, 2016. 50 min.
15. Episode 2: "Para el alma no hay encierro" (There is no confinement for the soul); episode directed by Patricia Arriaga-Jordán and Emilio Maillé, written by Patricia Arriaga-Jordán and Monika Revilla, release date April 2, 2016. 50 min.
16. Episode 3: "Lágrimas negras de mi pluma" (Black tears from my pen); episode directed by Emilio Maillé, written by Patricia Arriaga-Jordán and Monika Revilla, release date April 9, 2016. 50 min.
17. Episode 4: "Este amoroso tormento" (This lovely torture); directed by Emilio Maillé, written by Javier Peñalosa and Monika Revilla, release date April 16, 2016, 51 min.; Episode 5: "Divina Lysi" (Divina Lysi); directed by Emilio Maillé, written by Monika Revilla, release date April 23, 2016, 50 min.; Episode 6: "Detened la mano" (Hold the hand); directed by Emilio Maillé, written by Javier Peñalosa and Monika Revilla, release date April 30, 2016, 51 min.; Episode 7: "La vida con que muero" (The life

I die); directed by Julián de Tavira, written by Patricia Arriaga-Jordán and Monika Revilla, release date May 7, 2016, 51 min.
18. Whereas in later episodes Arriaga-Jordán explores her protagonist's lesbian identity, this is not clear in the early episodes when the protagonist is younger. Based on Octavio Paz's examination of Sor Juana, Bemberg's film, for example, highlights Sor Juana's sensual relationships with the second vicreine who arrives. In later episodes of her series, Arriaga-Jordán explores this part of the character's identity, as well. However, the adolescent protagonist in *Juana Inés* rejects the first vicereine's advances and has a male love interest.
19. Access to books is a theme that runs throughout Arriaga-Jordán's series as well as Bemberg's films. For example, Bemberg explores the issue of access to books and knowledge in her film *Yo, la peor de todas*, as well as in her historical melodrama *Camila*, in which the main character secretly trades books with a friend who is later hung for having subversive materials.
20. As Sor Juana continues to be such an important figure and subject of study, there is an extensive body of work that focuses on her writings and biography. For the purposes of this chapter, I have chosen to reference those that relate directly to the issue of indigeneity in her poetry as well as studies that elucidate relevant elements of her biography.
21. Kirk, *Sor Juana Inés de la Cruz*, 15.
22. Kirk, 15.
23. Kirk, 19.
24. Kirk, 19–20.
25. Kirk, 22.
26. "From my first glimmers of reason, my inclination to letters was of such power and vehemence, that neither the reprimands of others—and I have received many—nor my own considerations—and there have been not a few of these—have succeeded in making me abandon this natural impulse which God has implanted in me." de la Cruz, *Florilegio*, 737. English translation is from Trueblood, trans., *A Sor Juana Anthology*, 210.
27. de la Cruz, *Florilegio*, 738.
28. Kirk, *Sor Juana Inés de la Cruz*, 62.
29. Kirk, *Sor Juana Inés de la Cruz*, 62. Later, Kirk explains: "Latin, the common language of scholarship in Europe, served as an indication of the successful implementation of Western cultural ideals in the Americas and also stood as a barrier against the perceived barbarism of New

World cultures" (75). In another section, she reminds us: "Sor Juana was one of a very few non-aristocratic women in the early modern world who went beyond the possession of passive knowledge of Latin" (85).

30. Kirk, *Sor Juana Inés de la Cruz*, 80.
31. Kirk, 80.
32. Kirk, 191.
33. Kirk, 339.
34. de la Cruz, *Florilegio*, 738. Translation from Trueblood, trans., *A Sor Juana Anthology*, 94–95.
35. Francesca Gargallo discusses Sor Juana's proto-feminist status in "Philosophical Feminism in Latin America," a chapter in Pitts, Ortega, and Medina's *Theories of the Flesh*. Likewise, Alicia Gaspar de Alba examines "Colonial feminism" in "An Interview with Sor Juana."
36. de la Cruz, *Florilegio*, 124. "clear honor of women, / of men learned outrage, / that you prove it is not sex / of intelligence a part" (translation mine).
37. de la Cruz, *Florilegio*, 58. "Who arrives foolish to tread / of old age the confines, / shame they comb and not gray hairs; / not years, affronts they repeat" (translation mine).
38. In a beautiful edition by the Fondo de Cultura Económica in Mexico City, Américo Larralde Rangel published *El eclipse del Sueño de Sor Juana*, including several color illustrations and appendixes examining the poet's text and its relationship to astrology, the constellations, and the mastery with which Sor Juana describes a celestial event in the form of poetry.
39. Paz, foreword, viii.
40. Fernández Chagoya, "El Claustro femenino," 62.
41. This scene is comparable to a key moment in the first episode of Netflix's *The Queen's Gambit* (2020, directed by Scott Frank). The young protagonist stands alone at one end of a high-school classroom where chess boards are set up around the desks. A group of high-school boys walks in and stares at her from the other end of the room. The idea is that she will be playing them all simultaneously and it is clear that they do not think much of her. However, as viewers, our feminist desires are fulfilled as she quickly dispatches each of them on the chess boards. The feeling is similar to the one we experience when Sor Juana's intellect shines in this scene in *Juana Inés*.
42. Paul Julian Smith explains the overarching reach of Arriaga-Jordán in the series: "the queer theme prominent in the series also pointed to the

auteur status of Arriaga as executive producer. One of her earlier series for Canal 11 was a workplace drama on the theme of modern masculinity that also provoked controversy for its gay male love scenes." Smith, "Screenings," 86.
43. Smith, "Screenings," 83.
44. Smith, 83.
45. Smith, 87.
46. The actress Arcelia Ramírez, who played the older Sor Juana, commented in an article in *El Universal* that the historical figure fought for her right to knowledge and to have an intellectual life and, in this way, she overcame the boundaries of her gender. Janet Mérida, "Sor Juana, hábito de Arcelia," *El Universal*, Nov. 7, 2015, https://www.eluniversal.com.mx/articulo/espectaculos/teatro/2015/11/7/sor-juana-habito-de-arcelia.
47. Following many creators before her, Arriaga-Jordán uses her series to examine both the historical context of her protagonist as well as the contemporary society in which the series was created. Film and literature are typical avenues through which directors and authors critically analyze their own place and time by use of historical figures and societies. Furthermore, Arriaga-Jordán takes an openly feminist approach to the telling of Sor Juana's story, thus justifying another contemporary lens—intersectionality—in studying the series and historical figure.
48. Muñiz-Huberman, "Las claves de Sor Juana," 315. Stephanie Kirk identifies Sor Juana as unique among women in her knowledge of Latin. Kirk, *Sor Juana Inés de la Cruz*, 85.
49. Muñiz-Huberman, "Las claves de Sor Juana," 322.
50. Muñiz-Huberman, "Las claves de Sor Juana," 322.
51. Tabuenca, "Lo precolombino," 32. Francesca Gargallo contends that Sor Juana learned the Nahuatl language "in which she wrote from the age of seven." "Philosophical Feminism," 98.
52. *Tocotín* #1 (lines 83–118) in de la Cruz, *Obras completas*; English translation in Townsend, "Sor Juana's Nahuatl," 8–9).
53. Baudot, "La trova náhuatl," 850.
54. Tenorio, *Los villancicos de Sor Juana*, 149.
55. Leal, "El hechizo derramado," 198.
56. Sabat-Rivers, "Sor Juana Inés de la Cruz," 41.
57. "The necessary adjustments would have to be made that the cathedral performative space would merit, but could not be missing authenticity by any means, since the true critics of the performative moment were

those very Indigenous peoples." Robinson, "Sor Juana Inés de la Cruz," 166.
58. Baudot furthers this by saying: "Los dos textos, efectivamente, traducen, cada uno a su manera, el eco de una queja india, insinuada o declarada, pero reconocible y audible" (The two texts, effectively, translate, each one in its way, the echo of the Indian complaint, insinuated or declared, but recognizable and audible). "La trova náhuatl," 856. For an examination of linguistic legislation in New Spain, see Wright Carr, "La Política lingüística en la Nueva España."
59. The critical debate over Sor Juana's grasp of Nahuatl is not the only mystery regarding her work. In his book, José Pascual Buxó makes the case for Sor Juana's authorship of *El oráculo de los preguntones*.
60. Díaz Cintora, "'*Yoqui in Tlahuépoch* Medea.'"
61. Egan, "Lyric Intelligiblity," 201.
62. Baudot, "La trova náhuatl," 852.
63. Muñiz-Huberman, "Las claves de Sor Juana," 316.
64. Muñiz-Huberman, "Las claves de Sor Juana," 322.
65. Baudot, "La trova náhuatl," 849. Camilla Townsend proposes three "suppositions" in her study of Sor Juana's Nahuatl texts: 1) she was already bilingual by eight as evidenced by a newly discovered *loa*; 2) others such as Garibay supported her talents in the Indigenous language; or 3) she worked with a native speaker of Nahuatl. Townsend concludes the article by asserting that Sor Juana did, in fact, write the poems we have in Nahuatl; however, the errors they contain prove that she was not bilingual and was also not working with a native speaker. On the other hand, Townsend commends the poet for the level of knowledge she presumes that she reached even to be able to write at the level she wrote in the language. Townsend, "Sor Juana's Nahuatl."
66. Tabuenca, "Lo precolombino," 34.
67. Sabat-Rivers, "Sor Juana Inés de la Cruz," 41.
68. Sabat-Rivers, "Sor Juana Inés de la Cruz," 43.
69. Leal, "El hechizo derramado," 199–200.
70. Bravo Arriaga, "Sor Juana Inés de la Cruz," 15.
71. Bravo Arriaga, "Sor Juana Inés de la Cruz," 16.
72. "For I, my Lady, was born / in abundant America, / compatriot of gold, countrywoman of metals / where common sustenance / is given almost for nothing, / that in no place more / does Mother Earth show off. / Of the common curse / free they seem to be born / the children, as bread / does not cost sweat and toil" (translation mine). de la Cruz, *Florilegio*, 126.

73. Antonio Rubial García asserts: "al final de su comedia *Los empeños de una casa*, la monja jerónima no pretendía incluir dentro de los mexicanos a todos los habitantes de la Nueva España, sino sólo a los indios. Éstos eran ciertamente los que hacían al territorio distinto a Europa" (at the end of her comedy *Los empeños de una casa*, the Jerome nun did not pretend to include as Mexicans all of the inhabitants of New Spain, but only the Indians. These were certainly those that made the territory different from Europe). Rubial García, "La patria criolla," 382.
74. Carrillo Trueba, *El racismo en México*, 6.
75. For the Indigenous peoples she is definitely the owner of the discourse, and he, Cortes, Captain Malinche, chief of all the Spaniards, a man suddenly stripped of his virility; lacks language because his words lack force, that is to say intelligibility, only the words that a woman emits who complies with excellence her job as interpreter . . . arrive at their target: that operation of language acts on the virility and muddies what should be a strict category, that of masculinity. Glantz, *Obras reunidas I*, 71.
76. The Dover introduction to *An Aztec Herbal: The Classic Codex of 1552* traces the history of the manuscript later known as the *Libellus de Medicinalibus Indorum Herbis*. The *Libellus*, prepared by Juan Badiano, is the Latin version of a Nahuatl herbal codex written by an Aztec physician named Martín de la Cruz. As Gates states, this codex was "the first herbal and the first medical text known to have been written in the New World" Gates, *An Aztec Herbal*, iii. William Gates translated the text into English in 1939. The original text included drawings of medicinal plants and descriptions in Nahuatl of how to use these plants for medicinal purposes. The depth of knowledge of the healing uses of plants displayed in the codex is testament to the centrality of natural healing in the Aztec world.
77. Sor Juana herself refers to her varying identity markers in her "Response," ironically asking how she could handle the theme in her "manos indignas" (unworthy hands): "repugnándolo el sexo, la edad y sobre todo las costumbres" (when my sex, age, and especially my way of life all oppose it). *Florilegio*, 736; Trueblood, trans., *A Sor Juana Anthology*, 209.
78. There is a scene in Bemberg's film about Sor Juana where the protagonist grabs the archbishop by the lapel and pulls him close to the bars of her cell, forcing him to smell her. She exclaims that he cannot stand the smell of a woman and fears her as the unknown.
79. Later in Arriaga-Jordán's series, the protagonist does have sensual relationships with women; however, in the beginning of the series, the sexual interest of the vicereine is unrequited.

80. Minh-ha, *D-Passage*, 73.
81. Minh-ha, *D-Passage*, 10–11.
82. Kirk, *Sor Juana Inés de la Cruz*, 175. Also see Mónica Díaz's book *Indigenous Writings from the Convent: Negotiating Ethnic Autonomy in Colonial Mexico*.
83. This example confirms Lugones's emphasis on the historical aspect of intersectional identity in Latin America. Sor Juana's European parentage would mean something different in contemporary Mexico, while her criolla identity placed her within a particular, oppressive structural system in Colonial New Spain.

CHAPTER 2

A portion of the Cordero section appeared previously in Traci Roberts-Camps, "El género y la interseccionalidad en las cineastas ecuatorianas Viviana Cordero y Tania Hermida" *Kipus: Revista andina de letras y estudios culturales*, no. 50 (2021) : 139–64.

1. Guerrero financed *Mosquita y Mari* mainly through Kickstarter. The film was shot in eighteen days and edited with grants from the San Francisco Film Society, Film Independent, and Sundance. Guerrero's other work includes the short films "Pura lengua" (2005), "Viernes Girl" (2005), and "Pandora's" (2008). She has directed episodes of many television series including Ava DuVernay's *Queen Sugar*; *13 Reasons Why*; *Gentefied*; and *Bel-Air* (2022 series).
2. Guerrero says in the Sundance "Press Kit": "The inspiration behind my debut feature-film, *Mosquita y Mari*, was my own adolescence. Initially, when I decided I wanted to write a feature-length script I kept coming back to a series of complex, same-sex friendships I had while growing up. When looking back, long before I identified as queer, I realized my first love was one of my best friends. It was the type of friendship that was really tender and sweet but also sexually charged. Despite the fact that we had the makings of a beautiful teen romance we never crossed that line. The beginnings of *Mosquita y Mari* was reflecting back on that time and asking myself the questions, why didn't we cross that line and what kept us in 'our place'?" She says that although her family never explicitly condemned such a relationship, "it was implied in society's expectations" that romantic relationships were heterosexual. Guerrero, "Press Kit *Mosquita y Mari*," 3.

3. In an interview in *25 Watts*, Ana Cristina Franco Varea comments: "Si yo pudiera elegir seguir actuando quisiera que toda la vida me dirija Viviana Cordero" (If I could choose to continue to act I would like Viviana Cordero to direct me the rest of my life). Franco Varea, "Cuatro miradas," 41. In the 1990s, Viviana Cordero began directing films. Cordero is also a prolific dramatist and novelist. She examines themes of gender and social class in her novels such as *Una pobre, tan, ¿qué hace?* (2001). Her filmography includes *Sensaciones* (Sensations; co-directed with Juan Esteban Cordero, 1991), *El gran retorno* (The great return; mid-length film, 1995), *Un titán en el ring* (A titan in the ring; 2002), and *No robarás . . . . . (a menos que sea necesario)*. *Sensaciones* is a feature-length film that follows a group of musicians searching for the essence of Andean music. The melody becomes the central theme of the film, while the characters seek out new sensory experiences that affect their songs. Cordero made the film with her brother, Juan Esteban Cordero, and they are both central characters. Cordero's brother composed the music, which won a prize in the Film Festival of Bogota and has been considered part of the New Age style in Ecuador from the early 1990s. Cordero's second feature-length film, *Un titán en el ring*, also takes place in the Andes and presents the story of a star fighter, "La Bestia Loca" (The Crazy Beast), from a small town, who is challenged by a new fighter, "El Argonauta" (Argonaut). At the same time, the new priest arrives and begins to confront the town's traditions and conventional beliefs. Even though the setting is similar to *Sensaciones*, *Un titán* is more of a narrative film that explores the encounter between modernity and tradition, as well as politics of identity in a small town.
4. Guerrero recognizes intersectionality directly in her note at the end of the film: "A mis comunidades" (To my communities). Thus, she highlights that she belongs to more than one community and presents more than one identity, just like her characters.
5. Other Latin American films that address working-class adolescents and young women also highlight the protagonists' lack of agency in the face of intersectional and structural oppression. These include *Lola* (1989) and *Danzón* (1991) by María Novaro; *La vendedora de rosas* (1998) by Víctor Gaviria; and *Las mantenidas sin sueño* (2005) by Martín Desalvo and Vera Fogwill. By no means an exhaustive list, these films join Guerrero's in addressing female adolescence, class, and agency in Latin American cinema.
6. Hurtado, "Intersectionality," 159.

7. Collins and Bilge, *Intersectionality*, 2.
8. Viveros Vigoya, "Intersecciones de género," 118.
9. The input of this type of work has been to highlight that domination is a historical formation and that social relations are interwoven in the concrete experiences that can be lived in a multitude of ways. Universal feminist parameters are inadequate to describe specific forms of domination in which the relations are interwoven and are experienced in diverse forms. Vigoya, "La interseccionalidad," 11.
10. Moraga and Anzaldúa's introduction to *This Bridge* reflects the concepts of intersectionality in their 1979 letter calling for contributions to the anthology: "We want to express to all women—especially to white middle-class women—the experiences which divide us as feminists.... We want to create a definition that expands what 'feminist' means to us." Introduction, xliii. This idea is clearly akin to what would be known as intersectionality theory, the concept of expanding the definition of feminism. In this anthology in particular, the editors gather voices and ideas not considered part of the feminist movement previously. For many, they had developed their own theories outside of the framework of mainstream feminism and Moraga and Anzaldúa were finally reuniting these contributions. In her own preface to the original edition, Moraga describes being at a meeting of mostly white women talking about racism and writes: "How can we—this time—not use our bodies to be thrown over a river of tormented history to bridge the gap?" "La Jornada: Preface," xxxvii. The metaphor of the bridge is central to the anthology and to the writers' expanded model of feminism. They have always been expected to be the bridge that covers the gap in knowledge between those at the center of mainstream feminism and those on the periphery. Moraga asks here why it must be this way, why they must always explain themselves and help others understand their histories.
11. Audre Lorde explains that "those of us who stand outside the circle of this society's definition of acceptable women; those of us who have been forged in the crucibles of difference; those of us who are poor, who are lesbians, who are black, who are older, know that *survival is not an academic skill*," and then Lorde proclaims the all-important phrase: "*For the master's tools will never dismantle the master's house*." Lorde, "The Master's Tools," 95. Lorde continues to explain how women are asked to "stretch across the gap of male ignorance" and decries that "it is the task of black and third world women to educate white women" as an "old and primary tool of all oppressors to keep the oppressed occupied

with the master's concerns" (96). Hence, *This Bridge* offers a space for an alternative vision of feminism, parallel to what would be coined intersectionality theory. This space is open to those Lorde mentions as not fitting in the traditionally accepted definition of woman.
12. Alsultany, "Los Intersticios," 107.
13. Guerrero, "Press Kit *Mosquita y Mari*," 4.
14. Guerrero, "Press Kit *Mosquita y Mari*," 4–5.
15. Guerrero comments on the music in the film: "The young people in the film mix their immigrant roots with other musical influences. Thus, they listen to mariachi, banda, norteño, and cumbia mixed with reggae, pop, punk, and Ska." "Press Kit *Mosquita y Mari*," 6.
16. "Huntingtin Park, CA," Data USA, accessed Oct. 22, 2024, https://datausa.io/profile/geo/huntington-park-ca. In 2019, Huntington Park was named California's "most miserable city" by *Business Insider* (CBS Los Angeles).
17. "Quito tiene la tasa más alta de pobreza a escala nacional," *El Comercio*, Oct. 26, 2019, https://www.elcomercio.com/actualidad/negocios/quito-tasa-economia-pobreza-inec.html.
18. Guerrero, "Press Kit," 4.
19. Alsultany, "Los intersticios," 107.
20. Mina Karavanta, "Community," 449.
21. Karavanta, "Community," 450.
22. Moraga, *Native Country of the Heart*, 205.
23. Antonia I. Castañeda discusses the foundational violence, centering on rape, that existed during the time of the Spanish Missions in the region and traces the history of violence against Indigenous women in the territory. Castañeda, "History and the Politics of Violence."
24. Aldama, *Latinx Ciné*, 3. See Aldama's introduction to *Latinx Ciné* for an overview of groundbreaking Latinx films and filmmakers of the twentieth century.
25. Chilean filmmaker Alicia Scherson uses music as a theme and technique in her film *Play* (2005). She also uses the idea of trying on another's clothing as a way of trying on their identity.
26. Rueda Esquibel, "Memories of Girlhood," 59.
27. Rueda Esquibel, "Memories of Girlhood," 94.
28. Aldama, *Latinx Ciné*, 7.
29. Aldama, *Latinx Ciné*, 7.
30. An early example of a Latinx film exploring issues of gender and sexuality is Darnell Martin's *I Like It Like That* (1994).

31. Of queer studies, David William Foster said: "Queer studies question patriarchal heteronormativity and the compact narrative of compulsory matrimony, compulsory heterosexuality, compulsory monogamy, and the unquestionable homologizing of romantic love, erotic desire, and individual fulfillment." Foster, *Queer Issues*, ix.
32. Clarke, "Lesbianism," 126.
33. Gloria Calderón Kellett and Mike Royce's Netflix streaming series *One Day at a Time* (2017–2020), a remake of Norman Lear's 1975 television series of the same name, also explores adolescent gender and sexuality through the character of Elena Alvarez (Isabella Gomez).
34. Ortega, "*Cámara* Queer," 264.
35. Ortega, "*Cámara* Queer," 269.
36. Sandoval, Aldama, and García, "Introduction," 19.
37. Sandoval, Aldama, and García, 20.
38. Sandoval, Aldama, and García, 20.
39. There are palpable similarities between Cordero's *No robarás* and the films of Mexican directors Marisa Sistach and María Novaro. *Perfume de violetas (nadie te oye)* (2001), directed by Sistach, also deals with themes of youth and different social classes. *Perfume de violetas* tells the story of two adolescents, Yéssica (Ximena Ayala) and Miriam (Nancy Gutiérrez), who meet and become friends when Yéssica moves to a new school. The two live in a working-class neighborhood in Mexico City; however, it is clear that Miriam and her mother have more money than Yéssica and her family, who live in a temporary construction next to a large building. Yéssica's family depends on the mother's boyfriend for a place to live and the young character is subject to the sexual desires of the boyfriend's son. *Perfume de violetas* and *No robarás* explore themes of abuse and scarcity as well as how the characters in both films experience grave injustices for which there is impunity because the victims are part of a socioeconomic class that is invisible to the justice system. The images that coincide between the two films include Lucía in *No robarás* sitting alone on the roof of her apartment building looking out at the city and Yéssica sleeping under the stairs of her friend's apartment building. Furthermore, the two films depict the deteriorated state of the schools and neighborhoods where the girls live, with graffiti covering the concrete walls. This also reminds the viewer of María Novaro's first feature-length film, *Lola* (1989), which captures the ruins of certain neighborhoods in Mexico City that were never repaired after the 1985 earthquake. Moreover, in the three filmmakers' films, there are

central images that contrast the protagonists' innocence and worldly knowledge.
40. Zorica Mrsevic asserts: "Patriarchal societies are often characterized by a lack of institutional response and an absence of legal provisions concerning domestic violence. Such a context is ripe for the proliferation of all types of violence. Thus, violence is both a symptom of patriarchy and its cause, both a typical consequence of patriarchy and one of the most effective means to maintain a patriarchal system." Mrsevic, "The Opposite of War," 42.
41. Vanegas León, "Criminología y género," 89.
42. Vanegas León, 90.
43. Vanegas León, 93.
44. Vanegas León, 93.
45. Moraga, "La Güera," 24.
46. Viveros Vigoya, "Intersecciones de género," 119.
47. Carlos Piñeiro Iñiguez questions certain assumptions about the Indigenous populations in Ecuador, including the idea that they remained intact since before the Conquest; he doubts: "que existiera un mundo aislado en su opresión que se habría mantenido más o menos entero en su sistema de creencias a lo largo de cinco siglos de obligada subalternidad" (that there existed a world isolated in its oppression that would have remained more or less whole in its system of beliefs during five centuries of forced subalternity). Piñeiro Iñíguez, *Pensamiento equinoccial*, 52. The critic questions the sole focus on Indigenous communities as victims of oppression rather than recognizing alongside of this a history of political coordination and cultural resistance (52–53). He continues: "Durante mucho tiempo, las bien intencionadas propuestas de los indigenistas para la superación del problema indígena no fueron afirmativas de su identidad propia—nacional o al menos comunitaria—sino la de integrarlos a una condición mestiza que, fuera lo que fuera, no era india. Para los indígenas, el orgullo mestizo no podía sino sonar a retórica huera. El abandono de la teoría de la asimilación indígena a las formas de sociabilidad dominantes muy lentamente va dejando paso a un reconocimiento de la pluriculturalidad" (For a long time, the well-intentioned proposals of indigenists for the overcoming of the Indian problem were not affirmative of their own identity—national or at least community—but that of integrating them into a mestizo condition that, whatever it was, was not Indian. For the Indigenous, mestizo pride could not sound like anything but empty rhetoric. The abandonment of

the theory of Indigenous assimilation to forms of dominant sociability very slowly leaves room for a recognition of pluri-culturalism (53).
48. Other Latin American women filmmakers who explore music and youth culture include Alicia Scherson in *Play* (2005)—where the protagonist listens to music through her headphones throughout the film—and *Il futuro* (The future; 2013)—in which the protagonist discovers the power of counter-culture and dress following the death of her parents—as well as directors such as María Novaro, who explores the importance of music in all of her films from *Lola* with "rock en español" (1989), to *Danzón* with dancehalls (1991), to *El jardín del Edén* (The Garden of Eden; 1994), and *Sin dejar huella* (Without a trace; 2000) with regional Mexican music, among her other feature-length films.
49. Lorde, "The Master's Tools," 95.
50. Podalsky, "Out of Depth," 109.
51. Podalsky, "Out of Depth," 111.
52. Narváez, "Rock y Punk," 62.
53. Narváez, "Rock y Punk," 78. *Mejor no hablar de ciertas cosas* (It's better not to talk about certain things; 2012) is a film by Ecuadorian director Javier Andrade, director of *Lo invisible* (2021).
54. Narváez, 76.
55. Narváez, 67.
56. Narváez, 73.
57. Moraga, preface, xxxvii.

CHAPTER 3

A portion of this chapter appears in *Contemporary Argentine Women Filmmakers*, edited by Mirna Vohnsen and Daniel Mourenza (Cham, Switzerland: Palgrave, 2023).
1. *La mosca en la ceniza* won the FIPRESCI Award at the Kerala International Film Festival (2009), and David won the award for Best New Director at the Huelva Latin American Film Festival (2009). The film was nominated for Best Screenplay Silver Condor Award at the Argentinean Film Critics Association Awards.
2. Collins and Bilge, *Intersectionality*, 2.
3. There are many films that portray this period in time. Some of them include *La historia oficial* (1985, Luis Puenzo); *Garage Olimpo* (1999, Marco Bechis); *Kamchatka* (2002, Marcelo Piñeyro); *Hermanas* (2005,

Julia Solomonoff); and allegorically, *Camila* (1984, María Luisa Bemberg); among many others.
4. Mexican director David Pablos' film *Las elegidas* (The chosen ones; 2015) deals with similar topics of sexual exploitation in the border town of Tijuana, a place where young women are tricked into joining prostitution rings.
5. *Santa* was a Mexican naturalist novel, a genre that explored how the protagonist was unable to escape her conditions. Antonio Moreno adapted the novel into a film of the same name, which was released in 1932 and was the first Mexican "talkie" (film that included sound).
6. Boris Tarré, "Hacia una construcción," 102.
7. Forcinito, "Lo invisible y lo invivible," 38.
8. McCabe, *Feminist Film Studies*, 66.
9. McCabe, 65.
10. McCabe, 87.
11. Hurtado, "Intersectionality," 159.
12. Hurtado, "Intersectionality," 167.
13. Collins and Bilge, *Intersectionality*, 2.
14. Collins and Bilge, *Intersectionality*, 2.
15. We live a mirage of equality that, leaning on real achievements and unequivocal advances, denies the existence of androcentric culture, the *machista* gaze and the stereotypical assessment of roles that are made to look determined by nature. . . . The World Bank report presented in Washington in 2014 puts figures on these matters: more than seven hundred million women are victims of different forms of gender violence in the world. Hendel, *Violencias de género*, 24.
16. Hendel, *Violencias de género*, 25.
17. Hendel, *Violencias de género*, 34.
18. Corbalán, "Cine de denuncia," 40.
19. Forcinito, "Lo invisible y lo invivible," 38. Forcinito examines the importance of sound in Gabriela David's film *Taxi, un encuentro* (2001). Forcinito, "Are You Listening?"
20. Nair and Gutiérrez-Albilla, eds. *Hispanic and Lusophone*, 6–7.
21. Forcinito, "Fugas y resistencias heroicas," 58.
22. *La historia oficial* portrays the kidnapping of children by the secret police, who then tortured and killed their parents. The children were adopted by military officials or the secret police officers themselves and most were never told they were adopted.
23. Forcinito, "Las batallas de la memoria," 94.

24. According to Johanna Higgs, "Human trafficking in Argentina became highly visible only about fifteen years ago. One notable case led, for example, to the creation of the Fundación María de los Angeles, an organization founded out of despair and hope by Susana Trimarco in 2007. Her twenty-three-year-old daughter, Marita Verón, was kidnapped in 2002 one morning on the street where the family lived in Tucumán, in northern Argentina. Verón has never been found." Higgs, "Argentina Has a Problem."
25. The spectator observes in numerous scenes the daily life of the street, where you even see a police officer maintaining order and the spectator senses that the people who pass by know what is happening behind those closed doors, but no one does anything about it. Even at the end of the film, when the prostitution ring is disarticulated, the camera focuses on a series of evading glances that avoid confronting reality. Corbalán, "Cine de denuncia," 41.
26. In an article in *Clarin*, one of the actresses (Vera Carnevale, who plays Rubia) says specifically: "Hay que decirlo: estas cosas suceden porque hay gente que lo permite" (It must be said: these things happen because there are people who allow it). Redacción Clarín, "El cine argentino."
27. Andermann, "Productions of Space," 228.
28. Andermann, "Productions of Space," 229.
29. This is similar to what happens in Marco Bechis's film *Garage Olimpo* (Olympic garage; 1999) in which the exteriors are represented as seemingly normal and peaceful while the inside of the parking garage is used as a torture chamber. A comparison can also be made to Chilean director Carmen Luz Parot's *Estadio Nacional* (National Stadium; 2003) where the documentary depicts the stadium at once as a sports venue and an internment camp by the military dictatorship of Pinochet.
30. Rocha and Seminet, eds., *Representing History, Class, and Gender*, 5.
31. Das and Kleinman, introduction, 1.
32. Hinterberger, "Agency," 7.
33. Collins and Bilge, *Intersectionality*, 166.
34. This is analogous to the grandmother in Gabriel García Márquez's short story "La increíble y triste historia de la candida Eréndira y su abuela desalmada" (The incredible and sad tale of Erendira and her heartless grandmother). Rural studies can shed light on the rural/urban dynamic in David's film; however, much of this discipline is from and about the global north. Mark Shucksmith and David L. Brown's *Routledge International Handbook of Rural Studies* (2016) focuses on "Europe, America,

and Australasia" and includes topics such as demographic change, food systems, environment and resources, gender, and social and economic equality, among others. While the focus of the handbook is on the global north, the same general ideas apply to the rural setting in the global south, with the clear understanding that the context is different.
35. Collins and Bilge, *Intersectionality*, 19.
36. David William Foster, in *Gender and Society in Contemporary Brazilian Cinema*, analyzes Macabea's imitation of magazine fashions in the city, noting the tragic inadequacy of this imitation. Foster, *Gender and Society*.
37. Brynne Voyles, *Wastelanding*, viii–ix.
38. Brynne Voyles, *Wastelanding*, 9.
39. de Lucía, *Entre cabezas y trash*, 56.
40. de Lucía, *Entre cabezas y trash*, 95.
41. Baker, "An Intersectional Analysis," 209.
42. Baker, "An Intersectional Analysis of Sex Trafficking Films," 221.
43. Once again, Argentina is in economic crisis and many critics contend that the election of Javier Milei in November 2023 and the subsequent devaluation of the Argentine peso will have catastrophic consequences as will his social policies.
44. Thomas et al., *Critical Rural Theory*, 2–3.
45. Thomas et al., 5.
46. Thomas et al., 7.
47. In *The Projected Nation*, Matt Losada discusses film representations of spaces that depict social marginalization. According to Losada, contemporary Argentine cinema has shifted its focus from rural spaces to urban neighborhoods to represent the social margins; however, "despite the decreased cultural visibility of rural space, contemporary films have on occasion examined how it is conceived in the distant metropoli and documented economic exploitation and violence." Losada, *The Projected Nation*, 134. In *Before Bemberg*, Losada examines films by Ana Katz, Lucrecia Martel, Lisandro Alonso, and Pino Solanas and their critiques of the traditional view of rural life as utopic.
48. Bachelard, *The Poetics of Space*, 211.
49. Bachelard, *The Poetics of Space*, 222.
50. Les Pibes is a group of young Argentines whose goal is gender inclusivity. Pañuelos Verdes (green handkerchiefs) is a movement for legal abortion. #NiUnaMenos is a movement that seeks to draw attention to the disproportionate number of women murdered, a movement that stems from

a case in Argentina but that has grown to include many other countries in Latin America.

CHAPTER 4

1. In "Through Female Eyes: Reframing Peru on Screen," Sarah Barrow places Llosa's work within the context of other women filmmakers in Peru, namely, Marianne Eyde and Rosario García-Montero. Regarding the protagonist's name, the only direct reference is a tag in her clothing that reads "Made in USA." "America" could be seen as a stand in for anything from the outside, away from the confines of the village.
2. Claudia Llosa is the niece of famed Peruvian author Mario Vargas Llosa. She has also directed the following feature-length films: *Aloft* (2014) and *Distancia de rescate* (Fever dream; 2021). *La teta asustada* was nominated in the Best Foreign-Language Film category at the 2010 Academy Awards. Llosa's films have won more than twenty awards and been nominated in numerous film festivals around the world.
3. Ángeles Cruz is a well-known actress and also director of the 2021 film *Nudo mixteco*. The actor portaying José is Jansen's son.
4. Other comparable contemporary films by Latin American women directors include María Novaro's *Sin dejar huella / Without a Trace* (Mexico), Marisa Sistach's *La niña en la piedra* (The girl in the stone; Mexico), and Alicia Scherson's *Play* (Chile). These films highlight Indigenous populations in one way or another; the Mayan communities in Mexico and the Mapuche in Chile. In *Sin dejar huella*, one of the protagonists speaks on the phone to a friend in Yucatan and they communicate in Yucatec Maya. Likewise, the film refers to the supposed Mayan antiquities that she transports. In *Play*, the protagonist comes from a Mapuche village in the south of Chile and when she talks to her mother on the phone, she speaks in Mapundungun. In *La niña en la piedra*, workers find an artifact in the dirt that belongs to the corn goddess. In the film's narrative, the stone helps the protagonist survive because she steps on it, avoiding drowning in a swamp. While these films make reference to Indigenous communities or feature an Indigenous protagonist as in Llosa's films, the theme of the "other" varies in each. For example, in *Sin dejar huella*, the protagonist speaks a Mayan language but is not Mayan and the focus is not only on the Indigenous populations in Mexico. In *La niña en la piedra*, Sistach further explores the theme of the Mayan worldview

through the corn goddess, however, this theme is secondary to others such as gender and violence. In terms of theme and technique, perhaps the film that is closest to Llosa's is *Play* because the protagonist herself is Indigenous and there are fantastic elements. While *Madeinusa* and *La teta asustada* are not exactly fantastical, they examine Quechua culture from a Western perspective that some say orientalizes the Indigenous characters. *Play* is more fantastic in its technique, such as the sequence in which the protagonist becomes a fighter from the video game Streetfighter and fights with a mother who is mistreating her daughter. From a very different perspective, Mexican director Dana Rotberg explores indigeneity in her feature-length film *Tuakiri Huna* (White lies; 2013), filmed and produced in New Zealand. Rotberg tells the story of a healer and a young woman who hides her aboriginal identity, examining issues of gender, race, ethnicity, and class.

5. Salvador's name is ironic as it means "savior" in English. Madeinusa sacrifices him and saves herself in the end.
6. Kroll, "Between the 'Sacred' and the 'Profane,'" 120–21.
7. Similar images of incest appear in other Latin American films such as Dana Rotberg's *Ángel de fuego* (1992).
8. Kroll, "Between the 'Sacred' and the 'Profane,'" 120.
9. Kroll, 121.
10. Kroll, 116.
11. D'Argenio, "A Contemporary Andean Type," 40.
12. D'Argenio, "A Contemporary Andean Type," 40.
13. Carolina Rueda also emphasizes the problematic nature of this physical inspection. Rueda, "Memory, Trauma, and Phantasmagoria," 458. Rueda highlights the choice of location for Fausta and Aída's interactions; namely, the older woman's home is in a wealthy neighborhood that borders Fausta's working and subsistence class community, both divided by a wall that residents such as Aída see as protection against the "other" (458).
14. Anne Carruthers examines Llosa's film through the lens of the uterus; namely, she centralizes the protagonist's memories as a fetus within the narrative of the film and the story of the fear that is passed from one generation to the next through the rape of the mother. Carruthers, *Fertile Visions*.
15. Varas, "Posmemoria femenina," 35.
16. Varas, "Posmemoria femenina," 35. Varas identifies Fausta's songs and the use of the potato as a form of inherited post-memory as well as devices to regain social memory (38).

17. Vitelia Cisneros addresses the importance of Llosa's use of Quechua in *La teta asustada*, especially as it relates to the history of violence of which Fausta is a victim. Cisneros underscores the importance of the first sequence being in Quechua and in the form of singing, representing a community practice that juxtaposes itself against the spoken dialogue specific to Spanish-speaking Peru. Cisneros, "*La teta asustada* en el cine peruano," 125. Cisneros goes on to emphasize the importance of Llosa's focus on the Quechua language: "La relevancia del idioma para entender a quiénes afectó más el conflicto y por qué queda esclarecida en los datos ofrecidos inicialmente, que destacan que la mayor parte de las víctimas eran nativo-hablantes de las zonas más pobres del país. La presencia del quechua resulta entonces no sólo lógica, sino necesaria al abordar representaciones sobre este episodio, y pese a ello es excepcional, ya que gran parte de la producción cinematográfica peruana es básicamente limeña e hispana" (The relevance of the language for understanding who was affected most by the conflict and why it remains hidden in the facts offered initially, that underscore that most of the victims were native speakers from the poorest areas of the country. The presence of Quechua turns out to be not only logical, but necessary when approaching representations about this episode, and despite this it is exceptional, given that a great part of Peruvian cinematographic production is basically from Lima and Hispanic (Spanish-speaking). Cisneros, "*La teta asustada* en el cine peruano," 125).
18. Minh-ha, Woman, Native, Other, 87.
19. Minh-ha, D-Passage, 75.
20. Schroeder Rodríguez, *Latin American Cinema*, 282.
21. Schroeder Rodríguez, 284.
22. Schroeder Rodríguez, 287.
23. Schroeder Rodríguez, 289.
24. Mexico City is also referred to simply as Mexico.
25. Cesar Hernandez, "Exclusive: A First Look."
26. Hernandez, "Exclusive: A First Look."
27. Virtanen, "Amazonian Native Youths," 160.
28. Virtanen, 160.
29. Virtanen, 169.
30. In "La inscripción del autor," Jansen and Bautista recognize the multiple perspectives that encompass the Indigenous experiences in the Americas, partially due to the centrality of migration and Indigenous creators that navigate "entre diferentes espacios sociales y culturales

contradictorios" (between different contradictory social and cultural spaces) Jansen and Bautista, "La inscripción del autor," 298
31. McNelly, "Baroque Modernity," 9–10.
32. McNelly, "Baroque Modernity," 11. McNelly returns to José Carlos Mariátegui and his seminal text *Siete ensayos de interpretación de la realidad peruana* (1928) to show how the Peruvian Marxist viewed indigeneity differently and from an economic perspective: "Mariátegui's perspective transcends the perceived exceptionalism of the different guises of indigeneity (including urban indigeneity) and constructs spaces like El Alto as a dialectic part of a larger capitalist and colonial whole. It offers a way to approach the questions about the 'brutal' form assumed by capitalist modernity in El Alto highlighted by my interlocutor, a way of problematising the localised form of society in El Alto and its place in global capitalist dynamics. This helps us, for example, to view *cholets* as Aymara architecture with a different social function to the apartment blocks in La Paz and yet as being constructed by similar economic forces, namely a construction boom catalysed by increased hydrocarbon rents within the Bolivian economy" (14). The *cholets*, as McNelly explains, are a new type of building in El Alto, Bolivia: "*Cholets* are brightly coloured, multi-storied buildings which have come to dominate the skyline of El Alto, their name a playful nod to both *cholos* (discussed below) and alpine chalets. Comprised of several floors of commercial or events space topped with an apartment where the proprietor resides, they are considered a new Aymara or Indigenous form of architecture" (9). The term *cholo* has many meanings, depending on the context. For instance, it can mean an individual with Amerindian ancestry or anything related to Indigenous heritage and practices, mostly in the Andean region. In McNelly's study, this term also refers to dress and architecture in the city of El Alto; however, the author questions traditional uses of the term.
33. Postero, "Introduction: Negotiating Indigeneity," 108.
34. Postero, 110.
35. Postero, 111.
36. Minh-ha, *Woman. Native. Other*, 87.
37. D'Argenio, *Indigenous Plots*, 1.
38. D'Argenio, 43.
39. D'Argenio, 45.
40. D'Argenio, 46.
41. D'Argenio, 49.
42. D'Argenio, 49.

43. D'Argenio, 52.
44. Varas defends Llosa's respectful and creative filmic representation of a "vital" Peruvian syncretic community Varas, "Posmemoria femenina," 38–39.
45. Hernandez, "Exclusive," n.p.
46. Hernandez, "Exclusive," n.p.
47. In their essay on filmmaking and community, Jansen and Bautista confront the lack of Indigenous cultural representation by members of Indigenous communities: "La representación de los pueblos indígenas es producida principalmente por académicos, periodistas y cineastas no-indígenas. Es decir, la representación de los pueblos indígenas de las Américas generalmente no es producida por ellos mismos" (The representation of Indigenous communities is produced principally by non-Indigenous academics, journalists and filmmakers. That is to say, the representation of the Indigenous communities of the Americas generally is not produced by those same communities). Jansen and Bautista, "La inscripción del autor," 295. The authors even mention Claudia Llosa in their introduction as an example of this: "Estas representaciones mediáticas son enajenantes y muy distantes de la realidad que viven los pueblos indígenas en la actualidad" (These media representations are alienating and very different from the reality that the Indigenous communities live in the present) (295). They go on to criticize studies on cinematic Indigenous representation as describing these communities and characters as belonging to the past and rarely protagonizing the films in which they appear (295–96). Later in the chapter, the authors compare Llosa's Indigenous depictions in *Madeinusa* and *La teta asustada* to Ángeles Cruz's first short film, "La tiricia o cómo curar la tristeza" (2012). According to Jansen and Bautista, Llosa's representation of incest differs drastically from Cruz's and contributes to an image of Andean indigeneity as "radicalmente distinta, otra y monstuosa" (radically different, other, and monstruous) (308).
48. Schiwy, *Indianizing Film*, 9.
49. Canessa, *Natives Making Nation*, 3.
50. Canessa, 4.
51. Canessa, 24.
52. Canessa, 5.
53. Canessa, 8.
54. Canessa, 17.
55. Canessa, 19.

56. Elguera, "Antiracist Spatial Narratives," 188.
57. Elguera, 188.
58. Elguera, 192.
59. Arias, "What Indigenous Literatures," 151. "Previously, the *encomienda* system implemented by the Spanish crown in the colonies was not often referred to as slavery, and Spain's official rhetoric claimed that slavery was abolished with the Laws of Burgos of 1512 and then again with the New Laws of 1543. Nonetheless, Indigenous subjects' unpaid labor was mandatory and coerced" (151).
60. Arias, "What Indigenous Literatures," 152.
61. Arias, "What Indigenous Literatures," 166.
62. Kim Díaz also addresses race, socioeconomic class, and national identity, in this case in Peru. Giving context to Manuel González Prada, an Indigenist from Peru, Díaz discusses the Laws of the Indies, "established by the Spanish Crown to regulate the interactions between the American Indians and the Spanish settlers and *encomenderos*, Spanish men put in charge of the land, Indians, and other resources subject to the Spanish Crown. González Prada points out that during Spanish colonialism, even though the Spanish committed genocide and enslaved the American Indian, at least they had the Laws of the Indies and Las Casas, who advocated for the well-being of the Indians. Neither was the case under the Republic of Peru; even as a liberal state, Peru did not have laws intended to protect the Indians or an advocate like Las Casas. Instead of improving, the living conditions of the Indians actually worsened after Peruvian independence." Díaz, "Indigenism in Peru and Bolivia," 183–84. While González Prada's justifications are troubling, he does point to the conditions of Indigenous populations in Peru from the beginning of the Republic. Díaz goes on the explain González Prada's proposed solutions to the enslavement of Indigenous communities in Peru: "Either Spanish Americans have a change of heart and begin treating Indians with the dignity they deserve, or Indians claim their freedom by force" (184). According to Díaz, José Carlos Mariátegui paralleled González Prada's thoughts and also believed that the pre-existing ayllu system in Peru's Indigenous communities would allow for an economic solution to their oppression (187). As the ayllu system allowed for shared land and property, "Mariátegui believed that communism would find fertile ground in Peru given that the ayllu was the original economy of Peru and given that Indians made up the majority of the population" (187). As is evident, the history of national development is closely tied to the inclusion or

exclusion of Indigenous communities based on race, ethnicity, gender, socioeconomic class, language, as well as rural identity.

CHAPTER 5

1. One recent Venezuelan film that has garnered critical attention is *Pelo malo* (Bad hair; 2013) by Mariana Rondón. The film tells the story of Junior, a nine-year-old who worries about his tightly curly hair and wants to straiten it, while his mother worries that it is a sign of his sexuality. Rondón explores intersectional issues of race, gender, sexuality, and class in this film.
2. Interestingly, in his analysis of 1910s pre-industrial Argentine films made by women, Matt Losada sees a brief period in which "class, politics, and gender freely intersected on film before the eventual subsumption of the bulk of production under the aegis of the cinema industry." Losada, *Before Bemberg*, 12.
3. Schroeder Rodríguez, *Latin American Cinema*, 28.
4. See David William Foster's preface to *Latin American Documentary Filmmaking: Major Works* for a brief history of the genre in Latin America. See also Paulo Antonio Paranaguá's introduction to *Cine documental en América Latina*. In his analysis, Paranaguá distinguishes Latin American documentary filmmaking from outwardly imposed frameworks and touches upon the most important moments for the genre across the region.
5. Schroeder Rodríguez, *Latin American Cinema*, 167.
6. Schroeder Rodríguez, 168.
7. Schroeder Rodríguez, 168.
8. Flores Yonekura, "Director Q&A."
9. Flores Yonekura, "Director Q&A."
10. Kang, "Cecilia Kang." Kang tells the interviewers it took around five years to film and edit *Mi último fracaso*.
11. During the trip to Seoul, Kang films a parking garage sign that reads "Women-Only Parking" in a segment focusing on a group of sisters. Interestingly, the Korean government has decided to eliminate these parking areas in favor of family-only parking; according to the government, the designation was no longer needed.
12. Yoon, *Global Pulls*, 80.
13. Yoon, 80–81.

14. Yoon, 85.
15. Yoon, 85.
16. Yoon, xvi.
17. Yoon, xix.
18. Hurtado, "Intersectionality," 159.
19. Collins and Bilge, *Intersectionality*, 2.
20. Viveros Vigoya, "Intersecciones de género," 118.
21. Viveros Vigoya, "La interseccionalidad," 11.
22. Collins and Bilge, *Intersectionality*, 15. Emphasis in original.
23. Flores Yonekura, "Director Q&A."
24. Flores Yonekura, "Director Q&A."
25. Foster, *Latin American Documentary Filmmaking*, x.
26. Hopfenblatt and Flores, "Problematizing Film," 307.
27. Hopfenblatt and Flores, "Problematizing Film," 308.
28. According to Constanza Burucúa, film in Venezuela has been linked to state funding from the beginning, since the 1914 oil field discoveries and Juan Vicente Gómez's regime prompted the government to acquire "the technology needed for the production of short propaganda documentaries." Burucúa, "Young Women at the Margins," 173. As with other Latin American countries, Venezuela established a series of funds and centers to support national filmmaking (for example, the Fondo de Fomento Cinematográfico [FONCINE; Film Development Fund], and the Central Nacional Autónomo de Cinematografía [CNAC; National Film Center]). During Hugo Chávez's presidency, the government also created the Plataforma del Cine y Medios Audiovisuales (Platform of Film and Audio-Visual Media) to back films that expand representation and support the idea of the revolution (174). Burucúa traces the volume of Venezuelan film production to these forces as well as to co-productions with Spain's Ibermedia program. The author sees women filmmakers in Venezuela as central to the 1960s political documentary: "Throughout the 1960s, politically committed documentary became a privileged site for both artistic and political explorations across Latin America; a group of women were integral to the national iteration of this pan-regional movement in Venezuela. Between 1968 and 1973, three filmmakers with a clear political and feminist filiation formed the collective Cine Urgente (Urgent Cinema); its founders—Josefina Acevedo, Franca Donda, and Josefina Jordán—were militants of the MAS (Movimiento al Socialismo), as well as members of the Grupo Feminista Miércoles (Wednesday Feminist Group)" (175). Therefore, while Venezuelan film

production does not boast the same output as Argentine cinema, it was central for women filmmakers in the history of documentary filmmaking in the region. Documentarians such as Acevedo, Donda, and Jordán paved the way for more recent filmmakers such as Flores Yonekura to create socially conscious documentary films.

29. Brah, "Diaspora," 440.
30. Comparable to Flores Yonekura's documentary, Brazilian director Tizuka Yamasaki's fictional films *Gaijin: Caminhos da liberdade* (1980) and *Gaijin: Ama-me como sou* (2005) also explore the lives of Japanese descendants in Latin America, in this case Brazil. The first represents the arrival of Japanese immigrants in Brazil to work on coffee plantations in the early twentieth century, their early struggles, and their path to carving out a space for themselves in Brazilian society. The second is about the descendants of these Japanese immigrants in Brazil who decide to move to Japan to recover elements of their cultural identity and work in factories in the late twentieth and early twenty-first centuries. This fictional story of Nikkei and Nissei communities in Brazil and Dekassegui communities in Japan mirrors Flores Yonekura's own exploration in her documentary. All three focus on national origin and nationality as central to discussions of identity. At the same time, they problematize the idea of national identity, race, and ethnicity; a thought process akin to what happens in the theory of intersectionality where questions of identity are not simplified but made more complex. Yamasaki and Flores Yonekura both take the concept of nation within identity and turn it around. In other words, nationality is not binary; one is not either Venezuelan or Japanese but somehow a complicated mixture of both. At one point in the documentary, Flores Yonekura writes in her journal: "Ser Nikkei es ser un latinoamericano más: la combinación de naciones, culturas y pensamientos" (Being Nikkei is being another Latin American: the combination of nations, cultures, and thoughts). The director recognizes this non-binary nature of identity.
31. In 1989, US sociologist Arlie Hochschild published the book *The Second Shift: Working Parents and the Revolution at Home*. The title refers to the working mother's second shift she works when she arrives home and must take over the larger share of household duties, including cooking, cleaning, and childcare.
32. Three significant recent contributions to the study of affect in film are Cynthia Tompkin's *Affectual Erasure: Representations of Indigenous Peoples in Argentine Cinema* (2018); Inela Selimović's *Affective Moments in*

the Films of Martel, Carri, and Puenzo (2018); and Laura Podalsky's *The Politics of Affect and Emotion in Contemporary Latin American Cinema: Argentina, Brazil, Cuba, and Mexico* (2011).
33. Piedras, *El cine documental*, 22. Nicolás Prividera also addresses documentary filmmaking in Argentina as well as its connection to New Argentine Cinema in "El lugar del documental en los Nuevos Cines Argentinos."
34. Minh-ha, *D-Passage*, 158.
35. Minh-ha, *D-Passage*, 158–59. Minh-ha talks further about the idea of the "other" in her filmmaking: "In my work and its politics of naming: the inappropriate/d—woman, native, handicapped, abnormal, deviant, queer, foreign, refugee, not-yet-citizen, nonaligned, marginalized, silenced, dominated, oppressed—in other words, all those who stray from the norms of man, mankind, and human. And with these, the other withing: the West in me, or the Master, the dominant I, the sovereign subject, the Us versus Them, the omniscient, rational outsider, and more—all also inside me" (157–58).
36. Minh-ha, *D-Passage*, 75.
37. de la Cruz, *Florilegio*, 750.
38. de la Cruz, *Florilegio*, 750.
39. Minh-ha, *D-Passage*, 75. Minh-ha further develops her theory of filmmaking: "Making a film that shows and speaks with the subject of your inquiry as if she is listening and looking next to you would shift subtly but radically your mode of address, of forming and contextualizing. Whether this subject is actually present or not doesn't matter; you're committed to speaking nearby him, her, or it. What has to be given up is, first and foremost, the voice of omniscient knowledge. . . . In positioning your voice next to, you acknowledge that there's a space in between, an interval of possibilities, and you learn to speak with audible holes and gaps" (59). She later confirms: "raising the question 'Who's speaking?' is also asking 'Who's listening?' To be aware, without closing off, of where and from where one speaks, or else of how, when and by whom one can be heard" (73).
40. Sarlo, *Tiempo pasado*, 9. Sarlo speaks from the immediate context of post-dictatorship testimony and examines the rise of and significance given to testimonials as a public way of knowing the past: "Este libro se ocupa del pasado y la memoria de las últimas décadas. Reacciona no frente a los usos jurídicos y morales del testimonio, sino frente a sus otros usos públicos. Analiza la transformación del testimonio en un

ícono de la verdad o el recurso más importante para la reconstrucción del pasado; discute la primera persona como forma privilegiada frente a discursos de los que la primera persona está ausente o desplazada. La confianza en la inmediatez de la voz y del cuerpo favorece al testimonio. Lo que me propongo es examinar las razones de esa confianza" (This book focuses on the past and memory of recent decades. It reacts not to the judicial and moral uses of testimony, but to its other public uses. It analyzes the transformation of testimony into an icon of truth or a more important recourse for the reconstruction of the past; it discusses the first person as a privileged form in the face of discourses of which first person is absent or displaced. Confidence in the immediacy of the voice and of the body favors testimony. What I propose is to examine the reasons for this confidence) (23).

41. Sarlo affirms: "La Argentina todavía vive las consecuencias a largo plazo de lo que ocurrió en los años de la última dictadura. En términos culturales, se ha abierto el capítulo de la memoria" (Argentina is still experiencing the long-term consequences of what happened in the years of the last dictatorship. In cultural terms, the chapter of memory has been opened). *Tiempo presente*, 43. Sarlo sees the turn of the century (twentieth to twenty-first centuries) as the chapter of memory in Argentine history. She clearly speaks from the perspective of post-dictatorship Argentina and the efforts to remember and uncover the lived experiences of dictatorship. It is also evident that this "capítulo de la memoria" opened up a cultural and representational space for other memories. Thus, the memories of the many communities that arrived more recently in the country find an amenable place within national cultural production in which to explore their own lived experiences. Within this context of importance placed on testimony and memory, Kang presents the cultural practices and memories of her own family and community.

42. Piedras, *El cine documental*, 30. For an in-depth examination of Argentine film production and corresponding government funding and laws from 1996 to 2006, see Carolina Rocha's "Contemporary Argentine Cinema during Neoliberalism" in *New Trends in Argentine and Brazilian Cinema* (2011). For a detailed analysis of Nuevo Cine Argentino (New Argentine Cinema), including well-researched discussions of film schools, narrative mode and themes, production, audiovisual industry and laws, and local and international markets, see Osvaldo Mario Daicich's *El nuevo cine argentino (1995–2010): Vinculación con la*

industria cultural cinematográfica local e internacional y la sociocultura contemporánea.

43. Clara Kriger also addresses the rise in subjective documentaries after the turn of the century in Argentina, underscoring the tendency to mix the subject of study with the personal history of the documentarian: "Por lo tanto, lo inquietante y productivo del género sigue siendo su relación con lo real, siempre que se logre derivar de allí una asociación con la vida del espectador" (Therefore, what is disquieting and productive of the genre continues to be its relationship with the real, as long as it possible to derive from there an association with the life of the spectator). Kriger, "La experiencia," 35.
44. Paladino, "En torno," 58.
45. For her part, Argentine theorist Griselda Soriano asserts: "Si bien el cine se ha mirado a sí mismo desde sus comienzos, las últimas décadas han visto reaparecer con fuerza la cuestión de lo reflexivo" (If film has certainly looked back on itself from the beginning, the last decades have seen the reflexive question reappear with force). Soriano, "Reflexividad y autoreferencia," 83.
46. Lucía Rud has reflected specifically on Korean-Argentine film. Rud examines the question of transnationality in Argentine film from the perspective of cinematic co-productions and filmic depictions of the Korean diaspora. According to Rud, the "Argentine-Korean film connection is the largest and more intense film connection between an Asian and a Latin American country." Rud, "Transnationalism in Korean-Argentine Cinema." Rud attributes this to the fact that "their film industries boomed around the same time (in the late 1990s) product of film policies and the importance acquired at the same environment (European film festivals)" (np).
47. Collins and Bilge, *Intersectionality*, 167.
48. Collins and Bilge, *Intersectionality*, 167.
49. Minh-ha, *D-Passage*, 10–11.
50. Minh-ha, *D-Passage*, 11.

BIBLIOGRAPHY

Aldama, Arturo J., Chela Sandoval, and Peter J. García, eds. *Performing the US Latina and Latino Borderlands*. Bloomington: Indiana University Press, 2012.
Aldama, Frederick Luis. *Latinx Ciné in the Twenty-First Century*. Tucson: University of Arizona Press, 2019.
Alsultany, Evelyn. "Los Intersticios: Recasting Moving Selves." In Anzaldúa and Keating, *This Bridge We Call Home*, 106–10.
Andermann, Jens. "Productions of Space/Places of Construction: Landscape and Architecture in Contemporary Latin American Film." In *The Routledge Companion to Latin American Cinema*, edited by Marvin D'Lugo, Ana M. López, and Laura Podalsky, 223–34. Abingdon, UK: Routledge, 2018.
Anzaldúa, Gloria. "Speaking in Tongues: A Letter to Third World Women Writers." In Moraga and Anzaldúa, *This Bridge Called My Back*, 163–72.
Anzaldúa, Gloria. *Borderlands/La Frontera: The New Mestiza*. San Francisco: Aunt Lute Books, 1987.
Anzaldúa, Gloria. Preface to Anzaldúa and Keating, *This Bridge We Call Home*, 1–5.
Anzaldúa, Gloria, and AnaLouise Keating, eds. *This Bridge We Call Home: Radical Visions for Transformation*. New York: Routledge, 2002.
Arenal, Electa. "Sor Juana Inés de la Cruz: Reclaiming the Mother Tongue." *Letras femeninas* 11, no. 1/2 (1985): 63–75.
Arias, Arturo. "What Indigenous Literatures Tell Us about Race." In *Poetics of Race in Latin America*, edited by Mabel Moraña, 151–67. London: Anthem Press, 2022.

Arredondo, Isabel. *Palabra de mujer: Historia oral de las directoras de cine mexicanas (1988–1994)*. Madrid, Frankfurt, and Aguascalientes: Iberoamericana, Vervuert, and Universidad Autónoma de Aguascalientes, 2001.

Bachelard, Gaston. *The Poetics of Space: The Classic Look at How We Experience Intimate Places*. Boston, MA: Beacon Press, 1994.

Baker, Carrie N. "An Intersectional Analysis of Sex Trafficking Films." *Meridians: Feminism, Race Transnationalism* 12., no. 1 (2014): 208–26.

Barker, Cory, and Myc Wiatrowski, eds. *The Age of Netflix: Critical Essays on Streaming Media, Digital Delivery and Instant Access*. Jefferson, NC: McFarland, 2017.

Barker, Cory, and Myc Wiatrowski. Introduction to *The Age of Netflix: Critical Essays on Streaming Media, Digital Delivery and Instant Access*, edited by Cory Barker and Myc Wiatrowski. Jefferson, NC: McFarland, 2017.

Barrow, Sarah. "Through Female Eyes: Reframing Peru on Screen." In *Latin American Women Filmmakers: Production, Politics, Poetics*, edited by Deborah Martin and Deborah Shaw, 48–69. New York: I.B. Tauris, 2017.

Baudot, Georges. "La trova náhuatl de Sor Juana Inés de la Cruz." In *Estudios de folklore y literatura dedicados a Mercedes Díaz Roig*, edited by Beatriz Garza Cuarón and Yvette Jiménez de Báez, 849–59. Mexico City: El Colegio de México, 1992.

Bloch-Robin, Marianne. "De *Madeinusa* a *La teta asustada* de Claudia Llosa: La música en la visión del mundo de un autor." *El ojo que piensa: Revista de cine iberoamericano*, no. 3 (Jan 3, 2014). https://hal.science/hal-03883843.

Bordo, Susan. *Unbearable Weight: Feminism, Western Culture, and the Body*. Berkeley: University of California Press, 1995.

Boris Tarré, Marta. "Hacia una construcción psicológico-cultural de género en la mujer traficada en *La mosca en la ceniza* de Gabriela David." *Confluencia: Revista hispánica de cultura y literatura* 30, no. 2 (2015): 102–12.

Brah, Avtar. "Diaspora." In *The Bloomsbury Handbook of 21st-Century Feminist Theory*, edited by Robin Truth Goodman, 437–47. New York: Bloomsbury, 2019.

Brannon Donoghue, Courtney. "Globo Films, Sony, and Franchise Film-Making: Transnational Industry in the Brazilian *Pós-Retomada*." In Rêgo and Rocha, *New Trends*, 51–66.

Bravo Arriaga, María Dolores. "Sor Juana Inés de la Cruz, escritora barroca, su contexto y su obra." In *Sor Juana Inés de la Cruz: Vida y obra*, 9–23. Tlalnepantla, Mexico: Grupo Editorial Norma, 2006.

Brynne Voyles, Traci. *Wastelanding: Legacies of Uranium Mining in Navajo Country*. Minneapolis: University of Minnesota Press, 2015.

Burucúa, Constanza. "Young Women at the Margins: Discourses on Exclusion in Two Films by Solveig Hoogesteijn." In *Latin American Women Filmmakers: Production, Politics, Poetics*, edited by Deborah Martin and Deborah Shaw, 172–93. London: I.B. Tauris, 2017.

Butler, Judith. *Bodies that Matter: On the Discursive Limits of "Sex."* New York: Routledge, 1993.

Cade Bambara, Toni. "Forward to the First Edition, 1981." In Moraga and Anzaldúa, *This Bridge Called My Back*, xxix–xxxii.

Canessa, Andrea, ed. *Natives Making Nation: Gender, Indigeneity, and the State in the Andes*. Tucson: University of Arizona Press, 2005.

Carastathis, Anna. *Intersectionality: Origins, Contestations, Horizons*. Lincoln: University of Nebraska Press, 2016.

Carrillo Trueba, César. *El racismo en México: Una visión sintética*. Mexico City: Consejo Nacional para la Cultura y las Artes/Cultura Tercer Milenio, 2009.

Carruthers, Anne. *Fertile Visions: The Uterus as a Narrative Space in Cinema from the Americas*. New York: Bloomsbury Academic, 2021.

Castañeda, Antonia I. "History and the Politics of Violence against Women." In *Living Chicana Theory*, edited by Carla Trujillo, 310–19. Berkeley, CA: Third Woman Press, 1998.

Castellanos, Rosario. *Mujer que sabe latín . . .* Mexico City: Fondo de Cultura Económica, 1997.

Chen, Nancy N. "'Speaking Nearby': A Conversation with Trinh T. Minh-ha." *Visual Anthropology Review* 8, no. 1 (1992): 82–91. https://www.situated ecologies.net/wp-content/uploads/Trinh-Speaking-Nearby-1983.pdf.

Cisneros, Vitelia. "Guaraní y quechua desde el cine en las propuestas de Lucía Puenzo, *El niño pez*, y Claudia Llosa, *La teta asustada*." *Hispania* 96, no. 1 (2013): 51–61.

Clarke, Cheryl. "Lesbianism." In Anzaldúa and Keating, *This Bridge We Call Home*, 232–39.

Collins, Patricia Hill. *Black Feminist Thought: Knowledge, Consciousness, and the Politics of Empowerment*, 2nd ed. New York: Routledge, 1999.

Collins, Patricia Hill, and Sirma Bilge. *Intersectionality*, 2nd ed. Cambridge, UK: Polity Press, 2016.

Corbalán, Ana. "Cine de denuncia contra las redes globales de prostitución: Paralelismo entre Barcelona y Buenos Aires." *Letras femeninas* 39, no. 1 (2013): 33–47.

Daicish, Osvaldo Mario. *El nuevo cine argentino (1995–2010): Vinculación con la industria cultural cinematográfica local e internacional y la sociocultura contemporánea.* Ushuaia, Argentina: Editorial Universitaria Villa María and Universidad Nacional de Tierra del Fuego, 2016.

Danielson, Marivel T. "Loving Revolution: Same-Sex Marriage and Queer Resistance in Monica Palacios's *Amor y Revolución.*" In *Performing the US Latina and Latino Borderlands*, edited by Arturo J. Aldama, Chela Sandoval, and Peter J. García, 309–27. Bloomington: Indiana University Press, 2012.

D'Argenio, Maria Chiara. "A Contemporary Andean Type: The Representation of the Indigenous World in Claudia Llosa's Films." *Latin American and Caribbean Ethnic Studies* 8, no. 1 (2013): 20–42.

D'Argenio, Maria Chiara. *Indigenous Plots in Twenty-First Century Latin American Cinema.* London: Palgrave MacMillan, 2022.

Das, Veena and Arthur Kleinman. "Introduction." In *Violence and Subjectivity*, edited by Veena Das, Arthur Kleinman, Mamphela Ramphele, and Pamela Reynolds, 1–18. Berkeley: University of California Press, 2000.

de la Cruz, Juana Inés. *Florilegio: Poesía. Teatro. Prosa.* Mexico City, Promexa Editores, 1979.

de la Cruz, Juana Inés. *Obras completas de Sor Juana Inés de la Cruz II: Villancicos y Letras Sacras.* Edición y prólogo de Alfonso Méndez Plancarte. Mexico City: Fondo de Cultura Económica, 2016. Kindle.

de Lucía, Daniel Omar. *Entre cabezas y trash: Cine y clases subalternas en la Argentina: 1990–2016.* Buenos Aires: Editorial Metrópolis, 2017.

De Series 3–25–2016. "Juana Inés, estreno Canal Once," consulted Aug. 21, 2019. https://www.deseries.com/2016/03/juana-ines-estreno-canal-once.html.

Díaz, Kim. "Indigenism in Peru and Bolivia." In *Latin American and Latinx Philosophy: A Collaborative Introduction*, edited by Robert Eli Sanchez, Jr., 180–97. New York: Routledge, 2020.

Díaz, Mónica. *Indigenous Writings from the Convent: Negotiating Ethnic Autonomy in Colonial Mexico.* Tucson: University of Arizona Press, 2013.

Díaz Cintora, Salvador, "'*Yoqui in Tlahuépoch* Medea,' O el náhuatl en la obra de Sor Juana." In *Aproximaciones a Sor Juana*, edited by Sandra Lorenzano. Mexico City: Universidad del Claustro Sor Juana/Fondo de Cultura Económica, 2014.

D'Lugo, Marvin, Ana M. López, and Laura Podalsky, eds. *The Routledge Companion to Latin American Cinema.* Oxon, UK: Routledge, 2018.

Egan, Caroline. "Lyric Intelligiblity in Sor Juana's Nahuatl *Tocotines.*" *Romance Notes* 58, no. 2 (2018): 207–18.

Eguchi, Shinsuke, Bernadette Marie Calafell, and Shadee Abdi, eds. *De-Whitening Intersectionality: Race, Intercultural Communication, and Politics*. Lanham, MD: Lexington Books, 2020.
Elguera, Christian. "Antiracist Spatial Narratives in Daniel Munduruku's *Crónicas de São Paulo*: Indigenous Place-Names and Migration in the Paulista Capital City." In *Poetics of Race in Latin America*, edited by Mabel Moraña, 185–200. New York: Anthem Press, 2022.
Eseverri, Máximo, and Fernando Martín Peña. *Lita Stantic: El cine es automóvil y poema*. Buenos Aires: Eudeba, 2013.
Femenías, María Luisa. "From Women's Movements to Feminist Theories (and Vice Versa)." In *Theories of the Flesh: Latinx and Latin American Feminisms, Transformation, and Resistance*, edited by Andrea J. Pitts, Mariana Ortega, and José Medina, 38–52. New York: Oxford University Press, 2020.
Fernández Chagoya, Melissa. "El Claustro femenino o Juana Inés somos todas." *Inundación Castálida: Revista de la Universidad del Claustro de Sor Juana*. 5, no. 14 (2020): 60–64.
Flores Yonekura, Kaori. "Director Q&A with Kaori Flores Yonekura." Posted to YouTube by Japanese American Memorial Pilgrimages, Nov. 12, 2023. https://youtu.be/LI_KnUMKYw8.
Forcinito, Ana. "Are You Listening? Voices and Images in Gabriela David's *Taxi, un encuentro* (2001) and Lucía Puenzo's *El niño pez* (2009)." In *Contemporary Argentine Women Filmmakers*, edited by Mirna Vohnsen and Daniel Mourenza, 113–29. Cham, Switzerland: Palgrave Macmillan, 2023.
Forcinito, Ana. "Las batallas de la memoria: Violencia sexual y derechos humanos en Argentina." *Letras femeninas* 39, no. 2 (2013): 93–111.
Forcinito, Ana. "Fugas y resistencias heroicas: Entre la atrocidad y el encuadre de la trata de mujeres y niñas en Argentina." *Arizona Journal of Hispanic Cultural Studies* 17 (2013): 47–63.
Forcinito, Ana. "Lo invisible y lo invivible: El Nuevo Cine Argentino de mujeres y sus huellas acústicas." *Chasqui* 42, no. 1 (2013): 37–53.
Foster, David William. *Gender and Society in Contemporary Brazilian Cinema*. Austin: University of Texas Press, 2010.
Foster, David William. *Latin American Documentary Filmmaking: Major Works*. Tucson: University of Arizona Press, 2013.
Foster, David William. *Queer Issues in Contemporary Latin American Cinema*. Austin: University of Texas Press, 2003.
Fournier-Pereira, Marisol. "Feminismos e interseccionalidad: Aportes para pensar feminismos lésbicos los centroamericanos." *Cuadernos Inter.c.a.mbio sobre Centroamérica y el Caribe* 11, no. 2 (2014): 67–87.

Franco Varea, Ana Cristina. "Cuatro miradas sobre el oficio de la actuación en el cine ecuatoriano." *25 Watts* 3, no. 1 (2014): 37–43.

Gargallo, Francesca. "Philosophical Feminism in Latin America." In *Theories of the Flesh: Latinx and Latin American Feminisms, Transformation, and Resistance*, edited by Andrea J. Pitts, Mariana Ortega, and José Medina, 97–22. New York: Oxford University Press, 2020.

Gaspar de Alba, Alicia. "An Interview with Sor Juana." In *Living Chicana Theory*, edited by Carla Trujillo, 136–65. Berkeley, CA: Third Woman Press, 1998.

Gates, William, translator. *An Aztec Herbal: The Classic Codex of 1552*. Mineola, New York: Dover Publications, 2000.

Getino, Octavio, ed. *Cine latinoamericano: Producción y mercados en la primera década del siglo XXI*. Buenos Aires: DAC Editorial, 2012.

Glantz, Margo. *Obras reunidas I: Ensayos sobre literatura colonial*. Mexico City: Fondo de Cultura Económica, 2014.

Goldfine, Daniela. "Sex Trafficking in Argentina Now and Then: Keepers of Memory in *The Impure*." *Arquivo Maaravi: Revista Digital de Estudos Judaicos da UFMG*. 14, no. 27 (2020): 1–17.

González, Roque. "Cine latinoamericano: Entre las pantallas de plata y las pantallas digitales. Producción y mercados en América del Sur y México." In *Cine latinoamericano: Producción y mercados en la primera década del siglo XXI*, edited by Octavio Getino, 61–182. Buenos Aires: DAC Editorial, 2012.

Grzanka, Patrick R., ed. *Intersectionality: A Foundations and Frontiers Reader*. Boulder, CO: Westview Press, 2014.

Grzanka, Patrick R. Introduction to *Intersectionality: A Foundations and Frontiers Reader*, edited by Patrick R. Grzanka, 1–24. Boulder, CO: Westview Press, 2014.

Guerrero, Aurora. "Press Kit *Mosquita y Mari*." The Film Collaborative, 2012. https://www.thefilmcollaborative.org/films/img/epk/Press_Kit_Mosquita_y_Mari_011212.pdf

Haddu, Miriam. *Contemporary Mexican Cinema 1989–1999: History, Space, and Identity*. Lewiston, MD: Edwin Mellen Press, 2007.

Hancock, Ange-Marie. *Intersectionality: An Intellectual History*. New York: Oxford University Press, 2016.

Hendel, Liliana. *Violencias de género: Las mentiras del patriarcado*. Buenos Aires: Editorial Paidós, 2017.

Hernandez, Cesar. "Exclusive: A First Look at 'In Times of Rain,' a Mixtec Film by Indigenous Filmmakers Captures Audiences in Oaxaca." *L.A. Taco*, 22 Oct

2018. https://www.lataco.com/exclusive-a-first-look-at-in-times-of-rain-a-mixtec-film-by-Indigenous-filmmakers-captures-audiences-in-oaxaca.

Hershfield, Joanne, and David R. Maciel, eds. *Mexico's Cinema: A Century of Film and Filmmakers*. Lanham, MD: SR Books, 1999.

Higgs, Johanna. "Argentina Has a Problem: Sex Trafficking of Women and Girls." *PassBlue: Independent Coverage of the UN*. January 24, 2016. https://www.passblue.com/2016/01/24/no-longer-hidden-sex-trafficking-of-women-gets-more-attention-in-argentina.

Hinterberger, Amy. "Agency." in *Gender: The Key Concepts*, edited by Mary Evans and Carolyn H. Williams. New York: Routledge, 2013.

Hochschild, Arlie. *The Second Shift: Working Parents and the Revolution at Home*. New York: Viking Penguin, 1989.

Holling, Michelle A. "Intersectionality in the Fields of Chicana Feminism: Pursuing Decolonization through the Xicanisma's '*Resurrection of the Dreamers*.'" In *De-Whitening Intersectionality*, edited by Shinsuke Eguchi, Shadee Abdi, and Bernadette Marie Calafell, 3–24. Lanham, MD: Lexington Books, 2020.

Hopfenblatt, Alejandra Kelly, and Silvana Flores. "Problematizing Film and Photography." In *The Routledge Companion to Latin American Cinema*, edited by Marvin D'Lugo, Ana M. López, and Laura Podalsky. 297–315. Oxon, UK: Routledge, 2018.

"Huntington Park Named California's 'Most Miserable' City, Business Insider Says." *CBS Los Angeles*, Oct. 2, 2019. https://www.cbsnews.com/losangeles/news/huntington-park-named-californias-most-miserable-city-business-insider-says.

Hurtado, Aída. "Intersectionality." In *The Bloomsbury Handbook of 21st-Century Feminist Theory*, edited by Truth Goodman, 159–70. London: Bloomsbury Academic, 2019.

Jansen, Itandehui. "Interview with Director Itandehui Jansen." *VPRO Cinema*, August 15, 2019. https://www.vprogids.nl/cinema/lees/artikelen/interviews/2019/WCA-Presents--Tiempo-de-Lluvia--interview-met-Itandehui-Jansen.html.

Jansen, Itandehui, and Armando Bautista García. "La inscripción del autor en su comunidad por medio del cine." In *La producción afectiva de comunidad: Los medios audiovisuales en el contexto transnacional México-EE.UU*, edited by Ingrid Kummels, 295–315. Berlin: Edition Tranvía-Verlag Walter Frey, 2016.

Johnson, Derek, ed. *From Networks to Netflix: A Guide to Changing Channels*. New York: Routledge, 2018.

Kang, Cecilia. "Cecilia Kang." Interview on *Hablando de cine*, FM 106.5. Posted to YouTube by ngncomunicacion, Jan. 11, 2017. https://www.youtube.com/watch?v=vZ-hX1slQJo.

Karavanta, Mina. "Community." In *The Bloomsbury Handbook of 21st-Century Feminist Theory*, edited by Robin Truth Goodman, 449–62. New York: Bloomsbury Press, 2019.

Keating, AnaLouise. "Charting Pathways, Marking Thresholds . . . A Warning, An Introduction." In Anzaldúa and Keating, *This Bridge We Call Home*, 6–20.

Kirk, Stephanie. *Sor Juana Inés de la Cruz and the Gender Politics of Knowledge in Colonial Mexico*. New York: Routledge: 2020.

Kriger, Clara. "La experiencia del documental subjetivo en Argentina." In *Cines al margen: Nuevos modos de representación en el cine argentino contemporáneo*. Edited by María José Moore and Paula Wolkowicz, 33–49. Buenos Aires: Libraria Ediciones, 2007.

Kristeva, Julia. *Powers of Horror: An Essay on Abjection*. Translated by Leon S. Roudiez. New York: Columbia University Press, 1982.

Kroll, Juli A. "Between the 'Sacred' and the 'Profane': Cultural Fantasy in *Madeinusa* by Claudia Llosa." *Chasqui: Revista de Literatura Latinoamericana* 38, no. 2 (2009): 113–25.

Larralde Rangel, Américo. *El eclipse del* Sueño *de Sor Juana*. Mexico City: Fondo de Cultura Económica, 2011.

Leal, Luis. "El hechizo derramado: Elementos mestizos en Sor Juana." In *Y diversa de mí misma entre vuestras plumas ando: Homenaje internacional Sor Juana Inés de la Cruz*, edited by Sara Poot Herrera and Elena Urrutia, 185–200. Mexico City: El Colegio de México, 1993.

Ledesma, Eduardo. "Through 'Their' Eyes: Internal and External Focalizing Agents in the Representation of Children and Violence in Iberian and Latin American Film." In *Representing History, Class, and Gender in Spain and Latin America*, edited by Carolina Rocha and Georgia Seminet, 151–69. New York: Palgrave Macmillan, 2012.

Lené Hole, Kristin, Dijana Jelača, E. Ann Kaplan, and Patrice Petro, eds. *The Routledge Companion to Cinema and Gender*. London: Routledge, 2017.

Lillo, Gastón. "*La teta asustada* (Perú, 2009) de Claudia Llosa: ¿Memoria u olvido?" *Revista de crítica literaria latinoamericana* 37, no. 73 (2011): 421–46.

Lobato, Ramon. *Netflix Nations: The Geography of Digital Distribution*. New York: New York University Press, 2019.

Lorde, Audre. "The Master's Tools Will Never Dismantle the Master's House." In Moraga and Anzaldúa, *This Bridge Called My Back*, 94–97.
Losada, Matt. *Before Bemberg: Women Filmmakers in Argentina*. Newark, NJ: Rutgers University Press, 2020.
Losada, Matt. *The Projected Nation: Argentine Cinema and the Social Margins*. Albany, NY: SUNY Press, 2018.
Lugones, María. "Revisiting Gender: A Decolonial Approach." In *Theories of the Flesh: Latinx and Latin American Feminisms, Transformation, and Resistance*, edited by Andrea J. Pitts, Mariana Ortega, and José Medina, 29–37. New York: Oxford University Press, 2020.
Lugones, María. "Toward a Decolonial Feminism." *Hypatia* 25, no. 4 (2010): 742–59.
Lury, Karen. *The Child in Film: Tears, Fears and Fairy Tales*. London: I.B. Tauris, 2010.
Maguire, Geoffrey, and Rachel Randall, eds. *New Visions of Adolescence in Contemporary Latin America Cinema*. New York: Palgrave, 2018.
Marsh, Leslie L. *Brazilian Women's Filmmaking: From Dictatorship to Democracy*. Champaign: University of Illinois Press, 2012.
Martin, Deborah. *The Child in Contemporary Latin American Cinema*. London: Palgrave Macmillan, 2019.
Martin, Deborah, and Deborah Shaw, eds. *Latin American Women Filmmakers: Production, Politics, Poetics*. London: I.B. Tauris, 2017.
Martínez, Elizabeth. *De Colores Means All of Us: Latina Views for a Multi-Colored Century*. London: Verso, 2017.
McCabe, Janet. *Feminist Film Studies: Writing the Woman into Cinema*. London: Wallflower, 2004.
McNelly, Angus. "Baroque Modernity in Latin America: Situating Indigeneity, Urban Indigeneity and the Popular Economy." *Bulletin of Latin American Research* 41, no. 1 (2022): 6–20.
Mérida, Janet. "Sor Juana, hábito de Arcelia." El Universal, Nov. 7, 2015. https://www.eluniversal.com.mx/articulo/espectaculos/teatro/2015/11/7/sor-juana-habito-de-arcelia.
Minh-ha, Trinh T. *D-Passage: The Digital Way*. Durham, NC: Duke University Press, 2013.
Minh-ha, Trinh T. *Woman, Native, Other*. Bloomington: Indiana University Press, 2009.
Moraga, Cherríe. "Cherríe Moraga, Author—*Native Country of the Heart: A Memoir*." *One to One*, April 4, 2019. Posted to YouTube by CUNY TV, April 15, 2019. https://www.youtube.com/watch?v=X8AY9xPlSaU&t=1412s.

Moraga, Cherríe. "La Güera." In Moraga and Anzaldúa, *This Bridge Called My Back*, 22–29.

Moraga, Cherríe. "La Jornada: Preface, 1981." In Moraga and Anzaldúa, *This Bridge Called My Back*, xxxv–xlii.

Moraga, Cherríe. *Native Country of the Heart: A Memoir*. New York: Farrar, Straus, and Giroux, 2019.

Moraga, Cherríe, and Gloria Anzaldúa, eds. *This Bridge Called My Back: Writings by Radical Women of Color*, 4th ed. Albany: SUNY Press, 2015.

Mrsevic, Zorica. "The Opposite of War Is Not Peace—It Is Creativity." In *Frontline Feminisms: Women, War, and Resistance*, edited by Marguerite R. Waller and Jennifer Rycenga, 41–56. New York: Routledge, 2001.

Mulvey, Laura. "Visual Pleasure and Narrative Cinema." In *Feminisms: An Anthology of Literary Theory and Criticism*, 2nd ed., edited by Robyn R. Warhol and Diane Price Herndl, 438–48. New Brunswick, NJ: Rutgers University Press, 1997.

Mulvey, Laura. "Visual Pleasure and Narrative Cinema." In *Visual and Other Pleasures: Language, Discourse, Society*, 14–26. London: Palgrave Macmillan, 1989.

Muñiz-Huberman, Angelina. "Las claves de Sor Juana." In *Y diversa de mí misma entre vuestras plumas ando: Homenaje internacional Sor Juana Inés de la Cruz*, edited by Sara Poot Herrera and Elena Urrutia, 315–25. Mexico City: El Colegio de México, 1993.

Nair, Parvati and Julián Daniel Gutiérrez-Albilla, eds. *Hispanic and Lusophone Women Filmmakers: Theory, Practice and Difference*. Manchester, UK: Manchester University Press, 2013.

Narváez, Geovanny. "Rock y Punk en el cine ecuatoriano reciente: Discurso de la marginalidad y de la subjetividad." *Paralelo 31*, no. 12 (2019): 58–85.

Olson, Debbie, ed. *The Child in World Cinema*. Lanham, MD: Lexington Books, 2018.

O'Rouke, Ryan. "Quentin Tarantino Explains Why His Tenth Film Will Be His Last." *Collider*, Nov. 18, 2022. https://screenrant.com/quentin-tarantino-tenth-movie-last-why.

Ortega, Mariana. "*Cámara* Queer: Longing, the Photograph, and Queer Latinidad." In *Theories of the Flesh: Latinx and Latin American Feminisms, Transformation, and Resistance*, edited by Andrea J. Pitts, Mariana Ortega, and José Medina, 264–80. New York: Oxford University Press, 2020.

Page, Philippa, and Inela Selimovic, eds. *The Feeling Child: Affect and Politics in Latin American Literature and Film*. Lanham, MD: Lexington Books, 2018.

Paladino, Diana, ed. *Documental/Ficción: Reflexiones sobre el cine argentino contemporáneo*. Buenos Aires: Universidad Nacional de Tres de Febrero, 2014.
Paladino, Diana. "En torno a la primera persona." In *Documental/Ficción: Reflexiones sobre el cine argentino contemporáneo*, edited by Diana Paladino, 57–68. Buenos Aires: Universidad Nacional de Tres de Febrero, 2014.
Paranaguá, Paulo Antonio, ed. *Cine documental en América Latina*. Madrid: Cátedra, 2003.
Pascual Buxó, José. *El oráculo de los preguntones: Atribuido a Sor Juana Inés de la Cruz*. Mexico City: UNAM, 1991.
Paz, Octavio. Foreword to *A Sor Juana Anthology*, vii–x. Translated by Alan S. Trueblood. Cambridge, MA: Harvard University Press, 1994.
Piedras, Pablo. *El cine documental en primera persona*. Buenos Aires: Editorial Paidós, 2014.
Piñeiro Iñíguez, Carlos. *Pensamiento equinoccial: Seis ensayos sobre la nación, la cultura y la identidad ecuatorianas*. Quito, Ecuador: Editorial Planeta, 2005.
Pitts, Andrea J. Mariana Ortega, and José Medina, eds. *Theories of the Flesh: Latinx and Latin American Feminisms, Transformation, and Resistance*. New York: Oxford University Press, 2020.
Podalsky, Laura. "Out of Depth: The Politics of Disaffected Youth and Contemporary Latin American Cinema." In *Youth Culture in Global Cinema*, edited by Timothy Shary and Alexandra Seibel, 109–30. Austin: University of Texas Press, 2007.
Podalsky, Laura. *The Politics of Affect and Emotion in Contemporary Latin American Cinema: Argentina, Brazil, Cuba, and Mexico*. New York: Palgrave Macmillan, 2011.
Poot Herrera, Sara. "Sor Juana 325 (1695–2020)." *Inundación Castálida: Revista de la Universidad del Claustro de Sor Juana* 5, no. 14 (2020): 80–88.
Postero, Nancy. "Introduction: Negotiating Indigeneity." *Latin American and Caribbean Ethnic Studies* 8, no. 2 (2013): 107–21.
Prividera, Nicolás. "El lugar del documental en los Nuevos Cines Argentinos." In *La imagen argentina: Episodios cinematográficos de la historia nacional*, edited by María Iribarren, 221-230. Buenos Aires: Fundación CICCUS, 2017.
"Quito tiene la tasa más alta de pobreza a escala nacional." *El Comercio*, Oct. 26, 2019. https://www.elcomercio.com/actualidad/negocios/quito-tasa-economia-pobreza-inec.html.
Ramírez Rojas, Marco, and Pilar Osorio Lora, eds. *Growing Up in Latin America: Child and Youth Agency in Contemporary Popular Culture*. Lanham, MD: Rowman & Littlefield, 2022.

Randall, Rachel. *Children on the Threshold in Contemporary Latin American Cinema: Nature, Gender, and Agency*. Lanham, MD: Lexington Books, 2018.

Rashkin, Elissa J. *Women Filmmakers in Mexico: The Country of Which We Dream*. Austin: University of Texas Press, 2001.

Redacción Clarín, "El cine argentino aborda la 'trata': La prostitución, una forma de la esclavitud," *Clarín*, March 25, 2010, https://www.clarin.com/entremujeres/entretenimientos/cine-y-teatro/La_mosca_en_la_ceniza_0_Hk2e-y9DQg.html.

Rêgo, Cacilda, and Carolina Rocha, eds. *New Trends in Argentine and Brazilian Cinema*. Bristol, UK: Intellect, 2011.

Rivera Berruz, Stephanie. "Latin American and Latinx Feminisms." In *Latin American and Latinx Philosophy: A Collaborative Introduction*, edited by Robert Eli Sanchez, Jr., 161–79. New York: Routledge, 2020.

Roberts-Camps, Traci. "El género y la interseccionalidad en las cineastas ecuatorianas Viviana Cordero y Tania Hermida." *Kipus: Revista andina de letras y estudios culturales*, no. 50 (2021): 139–64.

Roberts-Camps, Traci. *Latin American Women Filmmakers: Social and Cultural Perspectives*. Albuquerque: University of New Mexico Press, 2017.

Robin, Diana, and Ira Jaffe, eds. *Redirecting the Gaze: Gender, Theory, and Cinema in the Third World*. Albany: SUNY Press 1999.

Robinson, Beatriz M. "Sor Juana Inés de la Cruz y la ensalada villanciquera: Performancias carnavalescas de eficacia/entretenimiento en la Nueva España." *Chasqui* 40, no. 1 (2011): 157–69.

Rocha, Carolina. "Contemporary Argentine Cinema during Neoliberalism." In Rêgo and Rocha, *New Trends*, 17–34.

Rocha, Carolina, and Georgia Seminet, eds. *Representing History, Class, and Gender in Spain and Latin America: Children and Adolescents in Film*. New York: Palgrave Macmillan, 2012.

Rocha, Carolina, and Georgia Seminet, eds. *Screening Minors in Latin American Cinema*. Lanham, MD: Lexington, 2014.

Rubial García, Antonio. "La patria criolla de Sor Juana y sus contemporáneos." In *Aproximaciones a Sor Juana*, edited by Sandra Lorenzano, 347–70. Mexico City: FCE, 2005.

Rud, Lucía. "Transnationalism in Korean-Argentine Cinema: International Co-Productions and Cinematic Representation." 9th World Congress of Korean Studies, Academy of Korean Studies, Sept. 12–14, 2018.

Rueda, Carolina. "Memory, Trauma, and Phantasmagoria in Claudia Llosa's *La teta asustada*." *Hispania* 98, no. 3 (2015): 452–62.

Rueda Esquibel, Catrióna. "Memories of Girlhood: Chicana Lesbian Fictions." In *Chicano/Latino Homoerotic Identities*, edited by David William Foster, 59–98. New York: Garland, 1999.

Sabat-Rivers, Georgina. "Sor Juana Inés de la Cruz: Barroco de Indias, feminismo y lenguaje transgresor." *Salina: Revista de lletre*, no. 6 (1991): 41–45.

Sanchez, Robert Eli, Jr., ed. *Latin American and Latinx Philosophy: A Collaborative Introduction*. New York: Routledge, 2020.

Sandoval, Chela, Arturo J. Aldama, and Peter J. García. "Introduction: Toward a De-colonial Performatics of the US Latina and Latino Borderlands." In *Performing the US Latina and Latino Borderlands*, edited by Arturo J. Aldama, Chela Sandoval, and Peter J. García, 1-27. Bloomington: Indiana University Press, 2012.

Sarlo, Beatriz. *Tiempo pasado: Cultura de la memoria y giro subjetivo: Una discusión*. Buenos Aires: Siglo XXI Editores, 2005.

Sarlo, Beatriz. *Tiempo presente: Notas sobre el cambio de una cultura*. Buenos Aires: Siglo XXI Editores, 2001.

Schiwy, Freya. *Indianizing Film: Decolonization, the Andes, and the Question of Technology*. New Brunswick, NJ: Rutgers University Press, 2009.

Schmidhuber de la Mora, Guillermo. "1695: Crónica verdadera de la muerte de Sor Juana Inés de la Cruz." *Inundación Castálida: Revista de la Universidad del Claustro de Sor Juana* 5, no. 14 (2020): 92–96.

Schroeder Rodríguez, Paul A. *Latin American Cinema: A Comparative History*. Berkeley: University of California Press, 2016.

Selimović, Inela. *Affective Moments in the Films of Martel, Carri, and Puenzo*. London: Palgrave Macmillan, 2018.

Shary, Timothy, and Alexandra Seibel, eds. *Youth Culture in Global Cinema*. Austin: University of Texas Press, 2007.

Shaw, Deborah. "Latin American Women's Filmmaking: A Manifesto." *Mediático*, Dec. 18, 2017. https://reframe.sussex.ac.uk/mediatico/2017/12/18/latin-american-womens-filmmaking-a-manifesto.

Mark Shucksmith and David L. Brown. *Routledge International Handbook of Rural Studies* (2016)

Smith, Paul Julian. "Screenings: Letter from Mexico City: *Juana Inés*, the Miniseries." *Film Quarterly* 70, no. 4 (2017): 83–87.

Smith, Paul Julian. "Mexican Film and Television in Transition: The Case of Club de Cuervos." *Film Quarterly* 71, no. 2 (2017): 72–77.

Soriano, Griselda. "Reflexividad y autorreferencia." In *Documental/Ficción: Reflexiones sobre el cine argentino contemporáneo*, edited by Diana

Paladino, 85–104. Buenos Aires: Universidad Nacional de Tres de Febrero, 2014.
Spivak, Gayatri Chakravorty. "Can the Subaltern Speak?" In *Marxism and the Interpretation of Culture*, edited by Cary Nelson and Lawrence Grossberg, 271–313. Urbana: University of Illinois Press, 1988.
Straayer, Chris. *Deviant Eyes, Deviant Bodies: Sexual Re-Orientation in Film and Video*. New York: Columbia University Press, 1996.
Tabuenca, María Socorro. "Lo precolombino: Notas sobre el diálogo disfrazado en sor Juana Inés de la Cruz." In "Número Extraordinario Conmemorativo 1974–1994," special edition of *Letras femeninas*, 1994: 31–38.
Tenorio, Martha Lilia. *Los villancicos de Sor Juana*. Mexico City: Colegio de México, 1999.
Thomas, Alexander R., Brian Lowe, Greg Fulkerson, and Polly Smith. *Critical Rural Theory: Structure, Space, Culture*. Lanham, MD: Lexington Books, 2011.
Thornton, Niamh. "Online Distribution and Access: The Case of Netflix." In *The Routledge Companion to Latin American Cinema*, edited by Marvin D'Lugo, Ana M. López, and Laura Podalsky, 370–74. New York: Routledge, 2018.
Tompkins, Cynthia Margarita. *Affectual Erasure: Representations of Indigenous Peoples in Argentine Cinema*. Albany: SUNY Press, 2018.
Townsend, Camilla. "Sor Juana's Nahuatl." *Le Verger* 8 (2015): 1–11.
Trelles Plazaola, Luis. *Cine y mujer en América Latina: Directoras de largometrajes de ficción*. Rio Piedras, Puerto Rico: Universidad de Puerto Rico, 1991.
Trueblood, Alan S., translator. *A Sor Juana Anthology*. Cambridge, MA: Harvard University Press, 1994.
Trujillo, Carla, ed. *Living Chicana Theory*. Berkeley, CA: Third Woman Press, 1998.
Truth Goodman, Robin, ed. *The Bloomsbury Handbook of 21st-Century Feminist Theory*. London: Bloomsbury Academic, 2019.
Vanegas León, Brenda Cielaika. "Criminología y género en el sistema económico del Ecuador." *Revista de la Facultad de Ciencias Económicas, UNNE* 10 (June 2013): 85–105.
Varas, Patricia. "Posmemoria femenina en *La teta asustada*." *Letras femeninas* 38, no. 1 (2012): 31–41.
Virtanen, Pirjo Kristiina. "Amazonian Native Youths and Notions of Indigeneity in Urban Areas." *Identities: Global Studies in Culture and Power* 17, no. 2–3 (2010): 154–75.
Viveros Vigoya, Mara. "La interseccionalidad: Una aproximación situada a la dominación." *Debate feminista* 52 (2016): 1–17.

Viveros Vigoya, Mara. "Intersecciones de género, clase, etnia y raza: Un diálogo con Mara Viveros." *Íconos: Revista de Ciencias Sociales*, no. 57 (2017): 117–21.

Viveros Vigoya, Mara, and Sergio Lesmes Espinel. "Cuestiones raciales y construcción de Nación en tiempos de multiculturalismo." *Universitas humanística*, no. 77 (2014): 13–31.

Vohnsen, Mirna and Daniel Mourenza, eds. *Contemporary Argentine Women Filmmakers*. Cham, Switzerland: Palgrave Macmillan, 2023.

Wright Carr, David Charles. "La política lingüística en la Nueva España." *Acta Universitaria: Universidad de Guanajuato* 17, no. 3 (2007): 5–19.

Yoon, Won K. *Global Pulls on the Korean Communities in Sao Paulo and Buenos Aires*. Lanham, MD: Lexington, 2015.

Zakaria, Rafia. *Against White Feminism: Notes on Disruption*. New York: W. W. Norton, 2021.

FILMOGRAPHY

Arriaga-Jordán, Patricia, pro. and dir., *Juana Inés*. Canal Once and Bravo Films, 2016.

Cordero, Viviana, dir. *No robarás . . . (A menos que sea necesario)*. Xpressmax, 2013.

David, Gabriela, dir. *La mosca en la ceniza*. INCAA and Pampa Films, 2009.

Flores Yonekura, Kaori, dir. *Nikkei: Un viaje extraordinario*. NO Film, 2017.

Guerrero, Aurora, dir. *Mosquita y Mari*. Indion Entertainment Group and Maya Entertainment, 2012.

Jansen, Itandehui, dir. *Tiempo de lluvia*. Lista Calista and Fidelio, 2018.

Kang, Cecilia, dir. *Mi último fracaso*. Misbelovedones, 2016.

Llosa, Claudia, dir. *Madeinusa*. Oberón and Wanda Visión, 2006.

Llosa, Claudia, dir. *La teta asustada*. Oberón and ICIC, 2009.

INDEX

#NiUnaMenos, 103, 195n50

A hora da estrela (Lispector and Amaral), 95
Abdi, Shadee, 12
ability, 4, 6, 18, 46, 54, 56, 66, 77–79, 81, 84, 92, 98, 102, 142, 165, 168, 176n36
active subject, 111
adolescence, 1–6, 17, 18, 20, 22, 54, 57–58, 68, 77–78, 93, 102, 165, 169, 178nn64–65, 179n65, 180n8, 186n2, 187n5
adolescent, 13, 2, 5–6, 18, 25, 52–54, 59–60, 62, 64, 75, 80, 91, 173n9, 181n18, 187n5, 190n33, 190n39
affect, 5–6, 91, 144, 158, 173n9m, 187n3, 204n32, 205n32
affective, 11, 19, 66, 72, 73, 77, 146–47, 150, 152, 155–56, 161, 164, 173n9, 204n32
age
 coming of age, 52, 60, 62
 and intersectionality, 1–2, 4–5, 11, 14, 20, 81, 137, 143, 165, 168, 176n36
 Juana Inés, 17, 23, 48, 167, 185n77
 Mi último fracaso, 136, 162, 164
 mosca en la ceniza, La, 18, 78, 80, 83–84, 91–92, 94–95, 98, 102, 167
 Mosquita y Mari, 52, 54, 59–60, 76–77, 167

Nikkei: Un viaje extraordinario, 19, 136, 162, 164
No robarás . . . a menos que sea necesario, 18, 52, 71, 75–77, 167
agency, 2, 5–6, 18–20, 22, 53, 76, 79, 92, 105, 118–20, 131–32, 135, 137, 165, 166, 173n9, 187n5, 194n32
Aldama, Frederick Luis, 18, 53, 61–62, 64, 189n24, 189nn28–29, 190nn36–38
Aloft (Llosa), 196n2
Alsultany, Evelyn, 55, 176n61
Alvario, Vanesa, 53
Amaral, Suzana, 95, 173
Andean cinema, 6
Andean region, 2, 70, 106, 165, 199n32
Andermann, Jens, 91, 194nn27–28
Andrade, Javier, 192n53
Anzaldúa, Gloria, 16, 24, 166, 175n30
Argentine economic crisis, 98
Arias, Arturo, 19, 134
Arredondo, Isabel,172
Arriaga-Jordán, Patricia, 174n19
Astorga Carrera, Laura, 179
autonomy, 75, 101, 186n82

Bachelard, Gaston, 101–2, 195n48, 195n49
Baker, Carrie N., 97–98, 195n41, 195n42
Balarezo, Ana María, 53

[225]

Barker, Cory, 7
Barrow, Sarah, 196n1
Baudot, Georges, 23, 35, 39–40, 180n9, 183n53, 184n58
Bechis, Marco, 192n3, 194n29
Bel-Air (DuVernay), 186n1
Bemberg, María Luisa, 22, 26, 32–33, 35, 42, 173n11, 180n7, 181n18, 185n78, 195n47, 202n2
Bilge, Sirma, 11–13, 17, 19–20, 54–55, 78, 81, 92, 94, 142–44, 148, 154, 163, 176nn36–38, 188n7, 192n2, 193nn13–14, 194n33, 195n35, 203n19, 203n22, 207nn47–48
Birri, Fernando, 138, 147
body
   Borderland Performance Studies, 66
   female body, 22
   identity, 1, 55
   Juana Inés, 32, 47–48, 55
   Mi último fracaso, 140, 163
   Moraga, Cherríe, 147, 167
   mosca en la ceniza, La, 101
   Mosquita y Mari, 59–60, 76
   Sarlo, Beatriz, 206n40
   teta asustada, La, 115, 118
   Viveros Vigoya, Mara, 148
borderlands, 16, 66
Borderlands / La Frontera: The New Mestiza (Anzaldúa), 16, 177n57
Bordo, Susan, 48
Boris Tarré, Marta, 19, 76, 80, 193n6
Brah, Avtar, 20, 142, 149, 162, 204n29
Brannon Donoghue, Courtney, 174
Bravo Arriaga, María Dolores, 23, 43, 180n10, 180n11, 184nn70–71
Brown, David L., 194n34
Brynne Voyles, Traci, 19, 79, 96, 195n37, 195n38
Burucúa, Constanza, 203n28
Butler, Judith, 48

Caccamo, María Laura, 79
caída, La (Puenzo), 179n65

Calafell, Bernadette Marie, 12, 176n39
Calderón Kellet, Gloria, 175n23, 190n33
Camila (Bemberg), 181, 193n3
Canal Once, 17, 22
Canessa, Andrea, 19, 132–35, 200nn49–55
Caracol Channel, 180n8
Carastathis, Anna, 11–12, 175n24, 175nn31–33, 176nn34–35
Carruthers, Anne, 197n14
Castañeda, Antonia I., 189n23
Castellanos, Rosario, 21, 179nn1–3
Cisneros, Vitelia, 198n17
citizenship, 94, 128
Clarice Lispector, 95
Clarke, Cheryl, 65, 190n32
class
   and gender, 6, 12, 52, 54, 56–57, 60, 133, 172, 173n9, 178n61, 179n65, 194n30
   and intersectionality, 11, 15, 20, 61–62, 66–67, 81, 99, 149–50, 168, 176n36, 197n4
   middle-class feminism, 55, 188n10
   socioeconomic, 4–5, 13, 15, 18–19, 48, 53, 68–72, 74–78, 84, 97, 104, 106, 117, 121, 129, 131, 134–38, 141–43, 162–66, 187n3, 190n39, 201n62, 202n62
classism, 53, 77
cognitive ability, 18, 77–78, 81, 84, 102
Collins, Patricia Hill, 9–13, 16–17, 19–20, 54–55, 68, 78, 81, 92, 94, 142–44, 148, 154, 163, 166, 175nn25–26, 176n36, 188n7, 192n2, 193nn13–14, 194n33, 195n35, 203n19, 203n22, 207nn47–48
comadrazgo, 63–64
coming-of-age, 18, 52, 60, 62
Contreras, Paloma, 79
Corbalán, Ana, 19, 79, 83, 90–91, 193n18, 194n25
Cordero, Viviana, 3, 5, 18, 51, 52–54, 56, 67–77, 165, 167, 187n3, 190n39
corporeally lived experiences, 54, 142
critical rural theory, 99, 195n44
Cruz, Ángeles, 106–7, 195n3, 200n47

Cuarón, Alfonso, 107
cultural expectations, 162

D'Argenio, Maria Chiara, 19, 104, 114, 130–33, 135, 197nn11–12, 199nn37–42, 200n43
Daicich, Osvaldo Mario, 200n42
Danzón (Novaro), 187n5, 192n48
Das, Veena, 92
David, Gabriela, 2, 18, 77–79, 104, 165, 193n19
de Asbaje, Juana Inés, 23, 40
de Góngora, Luis, 32
de la Cruz, Sor Juana Inés, 17, 21–23, 28–29, 180nn10–11, 180n13, 181n21, 182n30, 182n34, 182nn36–37, 183n48, 183n52, 183n56, 184n57, 184nn67–68, 184nn70–72, 185n76, 186n82, 205nn37–38
de Lucía, Daniel Omar, 19, 78, 97
de Palafox y Mendoza, Juan, 28
de Sigüenza y Góngora, Carlos, 28, 36
decolonial feminism, 13, 166–67, 175n33, 177nn45–48
decoloniality, 13
del Torre, Carlos J., 105
Desalvo, Martín, 187n5
disability, 149
diaspora, 142, 144, 148–49, 162, 204n29, 207n46
Díaz Cintora, Salvador, 40, 184n60
Díaz, Kim, 19, 201n62
Dirty War, 79, 88, 91
Distancia de rescate (Llosa), 196n2
documentary
 autobiographical, 2
 Cuban Revolution, 147
 history, 202n4, 203n25
 Latinx, 64
 Lesa humanidad, 88
 social documentary, 168, 194n29, 203n28
 Vidas privadas, 87
do Amaral, Tarsila, 14

Duchess of Aveyro, 32, 43
DuVernay, Ava, 186n1

eclipse del Sueño de Sor Juana, El (Larralde Rangel), 182n38
Ecuador, 2–3, 6, 17–18, 52, 67, 69–72, 74, 165, 179n65, 187n3, 191n47, 192n53
Egan, Caroline, 40–41
Eguchi, Shinsuke, 12, 176n39
elegidas, Las (Pablos), 183n4
Elguera, Christian, 134, 201nn56–58
En el nombre de la hija (Hermida), 179n65
En la puta vida (Flórez Silva), 83, 93
Eseverri, Máximo, 5, 172n8
Estadio Nacional (Parot), 194n29
ethnicity, 35, 52, 64–66, 145
everyday, the, 157–58, 161, 164

Fabián Bielinsky, 98
female adolescence, 1, 20, 165, 169, 178, 187n5
female body, 22, 48, 76
Femenías, María Luisa, 177n49
feminist studies, 8, 9, 12, 166
Fernández Chagoya, Melissa, 32, 182n40
Flores Silva, Beatriz, 93, 179n65
Flores Yonekura, Kaori, 3, 5–6, 19–20, 135–40, 142, 144–49, 152, 155–62, 164, 165, 167–68, 203–4n28, 204n30
Flores, Silvana, 147
Fogwill, Vera, 187n5
food preparation, 142, 150, 154, 158, 164
Forcinito, Ana, 19, 79–80, 85, 87–88, 91, 193n7, 193n19, 193n21, 193n23
Foster, David William, 18, 53, 147, 190n31, 195n36, 202n4
Foucault, Michel, 175n30
Fournier-Pereira, Marisol, 14–15, 177nn51–53
Franco Varea, Ana Cristina, 187n3
Frank, Scott, 182n41

Gaijin: Ama-me como sou (Yamasaki), 204
Gaijin: Caminhos da liberdade (Yamasaki), 204
Gamboa, Federico, 80
Garage Olimpo (Bechis), 192, 194n29
García Márquez, Gabriel, 194n34
Gargallo, Francesca, 182n35, 183n51
Garibay, Ángel María, 35, 184n65
Gaviria, Víctor, 187n5
gaze, the, 48, 83, 85–86, 112
gender expectations, 151
gender studies, 9, 69, 176n41
gender violence, 80, 91, 193n15
generational differences, 150
Gentefied (DuVernay), 186n1
girlhood friendship, 63–64
Glantz, Margo, 18, 35, 46, 185n75
Global South, 168, 195n34
Goldfine, Daniela, 90
gran retorno, El (Cordero), 187
Grzanka, Patrick R., 9–10, 12, 67, 175nn27–28
Guerrero, Aurora, 3–6, 18, 51–54, 56–57, 60–66, 68, 71, 72, 76–77, 165, 167–68, 186nn1–2, 187n4, 189nn13–15, 189n18
Gutiérrez-Albilla, Julián Daniel, 5, 86, 172n8, 193n20

Hancock, Ange-Marie, 10, 12, 175nn29–30
Hendel, Liliana, 19, 79, 82–83, 193nn15–17
Hermanas (Solomonoff), 193n3
Hermida, Tania, 179n65
Hernandez, Cesar, 126
Herrera, Alejandra, 106
Hershfield, Joanne, 5, 172
heteronormativity, 53, 77, 190n31
Higgs, Johanna, 194n24
Hinterberger, Amy, 92, 194n32
Historia oficial (Luis Puenzo), 91, 192n3, 193n22

Hochschild, Arlie, 151, 204n31
Hole, Lené, 68, 172n4
Hopfenblatt, Alejandra Kelly, 147, 203nn26–27
Hurtado, Aída, 16, 53–54, 81, 166

I Like It Like That (Martin), 189n30
Iglesias, Gabriel ("Fluffy"), 175n23
Il futuro (Scherson), 192n48
immigration, 154, 177n56
impunity, 18, 78, 82–83, 86–91, 102, 190n39
indigeneity, 19, 103–4, 107, 111–12, 114, 121, 125, 127–29, 131–33, 135, 181n20, 197n4, 199n32, 200n47
Indigenous culture, 18, 23, 25, 33, 35, 40–43, 50, 123, 135
Indigenous identity, 111, 123, 129
Indigenous language, 22, 33, 35, 44, 49, 51, 129–30, 184n65
inequality, 10, 81 94, 138
internationality, 19

Jansen, Itandehui, 19, 104, 165
jardín del Edén, El (Novaro), 192n48
Juana Inés (Arriaga-Jordán), 6, 17–18, 21–35, 37, 42–51, 167, 180n6, 180nn10–11, 180n13, 181n18

Kahnu, Nu, 106
Kamchatka (Piñeyro), 192n3
Kang, Cecilia, 2–3, 5–6, 19–20, 135–38, 140–42, 144, 149–65, 167–68, 202nn10–11, 206n41
Karavanta, Mina, 60–62, 189nn20–21
Keating, AnaLouise, 55, 178n61
Kirk, Stephanie, 18, 28–30, 50, 181nn21–25, 181nn28–29, 182nn30–33, 183n48, 186n82
Kleinman, Arthur, 92, 194n31
Kriger, Clara, 207n43
Kristeva, Julia, 48
Kroll, Julia A., 19, 104, 111, 113–14, 197n6, 197nn8–10

Larralde Rangel, Américo, 182n38
Leal, Luis, 35, 39, 41–42, 183n55, 184n69
Lesmes Espinel, Sergio, 14, 177n50
linguistic difference, 19, 104, 153, 163
lived experiences, 1–6, 15, 17, 54–55, 60,
    66, 76, 138–39, 142–43, 148–49, 156,
    162–64, 166, 168, 206n41
Llosa, Claudia, 2, 19, 104, 165, 196n2,
    200n47
Lobato, Ramon, 8, 174nn21–22
Lola (Novaro), 187, 190n39, 192n48
Lorde, Audre, 55, 72, 178, 188n11, 189n11,
    192n49
Losada, Matt, 195n47, 202n2
Lugones, María, 13–14, 22, 50, 166–67,
    176nn43–44, 177nn45–48, 186n83
Luis Puenzo, 88, 91, 192n3
Lury, Karen, 5, 173n10

MacGuire, Geoffrey, 5, 173n9
Maciel, David R., 5, 172n8
Madeinusa (Llosa), 104–5, 107–15, 117,
    119–20, 122, 125, 129–31, 135, 167,
    187nn4–5, 200n47
Malintzin, 46
mantenidas sin sueño, Las (Desalvo and
    Fogwill), 187n5
marginalization, 61, 69–70, 99, 143, 149,
    195n47
marginalized, 8, 41, 72, 76, 138, 166,
    205n35
Marsh, Leslie L., 5, 172n8
Martin, Darnell, 189n30
Martin, Deborah, 172n7
Martínez, Elizabeth, 177
Martínez, Virginia, 179n65
Matar a Jesús (Mora Ortega), 179n65
matrix of domination, 9–10, 17, 166,
    178n61
McCabe, Janet, 81, 193nn8–10
McCarthy, Sheryl, 1, 171n1
McNelly, Angus, 19, 104, 127
médico alemán, El (Puenzo), 179n65
Medina, José, 13, 182n35

Mejor no hablar de ciertas cosas
    (Andrade), 74, 192n53
Mi último fracaso (Kang), 19, 136, 140,
    149–50, 153–54, 156–57, 159, 161, 164,
    167, 210n10
migration, 98, 104, 106–7, 112, 121, 125–27,
    129, 137, 139, 144, 149, 154, 162, 198n30
Minh-ha, Trinh T., 18, 104, 164, 168
Mixtec, 104, 106–7, 121, 125–26, 128–30,
    165, 196n3
Mora Ortega, Laura, 179n65
Moraga, Cherríe, 1, 12, 15–18, 48, 53, 55, 61,
    66, 70, 76, 147, 166–67, 169, 171nn1–2,
    175n30, 177n55, 188n10, 189n22,
    191n45, 192n57
Moromisato, Doris, 145, 149
mosca en la ceniza, La, 18, 78–83, 85–91,
    93, 95, 97, 99, 101–4, 112, 167, 192n1
Mosquita y Mari (Guerrero), 3, 18, 52–57,
    59–67, 69, 76–77, 167, 186nn1–2,
    189nn13–15
Mr. Iglesias, 175n23
Mrsevic, Zorica, 191n40
Mulvey, Laura, 48, 83
Muñiz-Huberman, Angelina, 36, 40,
    183nn48–50, 184nn63–64

Nahuatl, 18, 22–24, 35–36, 39–44, 47,
    49–51, 106, 128, 183nn51–52, 184n59,
    189n65, 185n76
Nair, Parvati, 5, 86, 172n7, 193n20
Narváez, Geovanny, 18, 53, 74–75,
    192nn52–56
national imaginary, 132, 134, 137, 145, 149
national origin, 137–38, 142, 148, 150, 162,
    165, 168, 175n23, 204n30
nationality, 5, 40, 55, 66, 134–36, 144, 148,
    150, 204n30
    internationality, 19, 136, 142, 151,
        162–63
    plurinationality, 137
    transnationality, 4, 154, 207n46
Native Country of the Heart: A Memoir
    (Moraga), 1, 147, 171n1, 189n22

Netflix, 7–8, 17, 22, 174n16, 174nn19–23, 175n23, 179n65, 180n8, 182n41, 190n33
New Argentine Cinema, 80, 85, 205n33, 206n42
New Latin American Cinema, 138, 147
Night Passage (Minh-ha), 164
Nikkei
　communities, 148, 204n30
　Nikkei: Un viaje extraordinario (Flores Yonekura), 19, 136, 138–39, 144–47, 149, 156–59, 161, 164, 167
Niña, La (Triana and Uribe), 180n8
niña en la Piedra, La (Sistach), 196n4
niño pez, El (Puenzo), 179n65
No robarás . . . a menos que sea necesario (Cordero), 3, 18, 52–57, 59, 61, 63, 65, 67–77, 167, 190n39
Novaro, María, 187n5, 190n39, 192n48, 196n4
Nudo mixteco (Cruz), 107, 196n3
Nueve reinas (Bielinsky), 98
Núñez de Miranda, Antonio, 25–27, 30, 33–34, 46–48

Olson, Debbie, 173n10
One Day at a Time (Calderón Kellet and Royce), 175n23
Ortega, Mariana, 13, 18, 53, 65–66, 179, 182n35, 190n34–35
Osorio Lora, Pilar, 5–6, 173n9, 174n15
other, the, 104, 107, 110, 112, 114–15, 118–19, 121–22, 135

Pablos, David, 193n4
Page, Philippa, 173n9
Paladino, Diana, 20, 142, 160, 207n44
Palermo, Zulma, 177n49
"Pandora's" (Guerrero), 186n1
Pañuelos Verdes, Las, 103, 195n50
Paranagua, Paulo Antonio, 202n4
Parot, Carmen Luz, 194n29
passive object, 50, 111, 119
patriarchy, 14, 18, 80, 191n40

Paz, Octavio, 22, 32, 35, 181n18
Pelo malo (Rondón), 202n1
Peña, Fernando Martín, 172n8
Perfume de violetas (nadie te oye) (Sistach), 190n39
photography, 53, 57–58, 65–66, 139, 147, 157, 164, 180n6
Pibes, Les, 103, 195n50
Piedras, Pablo, 20, 142, 155, 160, 205n33, 206n42
Pineda, Fenessa, 53
Piñero Iñíguez, Carlos, 191n47
Piñeyro, Marcel, 192n3
Pitts, Andrea J., 13, 182n35
Play (Scherson), 189n25, 192n48, 196–97n4
plurinational, 71, 128, 134, 137
Podalsky, Laura, 5, 72–73, 173n9, 192nn50–51, 205n32
Polvo nuestro que estás en los cielos (Flores Silva), 179
Poot Herrera, Sara, 35, 180n13
pop culture, 71, 79, 157, 175n23
Por esos ojos (Martínez), 179n65
Portillo, Lourdes, 178n64
Postero, Nancy, 19, 104, 128, 134, 199nn33–35
power dynamics, 4, 14, 18, 92, 138
Princesas rojas (Astorga Carrera), 179n65
Prividera, Nicolás, 205n33
proto-feminist, 17, 24, 30, 32, 182n35
Puenzo, Lucía, 173n9, 179n65, 205n32
"Pura lengua" (Guerrero), 186n1
punk
　culture, 53
　music, 55, 71–73, 75

Quechua, 105–6, 108, 110–11, 114, 116–71, 120, 129–31, 197n4, 198n17
Queen's Gambit, The (Frank), 182n41
Queen Sugar (DuVernay), 186n1
queer studies, 53, 190n31

racism, 53, 77, 188n10
Ramírez Rojas, Marco, 5–6, 173n9, 174n15

Randall, Rachel, 5, 173n9
Rashkin, Elissa J., 5, 173n8
Rêgo, Cacilda, 174n17
repression, 3, 12, 71, 121, 147
resistance, 5, 10, 12–15, 45, 65, 75, 178n61, 191n47
Respuesta a Sor Filotea (Sor Juana), 29–30, 158
Rivera Berruz, Stephanie, 176n42
Robinson, Beatriz M., 39, 184n57
Rocha, Carolina, 5–6, 91, 173n9, 174nn13–14, 194n30
Roma (Cuarón), 107
Rondón, Mariana, 202n1
Rotberg, Dana, 197n4, 197n7
Royce, Mike, 175n23, 190n33
Rubial García, Antonio, 185n73
Rud, Lucía, 207n46
Rueda Esquibel, Catrióna, 63–64, 189nn26–27
Rueda, Carolina, 197n13
Ruiz, Arantza, 22, 42, 180n6
rural
 rurality, 94, 127–28
 rural otherness, 18, 78, 81, 93, 95, 102–3
 rural studies, 79, 98, 194n34
 rural/urban continuum, 19, 103, 104, 111, 121–29, 133, 135, 168
 rural/urban divide, 19, 103, 112, 125, 127, 129, 168

Sabat-Rivers, Georgina, 39, 41, 183n56, 184nn67–68
Sanchez Jr., Robert Eli, 171n3, 176n42
Santa (Gamboa), 80, 193n5
Sarlo, Beatriz, 20, 159, 205–6nn40–41
Scherson, Alicia, 189n25, 192n48, 196n4
Schiwy, Freya, 19, 104, 132, 200n48
Schmidhuber de la Mora, Guillermo, 180n13
Schroeder Rodríguez, Paul A., 19–20, 104, 120–21, 137–38, 198nn20–23, 202n3, 202nn5–7

Seibel, Alexandra, 5, 173n10
Selena, 175n23
self-determination, 18, 128
Selimović, Inela, 5, 173n9, 204n32
Seminet, Georgia, 5–6, 91, 173n9, 174nn13–14, 194n30
Señorita extraviada (Portillo), 178n64
Sensaciones (Cordero), 71–72, 187n3
sex trafficking, 18, 78, 80, 87–98, 102, 167, 195n42
sexism, 53, 77
sexuality
 and intersectionality, 1, 4, 9, 11, 13, 16, 20, 48, 54, 61, 81, 143, 149, 165–68, 175n23, 176n36
 Martin, Darnell, 189n30
 mosca en la ceniza, La, 80
 Mosquita y Mari, 18, 52, 57, 59, 62–66
 No robarás . . . a menos que sea necesario, 18, 52
 One Day At a Time, 190n33
 Pelo malo, 202n1
 Puenzo, Lucía, 179n65
Shary, Timothy, 5, 173n10
Shaw, Deborah, 4–5, 172n5-7
Shucksmith, Mark, 194n34
Sin dejar huella (Novaro), 192n48, 196n4
Sistach, Marisa, 190n39, 196n4
Smith, Paul Julian, 18, 35, 182–83nn42–45
sobremesa, 150, 155
social network, 19, 68, 94–95
solidarity, 63, 86, 101, 149
Solier, Magaly, 105
Solomonoff, Julia, 193n3
Soriano, Griselda, 207n45
Spanish Inquisition, 25, 27, 46
speaking nearby, 118–19, 129–31, 142, 168, 205n39
Spivak, Gayatri Chakravorty, 49, 118–19
Stantic, Lita, 172n8
Strayer, Chris, 48
streaming, 2–8, 17, 22, 165, 168, 190n33
structural oppression
 and agency, 2, 6, 105, 137, 166, 187n5

structural oppression (cont'd.)
   Collins, Patricia Hill, 9
   Collins, Patricia Hill and Sirma Bilge, 143–44
   Grzanka, Patrick R., 10, 12
   and historical oppression, 17
   and impunity, 18, 78–79
   Juana Inés, 22, 35, 186n83
   Moraga, Cherríe and Gloria Anzaldúa, 15
   mosca en la ceniza, La, 91
   No robarás . . . a menos que sea necesario, 67
   structural inequalities, 5, 121
   Tiempo de lluvia, 121
subjective cinema, 142
subjectivity
   and agency, 5–6, 18, 79
   and intersubjectivity, 13
   mosca en la ceniza, La, 92
   No robarás . . . a menos que sea necesario, 75

Tabuenca, María Socorro, 36, 40–41, 183n51, 184n66
Tenorio, Martha Lilia, 39, 183n54
teta asustada, La (Llosa), 19, 104–5, 107, 115, 117–20, 129, 130–31, 135, 167, 196n2, 197n4, 198n17
13 Reasons Why (DuVernay), 186n1
This Bridge Called My Back: Writings by Radical Women of Color (Moraga and Anzaldúa), 15–16, 76, 166, 177n55, 178n61, 188n10, 189n11
Thornton, Niamh, 7
Tiempo de lluvia (Jansen), 19, 104, 106–7, 121–35
Tire Dié (Birri), 138
tocotines, 36, 39–40, 183n52
Tompkins, Cynthia, 204n32
transculturality, 19, 137, 164
transnationality, 4, 154, 161, 207n46

Trelles Plazaola, Luis, 5, 172n7, 173n11
Tren Gaucho (David), 97
Triana, Rodrigo, 180n8
Troncoso, Venecia, 53
Trujillo, Carla, 178n60
Tuakiri Huna (Rotberg), 197n4
TV Globo, 174n17

Un titán en el ring (Cordero), 187n3
Uribe, Juana, 180n8

Vanegas León, Brenda Cielaika, 69–70, 191nn41–44
Varas, Patricia, 118, 197n15–16, 200n44
vendedora de rosas, La (Gaviria), 187n5
Venezuela, 2, 17, 19, 137, 139–40, 144–45, 147–49, 162, 165, 203n28
Viceroys, 23–25, 29, 33–34, 42–44, 46
"Viernes Girl" (Guerrero), 186n1
villancicos, 39, 41–42, 183n54
Virtanen, Pirjo Kristiina, 19, 104, 126–27, 198nn27–29
visual representation, 3, 5–6, 17, 90, 93
Viveros Vigoya, Mara, 14, 18, 20, 53–55, 60, 70–71, 74, 76–77, 142–44, 148–49, 164, 166–67, 177n50, 188n8, 191n46, 203nn20–21

Wiatrowski, Myc, 7–8, 174n20

XXY (Puenzo), 179n65

Yamasaki, Tizuka, 173n11, 204n30
Yo, la peor de todas (Bemberg), 22, 42, 181n19
Yoon, Won K., 20, 141, 163, 202–3nn12–17
young adulthood, 1–3, 17, 20, 165, 179n65
youth culture, 55, 71–72, 75–77, 173n10, 192n48

Zakaria, Rafia, 176n41
Zwi Migdal, 90

www.ingramcontent.com/pod-product-compliance
Lightning Source LLC
Chambersburg PA
CBHW030540230426
43665CB00010B/973